The Complete Family Scrapbook

All My Children

The Complete Family Scrapbook

By Gary Warner

GENERAL PUBLISHING GROUP

Los Angeles

Publisher: W. Quay Hays
Editor: Murray Fisher
Managing Editor: Sarah Pirch
Art Director: Kurt Wahlner
Production Director: Nadeen Torio
Production Assistants: Harry Pierson, Bryan Shirley, Catherine Vo Bailey and Sheryl Winter
Very special thanks to Dawna Kaufman

For information:
General Publishing Group, Inc.
2701 Ocean Park Boulevard
Santa Monica, CA 90405

Library of Congress Cataloging-in-Publication Data

Gary Warner, 1957–
    All my children : the complete family scrapbook / by Gary Warner.
        p.   cm.
    Includes index.
    ISBN 1-881649-45-8 : $25.00
    1. All my children (Television program)   I. Title.
    PN1992.77.A5W33   1994
    791.45'72–dc20   94-36408
                                                                         CIP

Printed in the USA
10 9 8 7 6 5

General Publishing Group
Los Angeles

Table Of Contents

Introduction

𝕿𝖍𝖗𝖔𝖚𝖌𝖍 𝖙𝖍𝖊 𝖞𝖊𝖆𝖗𝖘 it has often been noted that *All My Children* is an ensemble effort. It begins, of course, with a creation of a concept, characters and interwoven plots which are then developed into serialized script form. Important as this seminal level is, just as vital are the subsequent contributions of production, direction, acting, scenic design, casting, music, camera work, lighting and technical crews in bringing 260 episodes a year to the television screen.

Agnes Nixon

But the ensemble doesn't end there. All our efforts would be meaningless, indeed nonexistent, were it not for the viewers who have kept us on the air for the past quarter of a century. It is their acceptance and loyalty that allow Pine Valley and its people to survive and thrive. They are integral co-habitants in the real world of our collective make believe.

Now we are celebrating our 25th anniversary. I find that fact amazing! Yet pages of this book are testimony to those years and all the stories spun down the corridors of time.

On first reading the precis of plotlines, I wanted all the humanity and special individuality of each character as conveyed in the daily segments. Then I realized that to have such an experience would require watching the past 6500 episodes. A clear impossibility.

This written and pictorial album felicitously fulfills a dual function: to introduce new friends to the wealth and variety of entertainment which *All My Children* offers and, for the veteran viewers, to be the spur which allows them to relive, in vivid memory, all the warmth, humor, conflict and drama enjoyed for 25 years.

Finally, but primarily, I should like to restate the constant theme of our show which is the kinship of humankind under God:

The great and the least
The weak and the strong
The rich and the poor
In sickness and health
In joy and sorrow
In tragedy and triumph
You are All My Children.

—Agnes Nixon

Acknowledgments

Just as putting on *All My Children* takes a remarkable group effort, so does assembling a book about the show! I could never have written this magna-tome without the assistance of ABC's sharpshooting photo department, led by Peter Murray and Jill Yager, who made it easy for me to locate and select hundreds of historic photographs. ABC's incredible "in house" resource, Ann Limongello, who has been snapping photographs on the set of *All My Children* for over 20 years, is a walking encyclopedia, and (lucky for me) she never forgets a face. Doubly lucky for me, *All My Children*'s venerable Associate Producer, Carole Shure, never forgets a name! Without Philip Seldis, Connie Passalacqua and Melissa McNeill, it would have taken me 25 years to assemble "The Complete Stories." They somehow managed to research and compile 25 years of detailed soap-opera history in just two grueling months. And I owe a wealth of gratitude to the bleary-eyed ABC executive Regina DiMartino, who personally screened 140 hours of *All My Children* (not once, but twice!) and pulled memorable quotations that I was able to easily incorporate into the text. Extra-special thanks to the following people: Stacy Balter, Lisa Connor, Cody Dalton, Iris DeVita, Mary Alice Dwyer-Dobbin, Pat Fili Krushel, Sheryl Fuchs, Victoria Gleason, Quay Hays, John Holms, Donna Hornak, Maxine Levinson, Timothy Lund, Nancy Mattia, Maria Melin, Jennifer Minda, Sarah Pirch, Howard Rosenstein, Rodi Rosensweig, Sallie Schoneboom, Esther Swan and Belinda Waldman. And to Agnes Nixon, Felicia Minei Behr and the cast and crew of *All My Children*—thanks for bringing Pine Valley alive for all of us for 25 memorable years!

"The community of Pine Valley is almost as important a factor in our story as the characters themselves. A settlement whose roots go deep into pre-revolutionary soil, the Valley has a distinctive personality and charm that affects all who live in or near it. And though it is a self-contained community, its role as a suburb to a large eastern city, as well as its proximity to New York, makes it unique from most small towns or suburbs in other sections of the country. The Valley will be what everyone thinks of when they think of 'home.' Home because, whether living there or not, this verdant valley has, in some way, made them what they are and is, to some extent, a part of them."

Agnes Nixon
from her original story bible for *All My Children*

Chapter 1

THE COMPLETE STORIES

n January 5, 1970, we entered the small town of Pine Valley, where, while we were the strangers in this quiet suburban community, it seemed everyone knew everybody else. As we were introduced to the residents of the Valley, we soon became captivated by these richly drawn characters, and they became familiar to us as our own friends and family.

In its quarter century on the air, *All My Children* has never been afraid to confront social issues with immediacy, impact, illumination and unparalleled drama. It has continually distinguished itself by introducing socially relevant storylines. In fact, these character driven plots are among the most important aspects of the show. Viewers identify with these complex characters because they deal with genuine situations that touch people's lives. The program's commitment to social relevance confirms for all its diehard fans the merit of their favorite pastime.

Adding to the pleasure of watching *All My Children* is the program's willingness to travel outside the studio to add dimension to an exciting storyline. Since its inception, the show has treated viewers to a sightseeing tour of the globe, visiting locales as nearby as New York's Central Park and as faraway as picturesque Budapest, Hungary.

Over the years, some of our favorites characters have left us unexpectedly, and we can't help but feel grief and sadness. We remember them fondly, for our Pine Valley friends have left us with memories to last a lifetime.

After 25 years of heartbreak and heartache, Pine Valley remains a small town where everybody knows just about everything there is to know about everybody else. But now so do we. The people of Pine Valley are friends and neighbors. As viewers, we share in their joys, their sorrows, their tender romances and their troubling obsessions. Pine Valley is a part of us. May it go on forever!

"It's the profoundest celebration anyone has ever hosted!" proclaimed a proud Adam Chandler of his masked ball in 1989. Wearing elaborate one-of-a-kind masks, Pine Valley's most prominent citizens gathered at this gala occasion, among them Brooke English and Mona and Erica Kane.

1970

One of the best—and the worst—things about life in a small town is that eventually everyone knows everybody else's business. When we first entered the world of Pine Valley in 1970, we found out that everybody did indeed know everyone else. We were the strangers in town, but it didn't take long before we settled in and became familiar with and fascinated by the residents and their stories.

Most of those stories were love stories. The first lovers we met were young Phillip Brent and Tara Martin, solid, dependable, likable kids, busy with classes, sports, hobbies and plans for college during their senior year at Pine Valley High. In the midst of this activity, Phil and Tara were also experiencing the first blush of love. It was soon clear to everyone that these two were meant to be together. Even Chuck Tyler, Phil's best friend, accepted what seemed the inevitable, despite his longstanding crush on Tara. Their classmate, Erica Kane, who'd had her eye on Phil for some time, was not quite as understanding. After all, Phil was the most popular guy in school, and in Erica's mind she was the prettiest girl. She couldn't fathom what a guy like Phil could see in a plain Jane like Tara Martin. So Erica set out to break them up.

Phil and Tara's romance had the support of both their families. Tara had moved from California with her father Dr. Joe Martin after the death of her mother. They lived with Joe's mother Kate, whom Tara called "Gran." Tara could always turn to Kate for words of wisdom and motherly advice. Tara's older brother Jeff, like Gran, was supportive of Tara's newfound love. Jeff was home for summer vacation from Stanford Medical School. When he found love of his own that summer, his plans for returning to Stanford would become a distant memory.

For the first eighteen years of his life, Phillip had brought Ruth and Ted Brent much joy. But if Ruth was pleased to see their son so happy in love it was soon clear that her relationship with her husband was falling apart. Ted Brent was a former professional football player who, after an injury, was forced to give up the game he loved. Eventually Ted made a new career selling used cars. But with his passion thwarted, he grew into a bitter man who began to resent Phil's youth and his promise of a bright future. Combined with the truth he faced every day about Phillip's real father, this sent Ted to the bottle for comfort.

The Brents' marriage also suffered because of Ted's resentment toward Ruth's job as a nurse at Pine Valley Hospital. He felt neglected when her work schedule took away time he felt she should be spending at home with her family. For her part, Ruth realized how little she and Ted had to talk about these days and how much she enjoyed her time with Dr. Joe Martin. They shared a common interest in their work, as well as their children's budding romance. Regardless of this growing connection, Ruth remained devoted to her marriage, determined to tough it out with Ted.

Ted's intense dislike of Ruth's younger sister Amy added to the tension in the Brent home. He was galled by Amy's constant presence in Phil's life and felt inferior to her polished, wealthy husband, Lincoln Tyler. Despite their differences, Ruth sided with Ted about Amy's involvement in Phillip's life. Phil and his Aunt Amy had always been close, but it soon appeared that things were getting out of hand. Amy was obsessive in her attention to Phillip's everyday activities. She worked hard to keep her husband Linc from finding out why. Amy truly loved Linc, who she felt

Lincoln Tyler accepted his wife Amy's liberal politics. Amy loved Linc, but even he had limits to his understanding when Amy's anti-war protests got her into hot water.

was the kindest and most understanding man she'd ever known. But not even Linc could understand or forgive Amy for the true reason she bonded so strongly with Phillip. Amy struggled to be a good wife to Linc and tried to make him happy. She also did her best to put up with Linc's intolerable mother, Phoebe Tyler.

While Linc accepted Amy's liberal politics, Phoebe considered her daughter-in-law's anti-Vietnam War activities vaguely un-American. Phoebe felt Lincoln had married beneath him. They were, after all, Tylers, the pinnacle of Pine Valley society. It galled Phoebe to think her son had tied himself to someone so clearly unworthy of him. That her husband, Dr. Charles Tyler, could tolerate, even like, Amy was beyond Phoebe's comprehension.

Charles and Phoebe had three children. Their older son, Charles Tyler II, died in an automobile accident with his wife many years earlier, leaving them a grandson, Chuck, to raise. Chuck, who hoped to become a doctor someday, had become more son than grandson to them. Their younger son, Lincoln, had become a fine attorney, and Phoebe hoped that he would run for office one day— provided Amy's politics didn't get in his way. Their only daughter, Anne, was in New York City pursuing a fashion career. All the Tyler children were level-headed and down-to-earth, attributes which bespoke Charles's influence far more than Phoebe's.

Life with Phoebe Tyler, perennial busybody and society snob, had never been easy for Charles. But he remained loyal to her and learned to tolerate her faults. He also had an escape at Pine Valley Hospital, where he was chief of staff. As Phoebe's meddling antics increased, he began spending more and more time at the hospital. That meant his secretary was putting in more and more overtime. But Mona Kane didn't mind. She loved the way Charles had come to rely on her over the years. She seemed to be the only one who could cajole him out of a black mood and soothe him after a bout with Phoebe. She wouldn't dare admit it to anyone, but she was falling in love with Charles Tyler. She simply loved him. Before long, this unspoken emotion had become mutual.

Mona had divorced her philandering husband Eric after he deserted her when their daughter Erica was only nine. While he found fame in Hollywood as a film director, Mona dedicated her life to raising their child, going out of her way to please Erica. But no matter how much attention or how many gifts Mona lavished on the child, it was never enough. A true "Daddy's Little Girl," Erica blamed Mona for her father's departure, a rejection that left Erica filled with insecurity. No matter how pretty she had convinced herself she was, she was driven by the fear that someone else was prettier. She was consumed by a need to be better in every way than everyone else. She wanted to be Somebody! If she wasn't, it was only because she was stuck in this stupid small town with her dull, drab mother. Or so she told herself. Erica thought she was meant for more than the life her mother had carved out for the two of them, and she never stopped letting Mona know how dissatisfied she was.

Although she was vain and self-centered, Erica's popularity with the boys never suffered. For the most part, her steady was Chuck Tyler, who came from the social register she longed to enter. But Erica was well aware of Chuck's grandmother's feelings toward her. To Phoebe, Erica was the daughter of "that Kane woman" who worked for her husband and thus was unfit for her precious grandson. Erica vowed to show Phoebe Tyler and everybody else in Pine Valley that she was someone special. At

Fashion plate Phoebe Tyler considered herself among the elite of Pine Valley society.

school, the person she wanted most to prove this to was Phil Brent.

Erica was relentless in her efforts to get close to Phil and take him away from Tara. Erica appealed on numerous occasions to Phil's chivalry and played damsel in distress to lure him in. Tara confided to her father and Gran that she didn't trust Erica. She saw what Erica was up to and warned Phil to wake up. Phil reassured Tara that there was nothing to fear where Erica was concerned, and they began to discuss marriage. Phil also told Erica he was through coming to the rescue after her contrived calls for help.

Mona, trying to spare Erica heartache, encouraged her daughter to give up chasing Phillip. This only ignited Erica's rage and increased her feelings of rejection. She demanded that her mother stay out of her life. When Mona's friend Nick Davis reprimanded Erica for her disrespect, the girl lashed back that Nick would be just the sort of lowlife she'd expect her mother to have as a friend.

Nick Davis had left Pine Valley nineteen years earlier to join the Navy. He had just returned to town with what little he had managed to save to open his own dance studio. Nick, the ultimate charmer, wasn't above sweet-talking the "right people" to get what he needed. When Phoebe Tyler entered his orbit, Nick felt his ship had finally come in. Here was a wealthy society dame who needed someone with panache to help her organize a charity ball. Nick wasn't about to let her or her money get away. With Charles spending so much time at the hospital, Phoebe was sorely missing male attention, and Nick wasted no time filling that void.

While Nick was charming Phoebe, he renewed his friendship with Mona, thereby getting to know Erica and her friends. He seemed to take a special liking to young Phil Brent and couldn't understand why this young man seemed so strangely familiar to him. Phillip's friendship with Nick upset his Aunt Amy, who alerted her sister Ruth that Nick was back in town. Neither had ever expected to see him again. Nick had been Amy's first love, the one she never told her husband Linc about, the one who left town one morning leaving her nothing but a "Dear Amy" note, the one who left her alone and pregnant with Phillip. Ruth didn't think Amy should worry about Nick. She reminded her sister that she and Ted had become Phillip's parents. They had agreed that Phillip must never know that Aunt Amy was really his mother. Amy also agreed Nick must never find out Phillip was his son.

For Amy, the sight of Nick and the sound of his apologies weren't enough to rekindle their past romance. But his presence still upset her. Linc sensed a distancing from Amy but was met only with her silence when he questioned the reason for it. Her silence increased the rift in their marriage. Linc began to wonder and realize how much Amy's world revolved around her nephew. Even her anti-war marching seemed to stem from her obsessive fear that Phil could be drafted and sent to Vietnam.

Phil faced a more immediate peril the night there was a gas leak in the Brent basement. He was home alone studying when the fumes knocked him out. Nick Davis drove up to return a notebook Phil had left at his studio. When Nick arrived, he saw lights on in the house, but no one answered the bell. He became alarmed when he looked in the window and saw Phil lying unconscious on the floor. Finding the door unlocked, Nick entered and smelled gas. Panicked, he rushed Phil to Pine Valley Hospital.

Hearing what had happened, Ruth, Ted and Amy joined Nick at the hospital and kept vigil until Joe brought the news that Phillip would be all

Ruth Brent kept a troubling secret from her son, Phil. She wasn't his real mother. Aunt Amy was.

right. When Joe suggested that perhaps Phil's mother might like to see him, Ruth and Amy both stepped forward. Amy would not be denied anymore, not after almost losing Phillip a second time. Linc walked into the waiting area in time to hear Amy proclaim that she was Phillip's mother. Ruth was aghast. Ted was livid. Linc and Nick were in shock. In that moment, with one look between Linc and Amy, they both knew their marriage was over. Nick was overwhelmed by the knowledge that he had a son and wanted to go to Phillip to tell him. Ted threatened that he would kill Nick first. The decision was made that Phil was in no condition to be told anything now. If and when he ever was told would be up to his parents, Ruth and Ted.

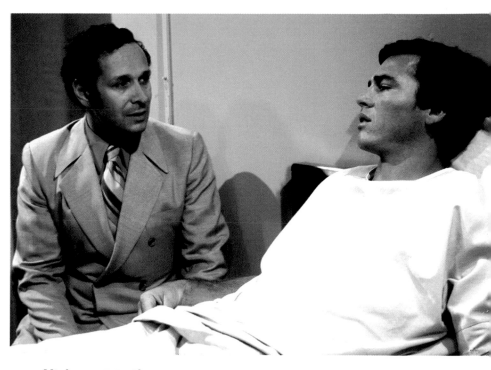

Phillip Brent owed his life to Nick Davis for more reasons than one. Not only did Nick rescue him after a gas leak at the Brent house caused him to pass out—Nick was also Phil's natural father.

Bursting with the need to tell someone, Nick went to the one person who knew about his long-ago affair with Amy—his best friend Mona Kane. As Nick recounted the story of Phil being his son, neither he nor Mona noticed Erica eavesdropping. Erica couldn't believe her mother and Nick would keep such a secret from her friend Phil. She privately decided the best way to show him just how good a friend she was would be to share this secret with him.

Phil reminded Erica of his decision not to see her anymore, but she was determined. She had news for him about his parents—his real parents. Erica hurriedly told him that his Aunt Amy and his friend Nick Davis had been lovers and Phil was their son. She waited for Phillip to be grateful. After all, Erica was the only person with courage enough to tell him the truth. Instead, Phil stormed out to confront the woman who had lied to him his whole life, the woman who decided that being his aunt was more convenient for her than being his mother. He was angry and confused, but mostly hurt. In Phil's mind, the woman who had pretended to love him had only done so to ensure no one would ever know about her dirty little secret.

Amy wept as she tried to explain and apologize, but Phil wouldn't listen and wanted nothing to do with her ever again. Her life in shambles, Amy left Pine Valley for Switzerland, where she joined an international peace organization dedicated to making the future safer for all the world's children. Once again, Phil was the motivating factor behind her devotion to this cause. She never returned to Pine Valley.

Then Phil confronted his parents over the lie they'd all lived with for eighteen years. Ruth was devastated. But Ted, who'd already been drinking, went ballistic when he was told Phil had learned the truth. He had warned Nick Davis he would kill him if Phil was told. A drunken Ted ran out of the house and into his car before Phil could explain it was Erica, not Nick, who had told him. Ted never reached Nick's. Unsteady at the wheel, too drunk to see clearly, Ted swerved to avoid a car and crashed into oblivion. In the hospital, Ted told Phil how much he loved him, how proud he was to have a son like him. Then he died.

The Complete Stories

Graduation day came for Phillip, Tara, Chuck and Erica. But their world had already changed. In the end, Erica had succeeded in breaking up Phil and Tara by revealing his family secret. But in doing so Erica had ruined any chance she might have had with Phil herself. Tara's brother Jeff was the only person she knew who wasn't angry at her for telling Phillip the truth. Jeff sympathized with Erica's friendless plight and became smitten with her. When Erica realized how much nabbing Jeff Martin would anger his sister, she charted a course to do just that. Erica entered Pine Valley University with her own agenda. According to her, books wouldn't give her anything she didn't already have—but being near Jeff Martin would. In the face of Tara's warnings, Erica worked her magic on the unsuspecting Jeff and won him over.

Phil had come to blame himself for all the pain and hurt in the lives around him, from the destruction of Amy and Linc's marriage to his adoptive father's death. He felt he would only bring hurt and pain to Tara if he married her as they'd planned. So Phil broke their engagement and announced he was leaving town. Tara insisted she would wait for him, but he asked her not to. Phil left Pine Valley determined to lose himself in New York City. And lose himself he did, when an accident caused him to suffer amnesia.

With Chuck feeling the loss of his best friend Phil almost as much as Tara, he did his best to lift her spirits. Tara had hoped to hear from Phillip, but when no letters or phone calls ever came from him, she began to lean on Chuck for support. He encouraged her to enter Pine Valley University with him that fall. The crush he had long tried to suppress began to blossom into something more.

With the death of her husband and the absence of her son, Ruth inevitably grew closer to her friend and colleague, Joe Martin. Their time together became more important to each of them, and they were happy to have found each other during such trying times. Joe had another reason to feel blessed. His brother Paul, presumed missing in Vietnam, turned up alive and returned to Pine Valley.

Phoebe Tyler's relentless harangue about Amy only succeeded in driving away her husband and son. With the dissolution of his marriage, Linc needed to get away from reminders of Amy, so he left town. Meanwhile, Charles became more involved with his work at the hospital. During this time, Phoebe and Charles's daughter Anne returned to Pine Valley. While it appeared she had moved back to open a fashion shop called The Boutique, other factors were drawing her home. She had become intrigued by a Pine Valley man she had met in New York: Nick Davis.

Nick had gone to New York City to find Phil and bring him back. During this search for his son he met Phoebe Tyler's daughter Anne. While his attention to Phoebe had been a means of acquiring money and gifts, his affection for Anne was genuine. Nick was changing. He wanted to be the kind of a man who would make his son proud.

Nick found Phil. When he learned Phil had amnesia, Nick talked him into returning to Pine Valley with the idea that perhaps, in familiar surroundings, Phil's memory would return. Nick also hoped Phil would revisit his past with Tara. He was convinced they could still have the life together that they'd planned. When Phil returned to Pine Valley, Tara was devastated that he didn't know her. She continued to seek consolation from Chuck, and their relationship finally became romantic. Grateful as Tara was to Chuck, and though she had grown to love him, she would never feel for him what she had felt for Phillip.

Tara warned that she wasn't going to just sit back and let Erica get her hooks in her brother. But Erica just smiled.

Anne Tyler was quite taken with Nick Davis, much to her mother Phoebe's chagrin. Phoebe believed Nick was the kind of man who used women like toys, manipulating their affections. Phoebe had conveniently forgotten her own flirtations with Nick. In her mind he wasn't fit for any woman, least of all her own daughter. But Anne had always had a mind of her own, and the more Phoebe railed against Nick, the more Anne defended him. Even Charles insisted Phoebe stay out of Anne's affairs, but to no avail. Anne tried to convince her mother that Nick had changed. He wasn't the same man who had walked out on Amy all those years ago. Anne saw Nick as a man who was truly sorry for his past mistakes. She witnessed his struggle to become something more than a stranger to his son. Her admiration and respect for him grew into a strong attraction.

Nick enjoyed Anne's attention—whether he thought he deserved it was another story. She was a true lady of considerable background, he was a drifter without roots. Nick agreed with Phoebe that Anne was too good for him. He was surprised when Anne didn't follow her mother's advice and be rid of him, but he was happy she didn't. Anne had the rare ability to bring out the best in Nick. He was honest about himself with her in a way he never had been before. They were an improbable couple: The daughter of society and the two-bit dance teacher. Despite their different backgrounds and the opposition of Anne's mother, Nick and Anne fell deeply in love.

Life wasn't as blissful for Tara. With Phil's failure to remember her, Tara had turned to Chuck even more. He confessed his love for her, and she acknowledged she loved him too, but not the way she loved Phillip. She longed for the day Phillip would come to her and they could resume their plans for the future. That day never came, so Tara accepted Chuck's proposal of marriage.

They were an improbable couple: The daughter of society and the two-bit dance teacher. But somehow Nick and Anne fell deeply in love.

But Phil's memory did come back. However, he chose to keep silent in the face of his friends' plans for the future. Only one word from Phil and Tara would be his. The feelings were still strong in both of them. When Phil confided in Nick about his feelings for Tara, Nick encouraged him to tell her and stop his misery. Phil refused. Chuck was his best friend, and Phil knew it would destroy Chuck to lose Tara. As for Tara, Phil believed he had brought enough pain and uncertainty into her world. He would not bring her more. So Phil remained silent and wished them both the best. Phil didn't know that Tara questioned her decision and was waiting for him to step in. If he had, she would have called the whole thing off. But Phil gave her no hints, so Tara forged ahead with wedding plans.

Phoebe was delirious. While her children continued to make disastrous choices in love, her grandson didn't. Phoebe heartily approved of Chuck's choice for a bride. Tara Martin was a lovely girl from a good, solid family. Phoebe busied herself with plans for a society wedding far more elaborate than anything the Martins could imagine. Meanwhile, Charles consoled Mona, who fretted over Erica's determination to marry Jeff Martin.

Erica wasn't nearly as in love with Jeff as she was with the idea of getting out of her mother's house. Erica saw Jeff as her escape from that mundane existence. Even if Jeff was only an intern, someday he would be a doctor. Being Jeff Martin's wife would mean something to people in

Pine Valley, and that was Erica's consuming goal.

Tara warned her brother against Erica, but Jeff was blinded by her beauty and her ability to make him feel important. Erica had convinced Jeff she needed him, that she leaned on him and depended on him to take care of her. Thoughts of Erica consumed Jeff. A pending date with her made his exhausting hours at the hospital bearable. Erica basked in his adoration. Though he wasn't sure whether it was his idea that they get married or Erica's, he was completely for it. The more time he could spend with her the better. But he wanted to wait until he was financially secure before they wed. Considering how hard Tara was working to keep them apart, Erica decided she'd have to act fast. As much as Jeff wanted to wait, when he eloped with Erica, he probably thought that was his idea too.

News of their marriage jolted both families. Still, Mona liked Jeff and felt Erica couldn't have picked a finer young man. Mona wished her daughter well, but Erica couldn't help hearing the apprehension in Mona's voice. While Jeff's family had strong reservations about the hastiness of the marriage, Kate and Joe welcomed Erica into the family, albeit reluctantly. Tara bit her tongue to keep from telling Jeff how angry she was that he'd fallen for Erica's phony charms.

Jeff and Erica moved in to a less-than-glamorous flat that was all Jeff could afford. Erica made it clear that if Jeff really loved her, he would find a more suitable place. This time Jeff was firm. They were staying put for the time being, and Erica must accept it. She was miserable. This marriage to Jeff was far from the idyllic image she had concocted. Again she felt trapped. She had fled her mother's provincial nest only to land in another. While Erica brooded in their tiny, drab apartment, Jeff spent most of his time at the hospital.

Jeff's work became even more demanding when he began his residency at Pine Valley Hospital. He wished he could make Erica understand how thrilling and challenging he found his work. But he couldn't ignore her stifled yawns whenever he spoke of it. He found a friendly, interested ear in Mary Kennicott, the new nurse at the hospital. Medicine fascinated Mary. And they spoke the same language.

Mary had impressed everyone at the hospital with her hardworking, down-to-earth attitude. Though she was a plain young woman, there was a sweetness about her that made her attractive. As one of the head nurses, Ruth Brent's job was to take Mary under her wing. As Ruth kept an eye on Mary, she couldn't help noticing how the young woman's face lit up whenever Jeff entered a room. Though Ruth knew Joe was doing his best to accept Erica as his daughter-in-law, Ruth had no doubt that Mary was a better match for Joe's son.

Ruth and Joe were becoming a familiar sight together in the hospital cafeteria as well as in and around Pine Valley. It was clear to onlookers that they were keeping company before they realized it themselves. Even though they found comfort in each other, there were problems. Ruth knew how much her son Phil still loved Joe's daughter Tara. She hoped Tara would break off her engagement to Chuck and longed to tell her of Phillip's true feelings. But Joe felt that he and Ruth should stay out of their children's lives. Besides, after the way Phil had hurt Tara, Joe wasn't too keen on Tara's picking up with him again.

Joe's mother Kate encouraged Tara to follow her heart. But without some encouragement from Phillip, Tara couldn't accept her Gran's advice. When the day of her wedding to Chuck finally arrived, she was nervous but determined. She would marry Chuck.

Phillip was miserable, and Nick hated seeing his son this way. Nick believed that marrying Chuck Tyler would be the biggest mistake Tara could make. The more he thought about what she was going to do, the angrier Nick became. He'd been drinking, and when the minister asked whether anyone had just cause for this marriage not to take place, Nick spoke up. His reason, he declared, was that Tara loved Phillip. A furious Chuck engaged Nick in a fight, but within moments Chuck collapsed.

Tara Martin visited Chuck Tyler during his hospitalization for kidney failure after he collapsed during their wedding ceremony.

The Complete Stories

Ruth pulled Tara from Chuck's side so that Joe, Charles and Jeff could minister to the stricken groom. Phoebe was terrified for her grandson and furious at Nick. The wedding she had planned and waited for ended when Chuck was rushed to the hospital with kidney failure.

That Anne continued to see Nick despite her mother's oft-stated objections incensed Phoebe. Especially when there was an infinitely superior candidate available for Anne's affection in Kate Martin's younger son Paul. With a promising career as a lawyer, he was the kind of man Phoebe had always hoped her daughter would find. She went so far as to let Kate know Anne was available. But Kate would not play matchmaker for her son and suggested to Phoebe that she use some restraint when it came to her daughter's life.

Kate wondered to herself how Charles ever had survived a woman like Phoebe. In truth, Charles rarely heard a word Phoebe said these days. He had learned to tune her out, preferring the company he found at the hospital to his wife. Charles wasn't sure exactly when he'd stopped loving Phoebe, but he knew he'd fallen in love with Mona Kane.

As Chuck hovered between life and death from his kidney problem, Tara and Phil kept a constant vigil at the hospital.

Phoebe was too busy trying to run Anne's life to notice Charles's increasing coolness. She turned out to be right about Paul Martin. Not only was he a perfect suitor for Anne, he was an eager one. Anne was still in love with Nick Davis though, just as Paul's niece was still in love with Phillip.

Ironically, it was Tara and Phil's mutual concern for Chuck that brought them back together. As Chuck hovered between life and death, Tara and Phil kept a constant vigil at the hospital. In reassuring glances and lingering touches, the strength of their feelings resurfaced. Tara knew Phil still loved her, and she could no longer pretend she didn't feel the same. They were finally back together. Then Chuck began to rally. The doctors informed Tara they believed his love for her had pulled him through and that his recovery would be a slow one. Joe told Tara that Chuck would need her more than ever and any upset could result in serious consequences. Hearing this advice, Tara realized she and Phil couldn't let anyone know they had reconciled. They agreed for the sake of their friend's life that Tara would remain Chuck's fiancée until he fully recovered.

While Chuck slowly convalesced, Phil received his draft notice. Having failed to enter college with the rest of his friends, he'd lost his student deferment. Phillip Brent was in the Army now, and all signs indicated he was headed for Vietnam.

While Phil cursed himself for not starting college, Erica was dropping out. She saw no purpose in studying and improving her grade point average. But with a workaholic husband, an apartment she hated and no direction, she had too much time on her hands. Erica was restless, she wanted something more from life. Then she found the perfect job at Anne Tyler's boutique. Part of her duties involved buying trips to New York. Erica Kane Martin had met her destiny at last.

Tara stalled whenever Chuck brought up the subject of setting a new date for their wedding, telling him she didn't want him to concern himself with wedding plans until he was completely well. What she didn't tell him was that she and Phillip were secretly dating. Phil's induction into the Army terrified her. She didn't want to let Chuck down or cause a relapse, but she had an ominous feeling that every moment she spent with Phillip was precious because they didn't have many left. Her fears were confirmed when he got his orders to leave for Vietnam.

During his final days before shipping out, Phil made his round of good-byes. Chuck was sorry Phil wouldn't be by his side as best man when he married Tara. Feeling guilty, Phil wished his friend a speedy recovery. Phil and Tara couldn't bear even the thought of hurting Chuck. With their love for each other stronger than ever, they didn't want to say good-bye with their situation still unresolved. Finally, the night before he had to leave, Phil asked Tara to marry him. Willing to wait for him if she could do so as his wife, she accepted. They made a secret trip out of town to find a justice of the peace. It was a treacherous night; a blizzard had all but buried the roads out of Pine Valley. As they crept along in the storm, they noticed a tiny roadside chapel and went inside. It was as if they were the only two people in the world on the last night of their lives together. Heartbroken that their plans to marry had been thwarted, they held each other and prayed for an answer.

Then an idea came: they would perform their own ceremony. Phillip and Tara lit candles on the small altar and exchanged vows. With only God as their witness, they became husband and wife.

They spent the night at a nearby country inn and made passionate, tender love for the first time. The next day, Phil Brent headed off to war.

After a few weeks, Chuck had recovered enough to leave the hospital, but Tara told no one she considered herself married to Phillip. Soon she began to feel queasy and suffer dizzy spells. Tara realized she was going to have a baby: Phillip's baby. She was eager to share the news with Phil but dared not tell anyone else yet. First, she had to tell Chuck she couldn't marry him. She was scared and excited at the same time. Then Ruth Brent got the news: her son, Phillip Brent, was missing in action and presumed dead.

Tara was as devastated as Ruth. Phillip was gone forever. All she had left was his baby. Finally, she confessed the truth to Chuck. Putting aside his own hurt, he again found himself in the awkward position of comforting the woman he loved over the loss of the man she loved. As they both mourned the loss of Phil, Chuck came up with the perfect solution.

Chuck proposed that he and Tara go ahead with their plans to marry. He suggested they tell everybody they had eloped a few weeks back, after his release from the hospital. When she had the baby, everyone would assume it was Chuck's. He promised to love the child as if it were his and vowed to make Tara happy. Tara felt Chuck deserved better than being second best to her and her child. He only knew he loved her and wanted to take care of her. He insisted Phil would want this, too. So Chuck and Tara went ahead with their plans, announcing their marriage and her pregnancy.

Phoebe was ecstatic, and she toasted the happy couple with champagne. Phoebe's fondness for a little drink now and then was beginning to get out of hand. Charles accepted some of the blame for spending so

Issues and Answers

Anti-war sentiment

During the height of the Vietnam War, All My Children *chronicled how the town of Pine Valley, like the rest of the country, was divided between those who supported the U.S. government's position and those who opposed and protested it. Ruth Martin, whose son Phil was reported missing in action, gave a stunning anti-war speech, the first of its kind on daytime television.*

much time at the hospital and leaving her with only a glass of sherry for company. Aggravating the situation was Phoebe's upset over her daughter Anne's relationship with the contemptible Nick Davis. Any efforts Phoebe made to end that union only brought the two closer.

Marriage was in the air in Pine Valley. Anne and Nick. Chuck and Tara. And, at long last, Joe and Ruth, who had already become the couple almost everyone in Pine Valley turned to for comfort, advice, and friendship. Even before they married, everyone took it for granted that one day they would. When Ruth moved into the Martin house, she was welcomed by Kate with open arms. Kate told Ruth it was her home now, and Ruth should feel free to run it as she saw fit.

Marriage was in the air in Pine Valley. Chuck and Tara. Anne and Nick. And at long last, Joe and Ruth.

Ruth, Joe and Kate helped Joe's brother Paul deal with his unrequited love for Anne Tyler Davis as she settled into her marriage with Nick. Anne was on top of the world. Her business was successful, and hiring Erica had given her more time to devote to Nick. She felt he needed her even more after he received the news of Phillip's death. Anne wanted more than anything to have a baby with Nick. She knew they would be wonderful parents, but pregnancy never occurred. Anne became increasingly despondent.

Secretly, Nick consulted a doctor, who told him Nick's sperm count was so low it was unlikely he could father a child. Nick knew that if he told Anne, she'd tell him not to worry about it. But he also knew how desperately she wanted a baby. It killed Nick knowing he could never give her one. All he could give her, Nick decided, was freedom to find someone who could give her children—someone who was more of a man than he was.

Driven by his feelings of shame and inadequacy, Nick began to provoke fights with Anne until they separated. Unwilling to give up on her marriage, Anne seduced him into one last night of love. Regretting the weakness of his resolve, Nick asked her for a divorce, never telling her why. Convinced that somehow Nick had fallen out of love with her, Anne was heartbroken and agreed to the divorce. She might have stopped it when she discovered she was pregnant, but she loved Nick too much to tie him down to a woman he didn't love. When their divorce became final, Phoebe tipped a glass in delight.

Anne's lawyer, Paul Martin, held her hand through her ordeal. He sensed she liked and depended on him and he had long been in love with her. Paul began to hold out hope even though he knew she was carrying Nick's baby. He convinced Anne that Nick didn't have to know about it. Instead, Paul offered to be her husband and the baby's father. Anne was confused, but her mother had no doubt Anne could make a life with Paul. Phoebe rhapsodized about her hopes for their union and persuaded Anne, in her vulnerable state, to give in. The more Phoebe saw Anne and Paul together, the more she drank in triumph.

Phoebe had still more happy news: the birth of her great-grandchild. Tara had given birth to a little boy whom she and Chuck had named Phillip Charles Tyler. Phoebe questioned their choice of a first name, but Tara and Chuck were adamant. They wanted to honor their late friend Phil—much to Phoebe's distaste. Phil's mother Ruth, in turn, was overjoyed to rock her new step-grandson in her arms. She had learned the truth that Phil, not Chuck, was little Phillip's father. When she looked in little Phillip's eyes, she saw her son. She kept this secret from Joe.

Tara's brother Jeff was ecstatic to be an uncle, while his wife was less than enthusiastic. Being a small-town doctor's wife was no longer Erica's goal. Everything about Jeff bored her.

Erica's job at Anne's fashion boutique had given her a taste of a far more glamorous life than she could ever have with Jeff.

Erica always wanted more. On a buying trip in New York City, she finally met someone who could give it to her. From the moment Erica met Jason Maxwell, she wanted him to sign her up as a model at his agency. Jason wanted her from the very first moment, but not necessarily as a model. He flirted with her, and she flirted back. If he would work with her, she was determined to learn. She was confident she could make money for his agency and persuaded him to give her a modeling assignment.

As Erica entered the fast lane, she made new friends. Margo Flax, an

Mona Kane shared a deep friendship with Nick Davis, whom she could always count on to lend an ear to the never-ending problems she had with her incorrigible teenage daughter Erica.

older woman whose best days as a model were far behind her, offered to teach her the business. By doing so, Margo realized she could keep an eye on Erica, because she had observed Jason's more than passing interest in his young discovery. Margo had long ago learned to tolerate her competitors, but that didn't mean she had to like them.

Jeff made himself believe he and Erica could live with her career as long as it didn't interfere with their life. But when it took her away from him, he always enjoyed catching a quick dinner with Mary Kennicott.

Jeff had his doubts about Erica's latest venture and her new friends but tried to be open-minded. Erica's mother wasn't so willing. She wondered why Erica couldn't be content with life in Pine Valley. Erica wondered why her mother could never be happy for her.

Mona wasn't happy at all, and as she observed Jeff at the hospital, she saw he didn't seem happy either. He confided to his friend and fellow resident, Frank Grant, that he was waking up to the fact that he'd married a very selfish young woman. But he loved Erica. Frank explained that his wife Nancy had a career, and they still had a happy marriage. Jeff wanted to believe he and Erica could live with her career. He just wished it didn't take her away from him so often. When it did, Mary Kennicott's company comforted him. Mary had fallen in love with Jeff and hated the way his wife took him for granted. But Mary could not bear to be the "other woman." So, she remained silent, happy just to be near Jeff in his loneliness.

Nick Davis's own loneliness drove him into the arms of Kitty Shea, a new dance teacher he'd hired for his studio. On the rebound after his divorce from Anne, Nick wanted companionship, and Kitty was a willing substitute. She had always had a low opinion of herself and was grateful for Nick's attention. Even if he wouldn't stop talking about his ex-wife, Kitty convinced herself Nick would come to love her. They fell into an affair.

Nick wanted to forget his affair with Kitty Shea, but he couldn't. She was pregnant.

𝕹𝖎𝖈𝖐 𝕯𝖆𝖛𝖎𝖘'𝖘 𝖆𝖋𝖋𝖆𝖎𝖗 with Kitty Shea was brief, and he wanted to forget it as soon as possible. Kitty felt differently. The more he pulled away, the harder she held on, which only convinced Nick what a mistake their affair had been. But it wouldn't be easy to walk away, because Kitty was pregnant. When she told Nick, he realized that if he wasn't sterile, as he'd believed, he had given up the love of his life for nothing. Nick was through with Kitty, and she was stung by his flagrant rejection.

Meanwhile, convincing herself she could learn to love Paul Martin, Anne married him. His kindhearted plan to raise Nick's baby as his own proved to her how much he loved her. When she had a miscarriage, Paul gave her the sympathy and support she needed. Paul knew he could never block her thoughts of Nick, but he was steadfast and loyal. Despite her feelings, Anne vowed to make her new marriage work.

When Nick learned of Anne's pregnancy and subsequent miscarriage, he ran to her. He confessed his love and told her the real reason he'd pressured her to divorce him. Anne was angry at him for his lack of trust in her love and for what it had cost them. But she couldn't deny she loved him. When they began seeing each other

1973

The Complete Stories

behind Paul's back, Anne knew her marriage to Paul was doomed.

When Kitty realized she was losing Nick, she told Anne she was carrying his baby. This news hurt Anne deeply, but she knew Nick couldn't walk away from another child, not after he'd missed most of Phillip's brief life. Anne went to Nick and insisted that he marry Kitty. It was the right thing to do. Nick protested but eventually gave in.

Shortly after the wedding, Kitty had a miscarriage. She slid into a deep depression that prevented Nick from ending this sham of a marriage. The baby had been their only connection. With her low self-esteem and total dependence on Nick, she couldn't live without him. Kitty attempted suicide, and after failing at it, she lost all sense of reality.

In her delusional state, Kitty was convinced she was still pregnant. Her psychiatrist encouraged Nick to humor her until she could deal with her loss. Nick stood by her while he watched Anne, the woman he loved, make another attempt at her marriage to Paul Martin.

While Kitty wouldn't accept she was no longer pregnant, Erica Martin was dealing with the fact that she was. Erica begged Doctor Clader not to mention it to her husband, to let her tell him first. A baby was the last thing in the world she and Jeff needed, she rationalized. They barely had enough money for themselves. Jeff was so busy at the hospital that he would have no time for a child anyway. More important, Erica was on the verge of making it as a high-fashion model. Pregnancy would surely put an end to that. And she wasn't prepared to give a baby the love and attention it needed. The Supreme Court had just declared that women had a constitutional freedom to choose whether or not to have a baby. Erica decided to have an abortion. Because she knew Jeff and his family would never understand her decision, she decided they would never find out.

Issues and Answers

Abortion

In 1973, Erica Kane, then married to Dr. Jeff Martin, feared that her pregnancy would bring an untimely end to her thriving modeling career. Soon after the Roe v. Wade *decision was handed down by the Supreme Court, she underwent television's first legal abortion.*

At the clinic, a doctor explained he would need her husband's signed consent as well as her own. He wanted to speak to both of them together to describe the procedure and discuss the choice. He wanted them to have time to reevaluate their decision. In her most persuasive manner, Erica explained her husband was a very busy doctor and already knew all about the procedure. She lied when she told the doctor they had discussed the issue. She claimed they had come to the conclusion that having a baby so early in their marriage would not be a wise move for them or for the baby. She promised to have Jeff's signature on the consent forms when she came back. Returning with the "signed" form, Erica had the abortion without telling her husband. When she was supposed to have a follow-up appointment, Erica had more important things to do. She began to feel ill but chose to ignore it as long as she could. Jeff was sick with worry when she was hospitalized. He blamed himself for not anticipating this collapse from overwork.

Doctor Clader and Joe diagnosed Erica's condition as an infection resulting from an abortion. It was the first Joe knew that his daughter-in-law had been pregnant. He felt compelled to tell his son what had happened. Jeff was in shock over what Erica had done. When she recovered, he demanded an explanation. She insisted the abortion was done to preserve their marriage; Jeff exploded. He knew better. She had done it for herself and her precious career. Throughout the ordeal, Mary Kennicott stood by Jeff in silent support. She hated seeing what Erica was putting him through. It was incomprehensible to Mary that Erica could abort Jeff's baby.

Erica felt abandoned. Nobody was on her side, not even her mother. Mona had been heartsick when it looked as if Erica might die, but she was furious when she learned the truth. Still, Mona knew Erica was too much of a child to become a parent. If anyone could make Jeff listen to reason, it was Mona, and Charles encouraged her to speak to Jeff. Perhaps Mona could help him understand what had motivated Erica to have the abortion. Mona worried that Jeff might never forgive her daughter, but she followed Charles's advice. She told Jeff she didn't approve of what her daughter had done or the way she had gone about it, but hoped Jeff would consider Erica's age. He knew she was young when he married her, and she was likely to make foolish mistakes. Jeff eventually forgave Erica. He had married her, and he still loved her. As he reminded himself of that fact, he wondered how he was going to explain to Mary Kennicott that he was giving Erica a second chance.

There were no second chances for Nick and Kitty. As far as Nick was concerned, their marriage would last only until Kitty got well and not a minute longer. As she began making progress, Nick tried again to pick up with his ex-wife. But Anne Tyler Davis Martin was torn between Nick and her husband, the wonderfully kind and loving Paul.

Then came the best news of Nick Davis's life: his son Phillip was no longer missing and was coming home from Vietnam. Joe had never been so happy for his wife Ruth. Her tears of joy flowed with many prayers of thanks.

Phil's only thoughts upon returning home were of Tara. He had dreamed of coming back to Pine Valley, to his mom and Nick and all his

On Location

New York's Hudson River masqueraded as a Vietnamese tributary during the 1973 rescue of Phil Brent, who had been missing in action.

friends, but mostly he dreamed of coming back to his bride. Phil's memory of their candlelight "wedding" in the middle of a snowstorm was all that had sustained him in Vietnam.

Tara's world was rocked by Phillip's return. She wanted to run to him, but she couldn't. She was Chuck's wife, and to the world Chuck was little Phillip's father. He was a good father, too, and Tara had grown to love her husband. But in her heart, she knew Phil was the love of her life. While Chuck was delighted over Phil's miraculous return from the dead, he prayed that his happy home with Tara and their son wouldn't be destroyed. Ruth, meanwhile, tried to talk with Joe about the unresolved feelings between Phil and Tara. While Joe sympathized with Phil's unhappiness over Tara's marriage to Chuck, he felt Phil would have to move on just as Tara had. Feeling deep guilt, Ruth decided not to tell her son he was little Phillip's father.

Tara was rocked by Phillip's return. She wanted to run to him, but couldn't. She was Chuck's wife. And as far as the world knew, Chuck was little Phillip's father.

Phil was surprised by all the changes in Pine Valley while he was away. One change in particular was his father's marriage to Kitty Shea, which was nearing its end. When memories of her miscarriage returned, Kitty began to deal with the loss and agreed to a divorce. Without hesitation, Nick turned to Anne, who had since grown to care deeply for her husband Paul. She loved them both. When Anne agreed to meet Nick in New York City, he was certain he would be her choice. But Anne chose Paul, and Nick was brokenhearted.

Driving her back to Pine Valley in a blinding snowstorm, Nick was quiet, sullen, preoccupied with thoughts of losing Anne rather than the icy road they were on. The car skidded and they crashed. Nick suffered a scratch or two, but Anne was critically injured. Paul rushed to the hospital to be with his wife, as did her parents, Charles and Phoebe. While they all waited for Anne to rally, the others wondered what Anne was doing on the road with Nick Davis in the middle of a snowstorm. With their eyes coldly upon him, Nick admitted Anne had considered divorcing Paul to remarry him, and that she'd made her decision.

But Nick didn't tell them what her decision was. He knew they assumed Anne had chosen him. Nick saw the betrayed look on Paul's face. Nick knew exactly how Paul felt but he didn't care. After her recovery, Anne was confused by Paul's coldness. After all, he surely knew how much she loved him. Feeling rejected, Paul had stopped listening to Anne. Heartbroken, she slipped quietly out of the hospital and disappeared from Pine Valley.

No one was happier to leave Pine Valley than Erica, and her trips to New York City became more frequent. She found the city intoxicating. She loved modeling and the attention her boss Jason Maxwell showered on her. While she had never lacked for male attention, Jason was different. He was older and more sophisticated than the "boys" back home. Even her husband Jeff seemed so young in comparison. Erica enjoyed her time with Jason and kept him dangling, always promising him a little more than she intended to deliver. It amused him that she thought she could manipulate him.

Playing her game was fun, but Jason held all the cards. When he tired of her teasing, he'd hold back an assignment or two. When it was clear who was in control, Erica would wind up in his bed. In the meantime, if Erica was unavailable, he had other models to amuse him. Of course, there was always Margo Flax, the old flame who watched and waited for Jason to call on her again. The more Erica saw of Jason in New York City, the less interested she was in being Jeff Martin's wife. Although she flared with jealousy whenever Jeff mentioned his favorite nurse, Mary Kennicott, Erica finally convinced herself she and Jason were in love. After months of arguing with Erica over both Jason and her career, Jeff stopped caring.

He had grown even closer to Mary while the two of them administered to a little boy who had been hospitalized after his parents had abandoned him. Ten-year-old Tad Gardner charmed everyone at Pine Valley Hospital, and no one could believe Tad's father had just pushed him out of a car and driven off. As Tad cried out for his mother and his little sister Jenny, Mary and Jeff's hearts went out to him. While every attempt to find Tad's mother and sister failed, Joe and Ruth helped Jeff and Mary care for Tad.

Jeff barely remembered that he had a wife. When Erica finally told him she wanted a divorce, he didn't fight her. He had begun to wonder if he'd ever loved Erica. What he'd come to feel for Mary seemed so much more real. Erica had flattered and built up his male ego, but Mary had entered his soul, and he loved her deeply. When she told him she felt the same way, he welcomed the divorce.

Mona was terrified Erica was falling under the spell of the despicable Jason Maxwell. As always, her daughter turned a deaf ear to her warning. Even Margo Flax tried to warn Erica that Jason was only toying with her. Erica thought she knew better and pursued him in earnest. To make it more interesting, she led Jason to believe that her husband Jeff was very jealous of him.

Jason traveled to Pine valley to set things straight with Jeff. From his room at the Valley Inn, he phoned Jeff to come over and waited for him. Jeff wondered what business Jason Maxwell had with him. He'd already agreed to give Erica a divorce. When he arrived at Jason's door and knocked, there was no answer. He knocked again. Still no response. Testing the knob, Jeff found the door unlocked. He walked in to find Jason Maxwell on the floor, dead from a bullet wound. Jeff was arrested for murder.

> *Testing the knob, Jeff found the door unlocked and walked in. There was Jason Maxwell—on the floor, dead from a bullet wound. Jeff was arrested for murder.*

Phoebe had predicted Jeff Martin's fall from grace when he married Erica Kane. She remembered how Erica used to cling to Chuck. It was clear then she was only interested in their money, so she was grateful when Chuck had the good sense to marry Tara Martin. Charles had no patience with Phoebe's penchant for gossip. He knew the idea that Jeff murdered anyone was preposterous and wanted her to stop her speculation. Phoebe reminded him of the scandal Jeff had brought on the hospital. As chief of staff, Charles was not the least bit concerned with any problem Jeff's arrest might cause. He knew the hospital would weather this storm. He was certain Jeff would be exonerated. Besides, he worried more for Mona, who was consumed with anguish over her son-in-law and her daughter's effect on Jeff's life.

As Jeff's lawyer, Paul Martin wouldn't stand by and let his nephew get convicted for a crime he didn't commit. Paul had plenty of time to devote to the case. His marriage to Anne was over. He intended to ask her for a divorce as soon as she returned to Pine Valley. But clearing his nephew's name was the most important job he had now.

As Paul began looking into Jason Maxwell's affairs, one name kept resurfacing: Margo Flax. Paul decided he should get to know her. Margo was at loose ends. Her modeling career was long over, and her lover Jason was gone. As many times as Jason had hurt her by flaunting his affairs in her face, the finality of his death devastated Margo. But she recovered when she decided good-looking, honest and successful Paul Martin would be a change of pace from the Jason Maxwells of this world. So Margo packed her bags and moved to Pine Valley, renting a room from her dear friend Erica's mother, Mona Kane.

Paul found Margo refreshing. She knew he was vulnerable and on the rebound after the recent loss of Anne. She created reasons to see him, offering little tidbits about Jason that she thought might help his case. They began spending time together. Then Paul's wife Anne returned with her brother Linc. They had stayed long enough in Seattle, and both decided it was time to return home.

When Paul asked Anne for a divorce, Phoebe urged her daughter to fight for her marriage. This time Anne heeded Phoebe's advice. But Margo would not let Anne back into Paul's life so easily. She told Anne of Paul's condition shortly after Anne's departure. She had left him a hollow, broken man who made work his entire reason for being. But things were better now. For the first time in a long while Paul was happy. Margo wondered if Anne could take that away from him again. Margo cleverly used Anne's love for Paul to persuade her to give him a divorce. With the same tactics, Margo convinced Paul he loved her as much as she loved him.

Margo cleverly used Anne's love for Paul to persuade her to give him a divorce. Just as cleverly, Margo convinced Paul that he loved her as much as she loved him.

As Jeff's trial got underway, Paul was shocked to discover that the gun that had killed Jason Maxwell belonged to Margo. On that fateful night, she had followed Jason to Pine Valley, planning to shoot him for rejecting her in favor of Erica. Jason just laughed in her face and took away her gun. But Margo insisted she left the room without killing him. When Margo pleaded her innocence under oath, the question of who killed Jason remained unsettled.

Erica was devastated by Jason's death. The scandal of her husband's being accused of killing her lover in a jealous rage had ruined her modeling career. She was insulted when accused of sleeping with Jason, but in the end she would tell the truth to save Jeff—for a price. In exchange for testifying on her husband's behalf, she asked for a payoff from Jeff's father, Joe Martin. She didn't think it was too much to ask after the humiliation she would go through when people learned her husband wasn't jealous at all. Scared by what could happen to Jeff if Erica didn't testify, Joe gave in to her demand.

Mona, who stood by Jeff throughout the ordeal, was backing up her daughter's testimony on the witness stand when it all came back to her. She realized she had also been in Jason's hotel room the night of the murder. To help her remember more clearly, Mona agreed to an injection of sodium pentothal. With the help of the truth serum and with Charles at her side, she recalled the events of that terrible night. She'd gone to Jason's room to tell him to leave her daughter alone. He laughed and told her Margo had just been there with the same request, waving a gun around. He showed Margo's gun to Mona. According to Jason, no one would stop him from having Erica if he wanted her. He asked Mona if she wanted to give it a try. Then he pushed the gun into her hand. They wound up struggling and the gun went off. Mona broke down and admitted she had killed Jason Maxwell. Charles cradled her in his arms. The accidental shooting had been so traumatic she had blocked it from her memory. Jeff was cleared of all charges. Paul won his case.

The trial over, Margo went to extremes to make Paul fall in love with her, even resorting to having a face-lift without telling him. To explain her absence while recovering, she fabricated a trip to visit her grown daughter, Claudette Montgomery. This lie almost blew up in Margo's

In a medical "first," audiences witnessed Margo Flax's on-camera recovery from cosmetic surgery. *All My Children* allowed the viewers to witness the healing process of the actress Eileen Letchworth's real-life face-lift.

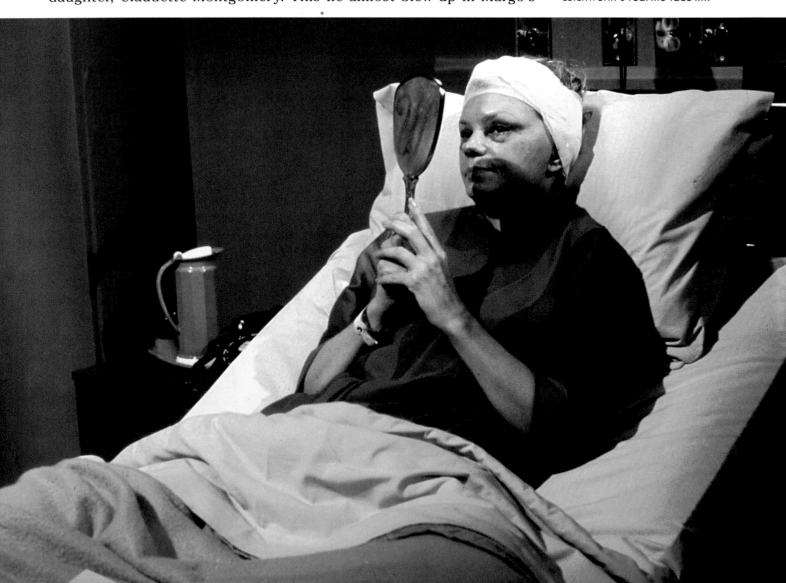

brand-new face when Claudette unexpectedly showed up in Pine Valley. But Margo's plan worked, and she finally persuaded Paul to marry her.

Jeff wasted no time divorcing Erica so he might marry his beloved Mary Kennicott. Blissfully, the newlyweds began talking about adopting young Tad Gardner, who had been living with Joe, Ruth and Kate. They all knew it would take time to work out the legalities. Aside from that, things seemed to be working out for everyone in Pine Valley.

Except for Erica. She was left with nothing. Everything she'd worked so hard to acquire was gone: her marriage, her career, her prospects for the future. Now it looked as if she'd be stuck for good in Pine Valley. Phoebe Tyler and her mother would surely hold over her head forever everything that had happened. Erica was alone. Everybody she knew had somebody to share their life with: Jeff had married his dear, sweet, plain Mary Kennicott; Margo, who Erica considered over-the-hill, had managed to catch the prominent Paul Martin; even Chuck and Tara were still together. Erica had never expected that marriage to last after Phil Brent returned to town. Erica began to think about Phil and got ready for her next acquisition.

With his mother married to Tara's father and strangely quiet about Tara's marriage to Chuck, Phil spent most of his time confiding in his father, Nick. Phil didn't understand how Tara could have married Chuck considering the way she and Phil felt about each other. Phil and Nick both seemed to be on the losing side of their respective love triangles. But Nick encouraged Phil not to give up on Tara as he had refused to give up on Anne. He now believed Anne had truly loved Paul and realized if he had never met Kitty Shea, things might have turned out differently. He and Kitty managed to remain friends as their marriage ended, and, though he doubted it could happen, Nick truly hoped Kitty would find happiness. She had begun seeing Anne's brother Linc, further exasperating Phoebe. Nick could well imagine Phoebe's fevered brain plotting how she could stop that coupling. Nick soon realized Phoebe was Phillip's nemesis as well. She would never allow her grandson's marriage to end in divorce and would do all she could to preserve it.

Phil took Nick's advice and did everything in his power to win Tara back. But she remained faithful to Chuck for the sake of their baby. She couldn't confide the truth to Phillip. The lie she and Chuck had told was going to stand. The old friendship the three of them had once shared was gone now. And Phil was odd man out. Even in Vietnam, he hadn't experienced the loneliness he was experiencing.

Erica and Phil had run into each other at the hospital where they were both visiting their mothers. Phil gazed at Erica and wondered if she wasn't even more beautiful than in high school. He remembered how jealous Tara had always been of her. Then he recalled how Erica had told him the news that had changed the course of his life. She tucked her arm in his and let him take her to dinner at McKay's. For the first time in ages, Phil was having a good time. It wouldn't be hard to fall for Erica. Nothing was holding him back.

When Erica began dating Phil Brent, he didn't take their relationship as seriously as she did. He was flattered by her attention, loved making love to her and chose to ignore all the warnings he received about her. Tara reminded him what Erica had done to her brother Jeff. Phil could see Tara was still jealous, and he was glad. Ruth warned her son Erica was not to be trusted. In truth, Ruth also felt a pang of guilt for the secret she continued about Phil's son. His father, Nick, had seen the worst side of Erica with her mother, Mona. To no avail, Nick tried to dissuade Phil from getting involved with Erica. Phil continued to see her, but even Erica realized he didn't love her and began to doubt he ever would. If anyone was in his heart, it was Tara. Erica couldn't believe she was still competing with such an unworthy opponent. She was tiring of second place.

By the time Erica decided to end her affair with Phil, she was pregnant. Again, she decided the sensible choice for her was abortion. Before she could act, Phil found out about the baby and was overjoyed. He persuaded Erica to marry him, and she let herself get caught up in his dream of a happy family life. The baby soon became real to her too. She loved it, and she loved Phil. With him, she saw a chance for real happiness. They were married, moved into their own house and started planning for the future.

While Phil's mother lamented that Erica was again a member of their family, her husband Joe was relieved that at least she was out of his son Jeff's life. Jeff had found happiness with Mary, and the newlyweds moved into a sunny apartment made even warmer by their love. They couldn't adopt Tad Gardner until the parents who had abandoned him were found. But Tad, who was staying with Ruth and Joe, visited often.

One afternoon Mary was home alone when Tad arrived for a visit. The boy didn't know that two thugs had broken in and were holding a terrified Mary at gun point. When Tad came to the door, she screamed at him to run, and Tad escaped. But the gunmen were trigger happy, and Mary was shot dead.

Mary's murder tore Jeff apart. He was haunted by happy memories of her and felt they'd been cheated of their time together. Jeff suffered tremendous grief and realized he could no longer stay in Pine Valley. Before moving away, he spoke with Joe and Ruth about Tad. They understood Jeff's need to leave the Valley and reassured him that Tad would be fine. They had come to regard Tad as a son and, if Jeff approved, wished to adopt him themselves. Jeff thanked them. Tad was thrilled and the Martins were overjoyed. They became his legal guardians until a formal adoption could be arranged. Not that any of them needed a piece of paper to feel he was part of their family.

It was little Phillip who worried the Martins when he suddenly became ill. They rallied to Tara's side when they learned her son desperately needed a blood transfusion. Tara and Chuck were frantic, because neither of their blood types matched little Phillip's. They soon learned that only Phil Brent's blood could save the child. Phil and Erica's happiness hadn't lasted long. Erica had a miscarriage and was so distraught over the loss that she suffered a nervous breakdown. Phil was forced to

Phil and Erica's happiness didn't last long. Erica suffered a miscarriage and was so distraught over the loss she had a nervous breakdown. Phil was forced to commit her to a mental hospital.

commit her to a mental hospital. While he and Mona prayed for Erica's recovery, the weeks became months.

During Erica's absence, Phil saved little Phillip's life with his blood, donating the instant he learned he matched the boy's blood type. He'd have done anything to help Tara's son. Chuck and Tara were grateful beyond words, but the blood match raised questions in Phil's mind. Things that never made sense to him began to clear up. Phil told Ruth he suspected she'd kept something from him since the day he returned from Vietnam. He demanded to know if little Phillip was his son.

Ruth confirmed what Phil already felt in his heart. The secret had to come out, and Ruth was relieved it had. She was wrong to have kept it from Phil for so long. Ruth felt justified when she explained her disclosure to Joe, but Ruth's interference angered him. He reminded her that Tara was still married to Chuck and the boy was their child. Joe felt it was wrong of Ruth to encourage Phil to pursue Tara. Kate watched uneasily as her son and daughter-in-law quarreled. She feared that a serious rift in their marriage could all too easily develop over what was best for their children.

Phil rushed to Tara. When he confronted her with his newfound knowledge, she tearfully told him the whole story of her pregnancy by him and subsequent marriage to Chuck. The confirmation gave Phil new hope. He asked Tara if she still loved him, and she broke down, confessing she had never stopped as they fell rapturously into each other's arms. Phil's mind was racing. He would divorce Erica, and Tara would leave Chuck. Then they could be together to raise their son. It was what they both wanted.

When Erica recovered and returned to Pine Valley, Phil asked her for a divorce. Seeing how much he wanted it, she emphatically refused. Before Tara could broach the subject of divorce with Chuck, he suffered a brief recurrence of his old kidney ailment. As little Phillip worried about his father, Tara rethought her plans. Tara couldn't help seeing how connected little Phillip was to Chuck. She felt the news that he wasn't little Phillip's real father would be too much for the boy. Phil was crestfallen. Ultimately, it wasn't Tara's decision to make. When Chuck discovered Tara still loved Phil and that he knew he was little Phil's father, Chuck sacrificed his own happiness for his friends' and granted Tara's request for a divorce.

Phoebe Tyler was heartsick that her grandson was giving up on his marriage. She reminded him of his son, Phillip, and the commitment Chuck had made with Tara for better or for worse. She turned to her own husband for support, but Charles was weary of Phoebe's incessant meddling. He wondered how she would feel if she knew how often the thought of divorce entered his own mind. As an image of Mona flickered into his thoughts, he left the room.

Phoebe's objections to her son Linc's involvement with Kitty Shea Davis were also ignored. To break them apart, she tried to promote a romance between Linc and Claudette Montgomery, the daughter of Paul Martin's new wife, Margo Flax. But Linc wasn't interested in Claudette. He'd fallen deeply in love with Kitty and nothing Phoebe could say or do—including falling into a dead faint in the middle of their wedding ceremony—could keep them from getting married.

Nick Davis was pleased that his ex-wife Kitty had found a man who could love and appreciate her as she deserved. Nick also remained friendly with his other ex-wife Anne, who was now Kitty's sister-in-law.

Anne gave Kitty a sales job in her fashion boutique. They became friends.

But when a stranger named Hal Short arrived in Pine Valley looking for Kitty, her stable world was shaken. Hal was Kitty's first husband. He thought Kitty had done very well for herself, marrying into money, and wanted her to help him set up an illegal drug operation in Pine Valley. Kitty wanted nothing to do with Hal's business. He showed her their final divorce papers, unsigned by him, and wondered how Kitty's brand new husband would feel about marrying a bigamist. Hal didn't think Linc would ever have to know as long as Kitty was agreeable to helping him. She had no choice. If she told Linc the truth, she'd lose him. She had to play Hal's game and allow him to traffic his drugs through shipments to The Boutique. He needed more help than the reluctant Kitty could provide for his operation, so Hal made Claudette Montgomery one of his associates. Anne's boutique was thriving, and it wasn't hard for Kitty, at Hal's insistence, to persuade Anne to hire Claudette, who didn't need money as much as she needed the drugs to feed her own addiction.

Paul's marriage to Margo turned out to be a loveless affair. He realized too late how he had been manipulated and that he never loved her. He had also never stopped loving Anne. As it turned out, Anne felt the same way. Slowly, they began to rekindle their romance from the embers of the past. Promising he would ask Margo for a divorce, Paul asked Anne to accompany him on a business trip. With Anne beside him, Paul had to force himself to keep his mind on the purpose of the trip.

Hal told Kitty he'd neglected to sign the final papers, so their divorce was never legal.

Margo felt her husband slipping away, and she didn't know how to hold on to him. She thought a baby might bind Paul to her, but she was too old to have one. Regardless, she liked the idea and began making plans. She found a baby broker, told him she needed a newborn and gave him the appropriate delivery date so it would appear she had been pregnant and given birth.

Paul returned from his trip with every intention of asking Margo for a divorce, but he never had the chance. She bombarded him with news of her pregnancy, how shocked she was that she could still conceive, what a miracle this would be for them. Paul was trapped. Anne couldn't believe the news but understood why Paul couldn't leave Margo. Anne had news of her own, which, under the circumstances, she wouldn't tell Paul. So she turned to her best friend, her ex-husband Nick Davis. When she told Nick she was pregnant with Paul's child, Nick came up with an idea: they could raise her child together. He'd always loved Anne and offered to marry her. Anne needed time to think about it and asked Nick not to tell Paul about the baby. Nick vowed to keep silent while he waited for her answer.

$\mathfrak{Anne}$ $\mathfrak{decided}$ she couldn't allow Nick to sacrifice his life for a baby that wasn't his. She looked so lost when she graciously declined his offer of marriage that Nick went to Paul and broke his vow of silence. He reminded Paul of their fight for Anne over the years and conceded defeat, urging Paul to go to her.

Paul wanted nothing more than to run to Anne, but he couldn't leave Margo. When he discovered her scheme to adopt a baby and pass it off as theirs he was outraged. Without hesitation, he walked out on her, demanding a divorce. Margo agreed to the split but made herself believe Paul would forgive and forget her little deception if his reason for a divorce no longer existed. Pretending to be Anne's friend, Margo offered to help her take inventory one evening at The Boutique. As soon as they began working, Margo made an excuse to leave Anne alone. Before she left, Margo turned the up thermostat, knowing the furnace in the basement was leaking carbon monoxide. Overcome be the fumes, Anne collapsed, but Paul arrived just in time and whisked her to the hospital. They both sighed with relief when they learned the poisonous gas hadn't harmed the baby she was carrying.

Her close call made Anne even more protective of her pregnancy—and more dependent on her sister-in-law Kitty Shea Tyler to run The Boutique. Kitty was overcome with guilt over her betrayal of both Anne and Linc. Linc still believed he was legally Kitty's husband, and Anne had no idea Hal Short was blackmailing Kitty into using the store as a front for his drug operation. Ultimately, Kitty couldn't live with herself and threw away a batch of cocaine-laced soap. She hoped to make Hal understand. But she never got the chance.

Claudette Montgomery, the troubled daughter of the troublesome Margo, was trying to keep an eye on Kitty, as Hal had instructed her to. But her eyes strayed to the cocaine. She burrowed into the "soap" Kitty had trashed and treated herself to an enormous high. It was a massive overdose, and Claudette was rushed to the hospital while the police rushed to The Boutique and arrested Kitty on drug charges. Claudette, who somehow survived, was arrested along with Hal Short, who was revealed to be Al Shea, Kitty's first and only legal husband. A scandalized Phoebe took action. Hoping no one would see her entering that sqaulid place, she paid a visit to the jail to see the woman who had bedeviled her son. Phoebe felt vindicated in her judgment of Kitty. She reminded Kitty of the shame she brought on Linc. Phoebe implored Kitty, for Linc's sake, to remove herself from his life. Phoebe had caught Kitty at her most vulnerable. It was easy to convince her she was no good for Lincoln Tyler.

Erica still refused to set Phil Brent free, long after Tara had gotten a quick Caribbean divorce from Phoebe's grandson, Chuck. But holding on to Phil just to spite Tara grew tiresome, even for Erica. Besides, Phil Brent had nothing and was going nowhere. Erica began thinking she deserved a higher caliber of man. Linc Tyler, one of the richest, most respected men in Pine Valley, had suddenly become available. Erica offered comfort to Linc after his separation from Kitty and became his most loyal friend.

Kitty was released from jail when Hal Short unexpectedly did the decent thing by clearing her of the drug charges and giving her a belated

Paul wanted to run to Anne, but he couldn't leave his pregnant wife Margo. Then he discovered Margo's scheme to adopt a baby and pass it off as theirs.

divorce. As he and Claudette Montgomery went to jail, Kitty realized she couldn't go back to the home she shared with Linc even though he wanted her back. Instead, she moved in with Erica and Mona.

While Erica was convincing Linc she was trying to persuade Kitty to reconcile with him, Erica told Kitty it was best for Linc if Kitty stayed away. And Erica kept Phoebe fully informed. For the first time in her life, Phoebe Tyler wasn't looking down her nose at Erica Kane. As Phoebe saw it, Erica was not only keeping Kitty away from Lincoln, she was keeping Tara and Phil apart, too. Every night, Phoebe prayed that Tara and her grandson Chuck would come to their senses and get back together. But Chuck's life no longer revolved around Tara. He had graduated from an accelerated program at medical school and was starting work at Pine Valley Hospital.

As Phoebe saw it, Erica was not only keeping Kitty from Lincoln, she was also keeping Tara and Phil apart.

At the hospital, Chuck met David Thornton, a physician's assistant. It was obvious to Chuck that David was a talented and skilled worker, and Chuck wondered why he had never become a doctor. David confided in his favorite nurse, Ruth Martin, that he did have a medical degree, but his experiences in Vietnam had so affected him that he'd stopped practicing. Ruth kept David's secret, flattered that such an attractive younger man had trusted her. She and her husband Joe had grown apart since his daughter Tara had chosen her son Phil over Chuck.

At the hospital, Chuck was able to work closely with his grandfather, Charles. He couldn't help noticing his grandfather had fallen in love with his secretary, Mona Kane. It was finally clear why Charles had moved out of the Tyler mansion and into his club. Knowing Phoebe wasn't easy to live with, Chuck gave his blessing to the relationship. Charles finally convinced Mona to see him socially.

Chuck's best friend was Dr. Frank Grant, who was experiencing upheaval in his own marriage. When Frank's wife Nancy accepted a job as a social worker in Chicago, Frank stayed behind. From his start as a poor black kid from the inner city, Frank was proud of the life he'd made for himself in Pine Valley. But with his wife living out of state, Frank was lonely, so he had plenty of time to spend with Chuck Tyler, showing him the ropes at Pine Valley Hospital.

Chuck's first patient was a young teenage girl, and he dedicated his time to helping her. She wouldn't talk about herself, but he learned she was Donna Beck, a high school dropout-turned-hooker. Before her pimp Tyrone tossed her out of his car, shattering her leg, she'd worked notorious Locust Street in nearby Center City. Chuck wondered how the life of someone so young could have gotten so tragically off track. He was determined to help Donna make a better life, so he encouraged her to get a high school equivalency diploma. To ensure her success, Chuck bought her books and hired a tutor. A skeptical Donna agreed to try.

Donna's tutor, Dan Kennicott, had come to Pine Valley University because his late sister Mary had told him how much she loved the town. When Dan looked up Mary's in-laws, Ruth, Joe and Kate Martin, they welcomed the friendly, good-looking, innocent young man into their home. Kate hoped Dan's presence would distract Joe and Ruth from their endless bickering about Phil and Tara.

Dan felt comfortable with the Martins and with Pine Valley, but he especially liked being around Phoebe Tyler's niece, Brooke English. In

Issues and Answers

Teenage prostitution

In this 1976 story, sixteen year old Donna Beck was lured into prostitution by a greedy Center City pimp, Tyrone. Through the love and support of her future husband, Dr. Chuck Tyler, Donna was able to get her life back on track.

her efforts to bring Chuck and Tara together, keep Linc and Kitty apart and mend her own damaged marriage, Phoebe really had no time for an extended visit from her brother Edward's daughter. But because Brooke was such a polite and well-behaved girl, Phoebe agreed to let her stay.

Brooke laughed when she told Benny Sago her aunt thought she was an angel. They both knew better. Benny had followed Brooke to Pine Valley. He was a ruffian with dirt under his fingernails, and Phoebe had instantly turned up her nose at him. She encouraged Brooke to date the clean-cut Dan Kennicott, and Brooke didn't mind. Dan was a pushover, and she could lead him around by the nose and use him to make Benny jealous.

Now that Brooke was matched up with Dan, Phoebe could concentrate on her own children. The happiness of Anne's remarriage to Paul was followed too quickly by tragedy. Everyone was shocked and frightened to learn that the mysterious flu Anne had contracted on their St. Croix honeymoon was toxoplasmosis, which could cause retardation or deformity in her unborn baby. When Anne rejected any thought of a therapeutic abortion, Phoebe felt helpless. All she could do for Anne was pray. But there was plenty she could do for Linc, and she directed her energies in his direction.

Despite the best efforts of Phoebe and Erica, Linc and Kitty had become closer than ever. Still refusing to divorce Phil, Erica realized there were other Tylers in Pine Valley besides Linc. She decided to remind Chuck of their long ago attraction. Meanwhile, Phoebe hatched a bizarre scheme to keep Linc from remarrying Kitty. Discovering that Kitty had never known her long-lost mother, Lucy Carpenter, Phoebe approached a destitute woman, improbably named Myrtle Lum, with a proposition that lifted the alcoholic haze from Myrtle's eyes. Myrtle had no use for a snob like Phoebe Tyler, but she had plenty of use for Phoebe's money. She listened as Phoebe told her of her son's involvement with a most unsuitable young woman and Phoebe's plan for an elaborate and phony reunion. Kitty's mother had left Pine Valley years ago. Phoebe thought it would work out nicely if Lucy Carpenter, who lived far from Pine Valley, contacted Kitty and convinced her to come and live with her. Myrtle realized Phoebe's plan was to break up Linc and Kitty and called her on it.

It was mutual dislike from the start, but Myrtle needed money and agreed to Phoebe's scheme. Setting her up as "Mrs. Lucy Carpenter" in Minneapolis, Phoebe warned Myrtle to stay away from Pine Valley or risk being exposed as a fraud. When Kitty heard from "her mother," she and Linc immediately went to Minneapolis, where Linc watched Kitty and "Mrs. Carpenter" develop a warm relationship. In time, Myrtle actually came to care for Kitty like a daughter.

Hating the deception, Myrtle phoned Phoebe to call off the ruse. That was the last thing Phoebe needed. Charles was flaunting that Mona Kane woman in her face and had just demanded a divorce. Phoebe assured him he would never have one. Adding to her misery was Phoebe's untamed niece. Brooke had proven to be so wild that Phoebe wanted to ship her home. When Myrtle Lum called to back out of their scheme, Phoebe held her to the agreement. Unfortunately, Benny Sago overheard the phone call. He used the information to blackmail Phoebe into letting Brooke stay on in Pine Valley.

When Kitty begged her "mother" to come to Pine Valley, Myrtle feigned a heart condition and had a friend of hers, Nigel Fargate, pose as a doctor and forbid any travel. Kitty decided to stay in Minneapolis permanently, prompting her friend Mona Kane to pay her a visit. When Myrtle opened the door to Mona and introduced herself as Lucy Carpenter, the deception was revealed. Mona had known the real Lucy Carpenter years ago, so Myrtle was caught. So was Phoebe when Myrtle related the entire scam to a furious Mona. Promising to let Kitty down easy, Myrtle begged Mona not to tell her the truth. Mona agreed and left to confront Phoebe.

Phoebe begged Mona not to tell anyone, that she would do anything to secure Mona's silence. Mona agreed to keep quiet on one condition: Phoebe must grant Charles a divorce. Mona shocked even herself when she resorted to blackmail, but she loved Charles and longed for him to be free of Phoebe. Phoebe agreed to the terms but was secretly determined that their fight over Charles was far from over.

On top of everything else, Phoebe had a new concern. Chuck was spending too much time with that teenage tramp, Donna Beck, and not enough with his son. Tara was also concerned. Little Phillip had developed an asthmatic condition the doctors believed was a psychological reaction to her divorce from Chuck and her plans to marry "Uncle" Phil. Feeling guilty, Tara took little Phillip to a clinic in Arizona for treatment. Phil was frustrated by all the obstacles he and Tara faced. He quit his job at his father's restaurant and joined the Pine Valley police force.

Brooke English and boyfriend Dan Kennicott enjoyed an amorous dip in Aunt Phoebe's swimming pool.

With his son out of town, Chuck devoted even more time to Donna. When her former pimp, Tyrone, found her, she was studying. He threw her books out the window, and Chuck threw him out of the hospital, thereby making a dangerous enemy. Tyrone's hired goons beat Chuck up. Even then, Chuck wouldn't turn his back on Donna. In another violent encounter in the hospital parking lot, Tyrone himself lunged at Chuck with a knife. But karate black-belt Frank Grant saved his friend, and Tyrone was hauled off to jail. Chuck became Donna's legal guardian, and they grew even closer.

As soon as Tara heard about Chuck's run-in with Tyrone, she rushed back from Arizona with her son and suggested that she and Chuck should get back together. Chuck gently told her no, encouraging her to marry her one true love, Phil Brent. Phil, meanwhile, was still stuck in his loveless marriage to Erica.

Nick Davis came up with an idea that would get Erica out of the picture. He offered "The Little Princess," as he liked to call her, a job as a hostess at The Chateau. Erica was thrilled at the prospect, until Nick made it clear that getting the job hinged on one stipulation: She had to grant Phil a divorce.

Erica didn't like the terms of this arrangement, but her need to be in the spotlight won. She took Nick up on his offer, finally freeing Phil to marry Tara. Ruth was thrilled for her son, but supporting Phil had damaged her own marriage, and Ruth had left Joe. When David Thornton told Ruth he loved her and could only become a doctor again with her at his side, Ruth decided she would seek a divorce. But the night Joe's appendix burst brought her back to earth, to the realization that she loved Joe more than she ever would anyone else. Joe almost died. David was the only staffer on duty capable of performing an emergency appendectomy, so he saved Joe's life. Ruth realized what she had almost thrown away and quickly reconciled with Joe.

Together they watched their children, Phil and Tara, say their vows and at long last become man and wife. Little Phillip resented "Uncle" Phil and stayed away from their wedding. As much as Phil wanted to announce that he was the boy's real father, he agreed with Tara not to tell him. Neither wanted to risk any more of little Phillip's asthma attacks.

With Phil out of her life, Erica began working for Nick at The Chateau. Their life-long feud continued. Whenever he called her on her selfishness, she pouted. Even so, she felt Nick was looking out for her, and that felt almost like having a father. But Nick wasn't Erica's father, and she wasn't his daughter. They were a man and a woman, a circumstance they couldn't ignore for long.

Eventually, Erica lured Nick into her bed, and they began an affair they kept a closely guarded secret. After all, he was not only old enough to be her father, he was her mother Mona's best friend.

The first time they kissed surprised them both. But Erica liked it, creating more opportunities to seduce Nick. Eventually, she lured him into her bed, and they began an affair they kept a closely guarded secret. After all, he was not only old enough to be her father, he was her mother Mona's best friend.

Mona had her own secret. She couldn't stand herself after blackmailing Phoebe into granting Charles a divorce, so she confessed the entire episode to Charles and waited for him to scold her. He couldn't believe her capable of such a thing. Mona cringed before his rage until he declared an even greater admiration for her. He only wished he could have been there to see Phoebe's face when Mona told her.

Charles, like Mona, chose not to tell his son Linc or Kitty of Phoebe's plan to break them apart. Her scheme had ended when Myrtle asked her friend "Doctor" Nigel to announce "Lucy's" death from a heart attack. Myrtle and Nigel left for Hollywood while Kitty returned to Pine Valley with Linc.

As much as he wanted to be free from Phoebe, Charles couldn't press the issue. He had to help her and their daughter Anne adjust to the terrible reality that Anne and Paul's newborn daughter, Elizabeth, was severely retarded. When they were advised to institutionalize their little Beth, Paul felt it was for the best. Anne adamantly opposed the idea. She insisted Beth needed a mother's love, something a cold institution couldn't provide. Paul reluctantly agreed to keep Beth at home.

Mental Retardation

During her 1976 pregnancy, Anne Tyler Martin developed toxoplasmosis, an illness often transmitted through raw meat. The tragic factor was that a pregnant woman suffering from the illness has a 50 percent chance of giving birth to a retarded or malformed child. Despite Paul's protests, Anne decided not to have a therapeutic abortion and gave birth to a retarded daughter, Beth. Their marriage suffered when Anne committed herself totally to the nurturing of the child, whose death the following year was attributed to Sudden Infant Death Syndrome.

Paul and Anne Martin struggle with the future of their retarded daughter, Beth.

December 1976

Anne:
You want to put our daughter in an institution!

Paul:
Darling, please, think of the child.

Anne:
The child, the child! You talk about her like she's some inanimate object. She's our daughter, she's a living breathing part of us.

Paul:
Look, do you think that this is what I want, I mean my God, don't you have any idea how painful this is to me, too? She needs proper care in a proper facility.

Anne:
She needs a mother's love. An institution can't give her that. You want her out of here, don't you? You're sorry I didn't have the abortion in the first place, aren't you?

Paul:
Look, you know that's not true.

Anne:
Are you sure?

Anne Tyler Martin was so obsessive in her devotion to Beth that she saw every smile of the baby's as a positive sign. But Paul saw little reason to hope, and neither did Beth's doctor, Christina Karras. She told Anne that Beth would never be a normal child. Anne refused to face reality and demanded Doctor Karras be taken off the list of Beth's physicians.

Anne's mother, Phoebe, worried as Anne shut herself and Beth off from the world. Phoebe understood why Anne had to do everything she could for her child. She herself had gone to extraordinary lengths to save her son Linc from his unfortunate fascination with Kitty Shea. If only Myrtle Lum hadn't betrayed their scheme by "dying," Linc and Kitty would have been history. Instead, they grew closer than ever.

Nothing was going right for Phoebe. Her husband Charles still wanted a divorce. Her grandson Chuck had long since separated from Tara, who had remarried that Brent boy. Phoebe couldn't bear the thought of her great-grandson being taken from Chuck. At least she had both Chuck and little Phillip staying at home with her while Tara honeymooned with her new husband. But Phoebe was slipping. After consoling herself with one too many sips of sherry, she went driving with little Phillip one afternoon. In her tipsy state, she had a serious accident. Phoebe wasn't hurt, but little Phillip's brief hospital stay caused Phil and Tara to cut short their honeymoon. Chuck wondered if he could ever trust his grandmother with his son again and was glad when the police revoked her license.

After refusing to attend Linc and Kitty's wedding, Phoebe nursed her misery with a bottle of vodka. Her estranged husband Charles, escorting Mona Kane, witnessed his son and Kitty exchanging their vows. Before leaving on their honeymoon, Kitty asked Linc to make peace with his mother. The newlyweds left the church to visit Phoebe, who was none too pleased to see them. Kitty wanted Phoebe's blessing, as she'd never have one from her own mother. When Linc explained this to his mother, a drunken Phoebe spilled the whole sordid mess. She tripped over her words as she told of Myrtle Lum posing as Lucy Carpenter only to get her hands on Linc's money.

In revealing the scheme to Kitty and Linc, Phoebe conveniently forgot to mention who'd created it. Mona later told them about Phoebe's part in it and that Myrtle truly loved Kitty like a daughter. She couldn't bear to hurt Kitty and had faked her death to end the charade. Linc angrily confronted Phoebe and vowed never to forgive her. Phoebe swore she'd never meddle again.

With her secret revealed, a humiliated Phoebe was no longer susceptible to blackmail—she told Mona that she'd never divorce Charles. By hiring Benny Sago as her lowly chauffeur, Phoebe stuck the interloper in his place, a role he accepted resolutely.

Meanwhile, Linc and Kitty tracked Myrtle Lum to Hollywood, where Nigel Fargate had deserted her. During their trip back to Pine Valley, Kitty began experiencing dizzy spells and bouts of temporary blindness. The doctors deemed her spells psychosomatic. Kitty wasn't concerned. She had her "mother" back and was happy with Linc.

With one father too many in his life, little Phillip Tyler was anything but happy. He told his mother Tara that he wanted to live with Chuck instead of her and his new stepfather, Phil Brent. When he didn't get his way, little Phillip blamed "Uncle" Phil. Things got worse when Phil found the boy playing with the revolver he carried as a cop and tried to spank him. Little Phillip screamed that only his father had the right to spank him. Phil bit his tongue to keep from telling the boy the truth.

When Tara became pregnant, she asked Phil to quit his dangerous job, but he refused. One afternoon, Tara received the call she always feared would come. Phil had been shot. She rushed to the hospital, where Phil was in critical condition. He told her how much he loved her and their family. When Chuck paid him a visit, Phil asked him to remarry Tara in case he didn't make it. Fortunately, Phil survived, because Chuck was no longer interested in Tara. Donna Beck filled his thoughts.

Donna had begun to dream about a life with Chuck. She was still insecure about herself, because, in her own eyes, she was a nothing, only an ex-hooker. Surely Chuck could never feel about her the way he did about his smart and upstanding ex-wife, Tara. While Donna worried about Tara, Erica Kane decided Chuck was the prize she really wanted. In Erica's mind, her first order of business was to get Donna out of Chuck's life.

To celebrate Donna's eighteenth birthday, Chuck took her to The Chateau. Erica was hostess that night, and a diner approached her regarding Donna, implying he knew her well. Erica gleaned that he must have been a client of Donna's in her hooker days. She couldn't let him leave without saying hello to his old friend. Erica escorted the man to Chuck and Donna's table. Recognizing her former "john," Donna bolted from the restaurant. Aching for Donna over this humiliation, Chuck realized for the first time he loved her.

Pleased with herself for shaming Donna, Erica went too far when she accidentally slipped and told Chuck's cousin Brooke that Phil Brent was little Phillip's real father. A furious Chuck ordered Erica to keep her mouth shut about his son, especially around his grandmother Phoebe. He also demanded she stay out of his life. Erica got the message and redirected her amorous attention to her first husband, Dr. Jeff Martin.

Jeff had just returned to Pine Valley after grieving over his beloved wife Mary's death. Quickly reestablishing himself at the hospital, he caught up with old friends. He was sorry to hear Frank and Nancy Grant had decided to divorce when their geographic separation strained their marriage. Nancy had begun dating a white man, Carl Blair. Jeff thought he was nice enough but was surprised by Nancy's choice. For his part, Frank was seeing Caroline Murray, a woman who was helping Chuck take care of Donna. When Frank told Jeff about Donna and Chuck, Jeff realized a lot had changed in his two years away from Pine Valley.

Friends Dr. Chuck Tyler and Dr. Frank Grant commiserated with each other over their turbulent love lives.

But one thing remained constant: Erica Kane. The same velvety voice, the same beautiful smile and the same old routine. Jeff wasn't interested in a second go-around with Erica, no matter how attractive she made the prospect appear. When Erica met Mark Dalton, a new music teacher at Pine Valley University, she forgot all about Jeff. Mark and Erica were instantly drawn to each other, and neither could explain why.

Jeff, in the meantime, was attracted to a colleague, Dr. Christina Karras, who was receiving mysterious, hateful, threatening notes. Jeff wanted to help Christina and hastened to her rescue. But it was David Thornton who discovered that Christina was tormenting herself, that she had written the death threats in a trance. Apparently her psychosis stemmed from her belief that she'd killed her own father. By finding proof of her innocence, David cured her. With her mind and conscience at ease, Christina would have married David instantly. In another twist, David's ex-wife Edna came to town with the explosive news that they were still legally married and that they had a seven-year-old daughter named Dottie. David asked Christina to wait until he could resolve the mess in his life. Jeff Martin told him to let Christina go. David resented the advice—and Jeff, who declared himself a rival for Christina.

Christina tried to lose herself in her work. She told Paul Martin about a support group for parents of handicapped children that might help Paul's wife. Anne was consumed with their retarded daughter's care. After weeks of trying, Paul persuaded Anne to attend a meeting, assuring her he'd take good care of little Beth. An uneasy Anne left Beth in his care for one evening. When she returned, Anne rushed past Paul to check on her child. When he heard Anne scream, he dashed in after her. Beth had died in her sleep, a victim of SIDS, Sudden Infant Death Syndrome. Paul tried to comfort Anne, but she was inconsolable.

When Anne began talking to Beth's picture and rocking it in Beth's crib, Paul was beside himself. Paul pleaded for Anne to face the fact Beth was gone. But deep depression led Anne to a suicide attempt with sleeping pills, soon followed by a total breakdown. Paul wanted to help his grieving wife but all he could do was sign the papers committing her to Oak Haven. Phoebe stood witness and cried.

Seeing how upset his mother was about his sister dissipated Linc's anger toward Phoebe. Besides, he had more important problems to deal with. Dr. Joe Martin had finally diagnosed his wife Kitty's bouts of blindness and dizziness as being caused by an inoperable and terminal brain tumor. Kitty had only a short time to live. During her final days, Linc and Myrtle Lum surrounded her with love. Kitty thanked Linc for being her husband, her lover and her dearest friend. She died in his arms. Shortly after Kitty's death, Myrtle said goodbye to Linc. Nigel Fargate had asked her to marry him and move back to Minneapolis.

Anne Tyler had given The Boutique to Kitty, and Myrtle sold it before she left town. She thought the new owner was someone both Anne and Kitty would have liked. Ellen Shepherd was recently divorced. She had come to Pine Valley with her daughter Devon, and they moved in with Ellen's father Harlan Tucker, a great old friend and next-door neighbor of Kate Martin. Ellen arranged for Devon to take piano lessons from Mark Dalton, who taught at the university that Devon was about to enter.

Mark was fascinated by Erica Kane and had no idea she'd also been seeing Nick Davis, her boss at The Chateau. It pleased Erica that Nick was jealous of Mark. She liked Mark, but not enough to go to bed with him. She told her mother of her feelings and Mona was desperate to separate them.

When Mona heard Mark was Maureen Dalton's son, she realized he was also Erica's half-brother. Maureen had been Eric Kane's secretary and lover early in Mona's marriage to him. She tried to tell her daughter, but Erica, loyal to the memory of her father, refused to hear a word that would sully her idealistic image of him. Mona asked Nick to reason with her, but when he tried to tell her that her father was less than honorable, Erica slapped him. Erica finally accepted the truth and was furious. Mark was a symbol of her father's infidelity and became her enemy. When she froze him out of her life, Mark didn't understand why at first. When Erica told him he was her own father's bastard son, her half-brother, Mark was shocked.

To recover from the bitter news, he devoted himself to his work. He especially enjoyed teaching piano to Devon Shepherd, whose mother Ellen always made Mark feel good. Ellen liked him, too, and it wasn't long before they fell in love. But Ellen was worried what people might think, because Mark was ten years younger than she. Her father Harlan told her to forget about other people. She deserved happiness as much as anyone.

Much of Ellen's daughter Devon's happiness had to do with Dan Kennicott, who lived next door with the Martins. As a favor to Harlan, Kate Martin had asked Dan to show Devon around the university. Dan complied, confiding in Devon about his relationship with Brooke English. He was crazy about her, but feared she was two-timing him with Benny Sago. Dan failed to notice Devon's growing crush on him.

Brooke teased Dan endlessly. She was sure he was a virgin, and deflowering him became her personal challenge. The moment she succeeded, she lost interest in him. She was on to a new challenge in one-time pro-football star Tom Cudahy. But with him Brooke English ran into competition: Erica Kane.

After one too many fights with Nick, Erica quit working for him at the restaurant. She wheedled her way into the hostess job at The Goalpost, the new restaurant Tom Cudahy had just opened. Tom became a hero in Pine Valley after rescuing young Phillip Tyler from kidnappers who had grabbed him leaving Tara and Phil's home. Nick hired Claudette Montgomery, newly paroled on her old drug conviction, to replace Erica. If Nick was jealous of Erica's interest in Tom, Erica was just as jealous of Nick's in Claudette.

Erica planted marijuana on Claudette to get her in trouble, but Nick thwarted her plan by replanting the grass on Erica. Erica and Nick didn't know whether they loved

Gone, But Not Forgotten
Kitty Shea Davis Tyler

Kitty Shea Davis Tyler found her knight in shining armor in handsome attorney Lincoln Tyler. Sadly, their time together was brief, because Kitty contracted a terminal illness in the summer of 1977. When she knew that the end was near, Kitty made an impassioned plea that she not be taken to the hospital to have her life prolonged by artificial means. In late summer, Kitty passed away peacefully in her sleep, with Linc by her side.

or hated each other, but they certainly enjoyed whatever it was. Finally, Erica decided she wanted to marry Nick and lured him back to her bed.

That night Mona Kane discovered their little secret. Mona was in shock. Nick was certain he'd been had, figuring Erica had seduced him just so Mona could catch them. He thought Erica was using Mona to pressure Nick into marrying Erica. He refused to be manipulated by Erica or any woman and left her vowing that he wouldn't be back. Erica didn't believe him, nor would she lose much sleep over his departure. Back at The Goalpost, Erica proceeded to vamp Tom Cudahy, who liked things the way they were. But Erica decided he was exactly the man she had been waiting for.

Brooke teased Dan endlessly. She was sure he was a virgin, and deflowering him became her personal challenge.

Little Phillip still wanted to move in with his father Chuck, and his mother finally gave in. Although Donna Beck enjoyed spoiling Chuck's son, her insecurities drove her to leave Pine Valley. She went back to her parents in Chicago, but they threw her out when she confessed she'd been a hooker. Stinging from their rejection, Donna felt the only place she belonged was back on Locust Street. On her way there, Donna was arrested for hitchhiking. Her old friend Estelle got her new pimp, Billy Clyde Tuggle, to bail Donna out. With a glint in his eye, Billy Clyde figured his stable of girls had just expanded by one.

Back on Locust Street, Donna refused to turn tricks for Billy Clyde. After he plied Donna with mind-altering drugs, Estelle let Chuck know where Donna was. Chuck and his grandmother's chauffeur, Benny Sago, stormed to Donna's rescue. After this incident, Benny became Estelle's friend, and Donna became Chuck's fiancée. Donna's dreams were coming true and so was Phoebe's worst nightmare.

Chuck's grandmother pressed a thick wad of bills into Donna's hand, urging her to take the money and leave Pine Valley for good. Phoebe warned Donna that if she married Chuck, he would lose his son. No court in the country would allow a common prostitute to raise a child. Because Donna loved Chuck, she threw the money in Phoebe's face. Phoebe went to Tara and harangued her mercilessly. She wanted Tara to take little Phillip back home and get him away from that common street walker. Phoebe upset Tara so much she suffered a miscarriage. If Phoebe felt bad about Tara's loss, it wasn't close to what she felt when she heard that Donna and Chuck had eloped. Chuck and Donna moved into a small apartment. When Tara was told that little Phillip was living with them, she suffered a setback. Phil held his wife's hand lovingly, but dropped it when she opened her eyes and, in her delirium, called him "Chuck." Phil was irate. He wanted to erase Chuck from his wife's thoughts and get him out of their lives. Phil arranged to have little Phillip move back with Tara and him.

Donna felt responsible for Chuck's losing his son, but Chuck reassured her. It wasn't long before Donna thought she was pregnant. She had all the symptoms, but Doctor Clader told Chuck that Donna was experiencing a "hysterical pregnancy." Her mind was playing tricks on her body. After an ecstatic Donna told Estelle she was pregnant, a confused Estelle revealed to Billy Clyde a secret. Years ago, Donna's pimp Tyrone had secretly had her sterilized so she wouldn't get pregnant turning tricks. Billy Clyde absorbed that information and immediately saw dollar signs. Chuck threw the pimp out of Phoebe's mansion before Billy Clyde could sell her the information.

Phoebe had her own trouble. Charles promised to divorced her if she didn't divorce him. In response, she threatened to brand Charles an adulterer and let the whole town know Mona Kane's true colors. When Charles refused to back down, an innocent Mona—knowing Phoebe meant business—threatened to leave town forever so Charles would give in to his wife's demand. Even so, Charles didn't move back home. Phoebe, having alienated most of her family, began drinking and driving again. When Phil Brent arrested her for it, she was sentenced to three weekends in the Pine Valley jail.

The first weekend was horrid. Benny Sago, the chauffeur she'd come to rely on, smuggled in a flask of vodka to get her through it. But before she could complete her jail sentence, Phoebe tumbled down the stairs at the Tyler mansion. She claimed the fall left her paralyzed. She turned to her lawyer son-in-law Paul Martin and pleaded that she not be sent back to jail.

Since institutionalizing his wife Anne, Paul had buried himself in work, and among other cases he handled Frank Grant's divorce from Nancy. Still in love with Frank, Nancy had moved back to Pine Valley. They shared one night of passion, but Frank went ahead with the divorce. Nancy learned she was pregnant with Frank's child the day he married Caroline. Unhappily, Nancy considered marrying Carl Blair.

Paul also tried to help his brother Joe and sister-in-law Ruth finalize their adoption of Tad Gardner. The good news was that Tad's father, Ray Gardner, had finally been located. Joe flew to Texarkana, where Ray told him Tad's mother was dead. Ray had no qualms about Ruth and Joe's adopting Tad, as long as they forked over $10,000. Joe refused to give in to extortion from this clearly dangerous character, leaving without telling Ray where he lived. Upon Joe's return, Ruth scolded him, feeling Tad was worth the money. She phoned Ray to renegotiate the deal and let slip that they lived in Pine Valley. Ray caught the next bus. Trouble was coming to town.

After an ecstatic Donna told Estelle she was pregnant, a confused Estelle told Billy Clyde that, years ago, Donna's pimp Tyrone had secretly had her sterilized so she wouldn't get pregnant turning tricks.

From the day Ray Gardner arrived in Pine Valley and darkened Ruth Martin's door, he made it clear he'd come to town solely to sell his son Tad. Ruth had raised Tad for years and was willing to negotiate. She quarreled with Joe over Ray's increased demand of $15,000. Ruth was willing to pay whatever Ray asked.

Tad and little Phillip were alone in the Martin home one day when Ray broke in. Ray opened his arms to Tad with the news he was his father. Ray laughed at Tad's panic when the boy saw this man who looked more demonic than fatherly. Ray left, satisfied to leave the boys shaken and scared. As soon as Ruth heard about Ray's intrusion, she read him the riot act, warning him he would never see Tad again nor would he ever get a dime out of the Martins.

Ray saw that Ruth meant business. Well so did he. No one ever spoke to him like that and got away with it. Ray began watching and waiting.

Ray saw that Ruth meant business. So did he. No one spoke to him like that and got away with it. He began watching and waiting. One evening, Ruth crossed a deserted parking lot and as she unlocked her car, Ray jumped her, robbing and raping her, then knocking her out. By the time her husband reached the scene, Ray had escaped.

Ruth lay in a coma for days before awakening to a clear memory of the attack. Her main concern was that Tad not learn what a monster his father was. She wondered if she should press charges while her police officer son, Phil Brent, vowed to apprehend the man who had raped and beaten his mother.

Ray hid out in David Thornton's cabin on the outskirts of Pine Valley. David's wife Edna and their daughter Dottie lived there while David was trying to convince the stubborn Edna to divorce him so he could marry Christina Karras. Ray persuaded a trusting Edna she needed protection in the deserted cabin, so she let him sleep on the couch. During his attack on Ruth, Ray had stolen a diamond pendant from her and set about trying to pawn it.

Down on Locust Street, Billy Clyde Tuggle considered himself much more than a mere pimp. When Ray Gardner showed up with that sparkler, Billy Clyde became an instant fence. One of Billy Clyde's hookers, Estelle La Tour, recognized Ray and called a cop. When Phil Brent showed up, Ray knocked him out and tried to escape, but Billy Clyde pulled a knife and stabbed Ray. Estelle was stunned to see the man who prostituted and beat her act so heroically.

Regardless, Estelle was far more interested in Benny Sago than Billy Clyde. They'd been seeing a lot of each other, and she hoped Benny would propose. But Billy Clyde popped the question first. He promised Estelle she'd never have to turn another trick if she became his wife. Billy Clyde sounded sincere in his declaration of love, but Estelle stalled him until Benny could propose. Billy Clyde told Benny Estelle had accepted his proposal, and before Benny could talk to her, a motorcycle accident put him in the hospital. He begged Phoebe to plead his case with Estelle, but Phoebe never contacted her. Phoebe considered a hooker just as unsuitable for her chauffeur as for her grandson. Eventually, Estelle became Mrs. Billy Clyde Tuggle.

Phoebe continued to fake her paralysis, which not only kept her out of jail, but brought her some long overdue attention from Charles. Wheeling about her estate, Phoebe rolled into the pool house to find her niece Brooke English and Dan Kennicott alone and naked. Aunt Phoebe decided it was time Brooke went home to her parents. But before she could ship Brooke out, Phoebe was caught out of her wheelchair. Brooke blackmailed dear Aunt Phoebe into an open-ended invitation to stay. Brooke had taken up with Dan Kennicott again after she realized Tom Cudahy was more interested in Erica Kane. Besides, Dan had been dating that insipid Devon Shepherd, and Brooke couldn't bear losing out to her. She told the virginal Devon that Dan was interested in Devon only for sex. Dan convinced Devon that he prized her purity, but secretly began seeing Brooke for sex.

While Devon happily dated Dan, her mother Ellen worried that her young lover, Mark Dalton, was becoming too serious. Ellen told herself she'd be better off with a man her own age, someone like Paul Martin. But with his wife Anne still institutionalized, Paul wasn't free to be anything more than a friend to Ellen.

Paul stood by his sister-in-law Ruth as she made the agonizing decision to prosecute Ray Gardner for raping her and filed a deposition against him. Ruth took Tad out of town while Joe testified at the trial. Only after Ray was convicted and sentenced to 25 years in prison did Ruth bring home an unaware Tad.

At last, Ruth and Joe were free to adopt Tad legally. Tad Gardner became Tad Martin. Ruth and Joe's grandson, little Phillip Tyler, also changed his name. He asked his teachers and friends to stop calling him "Phillip" and start calling him "Charlie" after his father, Chuck Tyler. When Phillip Brent learned his wife Tara and her ex-husband Chuck had approved the name change, Phil was furious. Angry and jealous that Tara consulted Chuck over every detail of his son's life, Phil felt his marriage crumbling.

Chuck had his own marital troubles. He had to tell his happily expectant wife Donna that her pregnancy was only her imagination. She went into therapy, remembered that her former pimp Tyrone had had her tubes tied and realized what it meant. The old feelings of worthlessness surfaced, and for his own good she left Chuck. Convinced Donna would never return, he redirected his interest to Tara and their son.

Billy Clyde Tuggle learned Donna's whereabouts from Estelle. He was already counting the greenbacks he would get from Phoebe Tyler to keep him from telling her precious grandson where his bride was keeping herself. But Estelle was one step ahead of Billy. She told Chuck where Donna was, and they persuaded Donna to return to have an operation that could reverse her sterilization. Chuck might have been completely happy if he could only stop thinking about Tara.

Tara's brother, Dr. Jeff Martin, felt no guilt in pursuing Dr. Christina Karras, even if she was engaged to Dr. David Thornton. But David was still married to the clinging Edna. David soon realized Christina was responding to Jeff, so he decided to get rid of Edna. In increasing doses, he slipped digitalis he'd stolen from the hospital into Edna's food. She went to Dr. Jeff Martin for treatment of her debilitating condition. Jeff diagnosed heart trouble just as Christina was returning her engagement ring to David.

David had to act fast. Edna's fatal heart attack had to happen now. After he spiked her wine with a lethal dose, David and Edna left the room for a moment. While they were gone, their daughter Dottie innocently switched the two glasses. As soon as David and Edna returned,

Little Phillip asked his teachers and friends to stop calling him "Phillip" and start calling him "Charlie" after his father, Chuck Tyler. When Phillip Brent learned his wife Tara and her ex-husband Chuck had approved the name change, Phil was furious.

they drained their glasses, and Edna left with Dottie. Almost immediately, David began to feel ill. Realizing he had drunk the fatal glass, he frantically called Christina to help him. But she arrived too late. David died. With her history of mental trouble, Christina became the prime suspect in his murder.

The widowed Edna mourned David no longer than a minute or two. Feeling healthier each day, she fell in love with and was in hot pursuit of Benny Sago, who was still pining for Estelle Tuggle. When Jeff saw Edna's heart symptoms had suddenly disappeared, he realized she had been poisoned. Jeff found proof that David had orchestrated the plot that caused his own death. Christina was released and quickly married Jeff. But being married to Christina proved almost as demanding and difficult as it had with Erica.

The widowed Edna mourned David no longer than a minute or two. Feeling healthier each day, she fell in love with and was in hot pursuit of Benny Sago, who was still pining for Estelle Tuggle.

Erica was already going after a third husband: Nick Davis. While working for Tom Cudahy at The Goalpost, Erica plotted to make Nick realize how much he loved her. Hinting that she'd kill herself if Nick didn't marry her, she disappeared, leaving clues suggesting a grisly demise in a Center City alley.

Nick and Mona panicked over Erica's disappearance. Meanwhile, Erica was enjoying herself in New York City—until she contracted viral pneumonia. When the doctors contacted Mona, they told her Erica had only a 50–50 chance of surviving. Mona told Nick only he could give Erica the will to live by asking her to marry him. Against his better judgment, but in an effort to save Erica, Nick proposed. Erica accepted and her slow recovery began. When her half-brother, Mark Dalton, flew to her bedside, his concern melted her antagonism toward him, and they began a warm brother/sister relationship.

While Erica was away, Tom Cudahy hired an overeager Brooke English to replace Erica. Brooke began to pursue Tom romantically even as she was dating Dan Kennicott. Dan was himself still dating the innocent Devon Shepherd, who didn't stay innocent for long. When Devon walked in on Dan as he was kissing Brooke, she felt betrayed, so Devon decided to lose her virginity.

After she seduced the equally virginal Wally McFadden in a motel, Devon felt degraded. She soon discovered she was pregnant from the encounter. Wally loved her and asked her to marry him, but Devon didn't love him. Her mother Ellen was distressed because she felt she had failed her daughter. Ellen had been so caught up in her own relationship with Mark Dalton she never heard Devon's cry for help. Mark had finally persuaded Ellen to accept his engagement ring, but with Devon pregnant, Ellen found herself pulling away from him. She found herself confiding more and more in Paul Martin. Ellen wasn't sure marriage was the right choice for either Devon or herself.

Meanwhile, Nick Davis was reconsidering his proposal to Erica. Although he loved her, he knew marriage would never work for them. Finally, he told her so. Erica made every attempt to change Nick's mind, including one last passionate seduction. But Nick was determined. When he walked out on Erica, she vowed revenge.

Erica wanted a man she could count on, and Tom Cudahy was about the most decent man she had ever met. She decided to do whatever she had to to make him fall for her. She began by reclaiming her hostess job at the Goalpost, ousting Brooke English with considerable relish. Knowing Tom loved children, Erica told him she'd broken her engagement to Nick because he was sterile and couldn't give her the children she'd always wanted. Before Brooke could make good her threat to tell Tom it was Nick who had dumped Erica, Erica told Tom the truth herself with such a dose of heartache in her voice that Tom melted. He asked her to go away with him for a weekend in the country, where they made passionate love. When she woke up in Tom's arms the next morning, Erica had convinced herself she was in love.

Tom was so bewitched by Erica that he asked her to marry him. The day of their wedding, Erica's mother Mona threatened to stop the ceremony. Mona knew Erica didn't love Tom, because she was still in love with Nick. She accused Erica of using Tom to hurt Nick. Erica warned her mother to stay out of it and threatened never to speak to Mona if she did anything to stop the marriage. So Mona sat silently as Erica married Tom. After a joyous reception at the Pine Valley Country Club, the bride and groom flew to St. Croix for their honeymoon. Mona looked to Charles Tyler for love and support. She hoped her daughter would be happy with Tom, but knew Nick Davis was still in Erica's heart. Nick had sold The Chateau to a multinational chain called Unirest and accepted a new job in Chicago. Before he left Pine Valley, he made sure Unirest would retain Claudette Montgomery as manager of The Chateau.

Before his marriage to Erica, All-American Tom Cudahy sought counsel from his wise clergyman, Father Tierney.

In 1978, *All My Children* became the first daytime drama to journey beyond U.S. shores when Tom and Erica took their glorious honeymoon on the exotic island of St. Croix. The happily couple took a romantic stroll along the beach at dusk.

Claudette had been dating Linc Tyler, who enjoyed her company but was still mourning the death of his wife Kitty. One night, in the middle of a sound sleep, Linc was awakened by a telephone call from a frantic Myrtle Fargate. She claimed to have seen Kitty. Linc couldn't believe what he was hearing. Kitty had died in his arms. Convinced that Myrtle's grief over the recent death of her husband Nigel was causing her to hallucinate, Linc dismissed her report. But Myrtle set out to look for "Kitty." The woman she had seen turned out to be an amazing double named Kelly Cole, an up-and-coming nightclub singer. Myrtle brought Kelly to Pine Valley to meet Linc. He was dumbfounded by her resemblance to Kitty and soon discovered Kelly was his dead wife's twin sister.

Myrtle moved back to Pine Valley. Kelly's manager and lover Eddie Dorrance booked her a singing engagement at The Chateau. Linc didn't trust Eddie and Kelly didn't trust Linc. She was convinced he saw Kitty whenever he looked at her. Linc understood she was Kelly and not Kitty, and he was falling for her anyway. Phoebe, Linc's mother, was not amused.

Phoebe offered Eddie Dorrance $50,000 to marry Kelly and take the girl away from Pine Valley. To Eddie that was easy money. Kelly was already dependent on him to supply her with the uppers and downers she needed to keep up the hectic pace of her career. Kelly was a pill head. As long as Lettie Jean, an old Locust Street friend of Donna's and Estelle's, supplied Eddie with the pills Kelly needed, Eddie could control Kelly. When he proposed, Kelly said yes.

Nancy Grant also said yes to Carl Blair's marriage proposal. With her ex-husband, Frank, married to Caroline, Nancy convinced everyone the baby she was carrying was Carl's. Tragically, Nancy married Carl on his deathbed after he'd been in a plane crash. Caroline soon learned Nancy's secret, but kept it from her husband, fearing he would leave her. Nancy gave birth to Frank's son, who she named Carl Junior. The love and attention Frank gave to Nancy's baby bothered Caroline, and she became distant.

As Frank and Caroline's marriage began to unravel, Phil and Tara Brent were at odds over their son, Charlie Tyler. After stealing hubcaps from Mona Kane's car, the troubled Charlie and his friend set fire to an abandoned car. When Phil realized what his son had done, he told Tara that Charlie had to face the consequences. Tara warned Phillip that if he turned in their son to the authorities, their marriage would be over. Phil did turn Charlie in and then moved out of his and Tara's home. Tara turned to her ex-husband Chuck to discuss Charlie's problems—and suddenly they weren't discussing Charlie at all. They were falling in love—and feeling very guilty about it.

Donna discovered proof of Chuck's infidelity and her insecurities grew. She was confiding her problems to her friend Estelle when their car stalled on the railroad tracks. The train couldn't stop in time, and the car was totaled. Neither woman was seriously hurt, but the impact left Donna with partial amnesia that erased the last three years of her life. In her injured state, Donna thought she was back in the hospital because her pimp Tyrone had thrown her out of his car. When she saw her husband Chuck, she greeted him as "Doctor Tyler." Her doctors told Chuck that telling Donna the truth might set her back further. She had to go through the process of remembering on her own. When Donna asked Estelle about Tyrone, Estelle told her Billy Clyde Tuggle had replaced him as top pimp on Locust Street. When Donna worried that she wasn't good enough to join Billy Clyde's stable, Estelle grew concerned. Chuck was torn. Donna needed him, but Chuck and Tara had fallen in love. Phil tried to win Tara back but suspected she and Chuck were having an affair. When they denied his accusation, he suggested they might as well have one, since they behaved like husband and wife. While Donna was recovering from her injuries, Chuck learned the operation to reverse Donna's sterility had worked and she was several months pregnant, which prompted Tara to end her relationship with Chuck.

Donna's amnesia sparked a meeting between Chuck's grandmother, Phoebe Tyler, and Billy Clyde Tuggle. Billy Clyde offered to lure Donna back to her life as a hooker if Phoebe would pay him for his trouble. Phoebe recalled all the schemes that had blown up in her

Myrtle Fargate was stunned but thrilled when, after Kitty's death, her twin sister Kelly Cole moved into her boarding house.

The Complete Stories

face, but a chance to remove Donna from her grandson's life permanently was an opportunity she couldn't pass up. Billy Clyde's wife Estelle discovered their plot and left him. She brought Donna with her to Chuck, who had no choice but to take them in. Phoebe was livid when she heard the news and was in no mood for an invitation to a social event staged by Erica Kane Cudahy.

Erica had never been more excited. With her husband Tom by her side, she was the hostess of a grand soiree in honor of Pine Valley's finest. *Tempo* magazine was covering it to spotlight Tom and Erica in their "Couples To Keep Your Eye On" feature. Phoebe tried to beg off, but Erica appealed to her ego and social standing. Erica promised Phoebe the night would be the social event of the season. It was important to Erica that the "First Lady" of Pine Valley be in attendance. Phoebe made a feeble excuse about having to take care of her great-grandson Charlie. Erica was desperate—she needed Phoebe there to prove how far she had come socially. Erica almost blurted out the biggest secret she knew, but managed to hold her tongue. Phoebe was intrigued by what Erica hinted at and agreed to attend.

The night of Erica's gala, Phoebe confronted the nervous hostess. She wanted to know what Erica knew about her grandson. Erica was trapped. As sensitively as she could with all of Pine Valley society about to arrive, Erica told Phoebe that Charlie was Phil Brent's son, not Chuck's. Erica left a shaken Phoebe and went to greet her other guests.

Phoebe found her voice in a bottle. When she was adequately stewed, she drew everyone around to announce the news Erica had told her and then publicly condemned her for revealing it. Tom couldn't believe what Erica had done and stormed out in fury, leaving her in the ashes of the social fiasco of the year. The *Tempo* photographers left as well. Without Tom Cudahy, there was no "Couple" for anyone to "keep their eyes on."

While Erica placated Tom and Phoebe nursed her latest hangover, Ruth and Joe Martin felt a mounting fear. The evil Ray Gardner, the man who had raped Ruth, had escaped from prison. They had no doubt he was heading back to Pine Valley to settle a score.

Hellbent on revenge

Ray Gardner was going to make Ruth and Joe Martin pay for sending him to prison. He would make them suffer by taking back what was rightfully his—his son Tad. After one failed attempt to snatch the teenager, Ray returned to his hiding place in Edna Thornton's cabin, where he held Edna and her daughter Dottie hostage.

An afternoon in the country with 'Doc' Tyler was all Donna expected when Chuck, the man she didn't remember as her husband, took her to Edna's cabin. When they arrived, Ray took them hostage, too. Chuck tried to wrestle away the gun he held on his captives, and in the struggle it fired. The shot reverberated in Donna's mind and triggered her memory's return. She recognized Chuck as her husband, and she knew she was pregnant with their baby. When she looked down and saw Chuck, bleeding, unconscious, she was terrified. Officer Phil Brent slipped into the cabin by pretending to be a doctor who could take care of Chuck. Phil arrested Ray and sent him back to prison. Chuck survived his wound but developed a fever that left him disoriented. At his bedside, Donna was shattered when in his delirium, Chuck called out for Tara. In his haze, he admitted he loved Tara and that his marriage to Donna had been a mistake.

Donna stifled her heartache and forced herself to believe Chuck would never leave her or the baby they were expecting. Tara made it easy for her. When Phil risked his life to save Chuck, Tara realized how much she truly loved Phil and went to him. They renewed their marriage vows in a touching ceremony with their son Charlie by their side. Because of Erica's and Phoebe's announcement, it was common knowledge that Phil was Charlie's real father, and Charlie finally began to accept him.

Charlie's Aunt Christina, his Uncle Jeff's wife, could never accept the Martin family as her own. After receiving a job offer from a San Francisco hospital, Christina told Jeff she was leaving whether he went with her or not. Jeff's father Joe urged him to save his marriage, and so did Jeff's friend, Frank Grant. The two of them persuaded Jeff to follow his wife to San Francisco. Frank himself was trying to win back his first wife Nancy. After learning that Carl Junior was actually his son, Frank divorced his second wife Caroline. Tara and Phil were leaving, too. Phil had gotten a mysterious job with the Federal Narcotics Bureau and moved with Tara and Charlie to Washington, D.C. Ruth and Joe shed tears saying good-bye to their children.

Before leaving Pine Valley, Tara and Phil congratulated Joe and Ruth on the unexpected good news that Ruth was pregnant. Their adopted son Tad worried that they might love the new baby more than him, but Ruth and Joe reassured him while Grandma Kate tried to calm Ruth's fears about having a healthy baby at her advanced age.

Donna happily awaited the birth of her own child, the symbol of Chuck's love for her and of their future together. As his dream of a life with Tara and Charlie crumbled, Chuck tried to share Donna's enthusiasm. He was with her when she gave birth. Donna was exhausted but deliriously happy when she asked about the baby. She was alarmed when Chuck hesitated and Donna demanded to know what was wrong. Chuck told her the baby was stillborn. They held each other in pain as the reality of the stillbirth clouded their future.

Newlyweds Devon and Wally McFadden's happiness was complete—for the moment—when they proudly held their daughter Bonnie after she'd been christened by Father Tierney.

Disoriented and child-like, Anne Tyler Martin remembered Paul as her beau, but nothing about her marriage to him—or their baby, who had died several years earlier.

While Chuck and Donna grieved over their loss, Erica and Tom were trying hard to conceive. At least that's what Tom thought. Actually, Erica was taking birth control pills. Erica was planning to be very busy opening a discotheque, which she failed to tell Tom about until it was about to open. When Tom found out, he was furious and forced Erica to return the seed money to her investors, Phoebe Tyler and Maureen Dalton, Mark's mother.

Maureen needed Erica's help in breaking up her son's engagement to an older woman, Ellen Shepherd. Ellen's own insecurities about their age difference increased when her daughter Devon gave birth to a baby girl. Mark would be marrying a grandmother. Ellen sought advice and friendship from Paul Martin. By the time Devon settled into her unhappy marriage to Wally, Ellen and Paul had begun to care for one another. Phoebe was appalled. She couldn't believe Ellen would chase her daughter's husband. Phoebe railed at Ellen after catching her on the dance floor with Paul, reminding him as well that he was still married to Anne. But Paul had already taken steps to divorce Anne.

Phoebe took her own steps to save her long dormant marriage to Charles. When she learned he was at a medical conference in Rome, she flew there to surprise him. She got a bigger surprise than she expected when she found him sharing a suite with Mona Kane. Phoebe fainted, but Charles had been married to Phoebe long enough to know she was faking. Phoebe got up with a renewed promise that she'd never consent to a divorce.

Phoebe had no use for divorce, whether her own or her poor, sick daughter's. She brightened when Anne started to make progress at Oak Haven, where Anne's doctors advised Paul to postpone divorcing her.

If Phoebe was unhappy about Paul's interest in Ellen, Ellen's ex-fiancé was miserable. Getting drunk one night, Mark ran into Phoebe's niece Brooke English. She liked Mark and easily seduced him. Brooke began a relationship with Mark, who made it clear to her that all they had together was sex, because he still wanted to marry Ellen. Brooke moved in with him anyway. Brooke's boyfriend Dan Kennicott got that message loud and clear. Heartbroken, he left town. Brooke was hopelessly in love with Mark, but Mark loved Ellen, and Brooke's constant jealousy began to wear thin. When Mark threw her out, Brooke began a reckless affair with Eddie Dorrance, who became obsessed with her.

Brooke's old boyfriend Benny Sago loved Estelle deeply. He kept trying to woo her away from her husband Billy Clyde Tuggle, who vowed he would rather die than lose her. But it was Benny Billy Clyde tried to kill. Even though Estelle returned Benny's love, Billy Clyde always managed to win her back.

Edna Thornton was interested in Benny, too, but his constant pursuit of Estelle left her alone at The Chateau once too often. Eddie Dorrance had manipulated himself into Claudette Montgomery's position as manager of the restaurant. He introduced Edna to Professor Langley Wallingford, an older man who seemed quite taken with her. She enjoyed

the professor's attention, but his interest wandered when Edna mentioned that Phoebe Tyler was the richest woman in Pine Valley. Edna didn't mind, because Benny had turned to her after Estelle and Billy Clyde moved to Sea City. Despondent and lonely, Benny figured marrying Edna wouldn't be the worst thing that ever happened to him. She hurried him to the altar before he could change his mind.

Meanwhile, Langley Wallingford asked Eddie, a con artist after his own heart, to introduce him to a lady of means. Eddie thought Edna was a rich widow. But in Phoebe, Langley had found himself a gold mine. The way she responded to his attention prompted him to propose. Phoebe accepted, offering her husband Charles his long-sought divorce. Eddie wondered if Langley wasn't actually falling for Phoebe. Langley realized that, despite himself, he was quite taken with her. Langley told Eddie how much he and Phoebe enjoyed their secret affair.

Phoebe's plan to pay Eddie to marry Kelly Cole fell apart when Kelly found out about it the morning of the wedding. Kelly called off the ceremony, and Phoebe's heart sank as she watched Kelly and her son Linc falling in love. Kelly never wanted Linc to find out about her drug addiction. She tried desperately to get off the pills, but one night she lapsed. Strung out after popping a few too many during a singing engagement, she fell apart on stage, publicly declaring her hatred of Eddie because he'd turned her into a pill head, then running out of the club. When Linc finally found her hours later, he brought her back to The Chateau, where they found Eddie in his office—dead. Eddie had blackmailed Langley over his conning of Phoebe. He had blackmailed Phoebe over her affair

Despite Estelle's feelings for Benny Sago, she constantly rebuffed him, insisting that she would never desert her husband, Billy Clyde Tuggle. In frustration, Benny allowed himself to be seduced by the man-hungry Edna Thornton.

The Complete Stories

The inimitable Ms. Kane dazzled Pine Valley with the opening of her disco, Erica's.

with Langley. He had skimmed money off the restaurant's profits. He had engineered Claudette's demotion. He had even threatened to murder Mark Dalton, his rival for Brooke. When Eddie was killed, Kelly's fingerprints were found on the gun, and she was charged with the murder. As her lawyer and fiancé, Linc vowed to Kelly that he would save her.

While she waited for Langley to visit, Phoebe prayed that her son Lincoln would fail to exonerate Kelly. One afternoon, Langley went to Myrtle Fargate's Boutique to buy a little bauble for Phoebe. Myrtle had the oddest sensation that she knew Langley, but she couldn't figure how. Langley recognized her, too, hoping she'd never recall he'd once snatched her purse at a carnival in Topeka, Kansas, where Myrtle knew him as roustabout Lenny Wlasuk. Langley didn't want Phoebe to find out about his past. She was oblivious, busying herself with plans to welcome her new neighbors to Pine Valley society.

The wealthy and aristocratic Palmer Cortlandt had moved to town with his innocent daughter, Nina. On the night of Phoebe's dinner party to welcome them, Nina suffered an acute attack of appendicitis and was rushed to the hospital, where young Dr. Cliff Warner operated and saved her life. When she recovered and Nina and Cliff looked into each other's eyes, it was love at first sight.

Palmer realized what was happening between Cliff and Nina. So did nurse Sybil Thorne, and neither one liked it. A possessive father, Palmer wanted to keep Nina by his side, and Sybil wanted Cliff. Father and nurse entered into an unholy alliance to break up the young lovers. Sybil told Palmer about Cliff's old girlfriend Janice Rawlins. After Palmer bribed Janice to lie and tell Nina that Cliff walked out on Janice when she was pregnant, Nina rejected Cliff. He was angry and confused. Nina, a diabetic, was so depressed she neglected her health, which alarmed Palmer's mysterious housekeeper, Mrs. Myra Murdoch. Realizing Palmer had orchestrated the situation, Myra ordered him to fix it. Palmer caved in to her demand, bridling at the thought of Nina's renewed infatuation with Cliff Warner. He began plotting how he could fix the damage he'd done, if only temporarily.

A more compassionate father, Joe Martin welcomed his daughter home when Tara and Charlie returned to Pine Valley. Happy to be home, she waited to hear from her husband Phil, who had disappeared on an undercover assignment out of the country. Tara's return stirred Donna's insecurities. Even though Chuck hadn't thought about Tara for months, Donna was driving him crazy with her jealousy.

Erica was driving her own husband Tom crazy in her endless quest for fame. After Tom refused to become the Adonis Cosmetics spokesman, Erica secretly sold the adman, Mr. Richmond, on hiring them as a husband–wife team, pleading with Tom to say yes. But Erica didn't know the lascivious Richmond expected her to sleep with him. As she was struggling to resist his attack, Tom broke down the door and saved her. The incident put an end to their modeling career and landed Tom in the hospital with an injured knee. While he recuperated, he dreamed of getting home to Erica so they could continue trying to make a baby. Erica let him dream on while she popped her birth control pills and opened her disco, which she proudly named "Erica's." Tom was flabbergasted that she could open a disco behind his back. But open it she did, and it was a success.

Tom hired Brooke to replace Erica at The Goalpost. Brooke was at a crossroads. She had been used badly, first by Mark Dalton, still lovesick over Ellen Shepherd, then by Eddie Dorrance. When Brooke learned that she was carrying Eddie's baby, she made a tough decision and secretly had an abortion.

Erica's darkest secret blew up in her face when Tom found her birth control pills. He waved them in her face, declaring that since their marriage was a lie, it was over. Erica couldn't believe Tom meant it, but he did. He wanted children and thought Erica did, too.

Tom wanted what Joe and Ruth Martin welcomed into their lives that peaceful Christmas morning: a healthy baby boy. They decided to name the baby Joseph Martin, Junior. He would be known as "Joey."

Tom Cudahy was livid when he discovered his wife Erica's birth control pills and realized she had deceived him

Issues and Answers

Pregnancy after 40

In 1979, Ruth and Joe Martin made the joyful discovery that Ruth was expecting. But their elation was tempered by reality: As a woman over 40, Ruth faced a greater risk of having a baby with health problems. With her husband Joe's help, she considered terminating the pregnancy for fear that the child would be born with Down's Syndrome. But after undergoing the relatively new procedure of amniocentesis, Ruth went through with her "Never Too Late" pregnancy, and gave birth to a healthy son, Joey, on Christmas Day.

The Complete Stories

1980

All My Children's second decade began in disaster for Erica Kane when business at her disco dropped suddenly after the opening of a hot, new competitor, The Steam Pit. The final blow came when the city rezoned the area, forbidding Erica's to play music after midnight. Alone and despairing, she was forced to close the disco. But the inimitable Erica would not accept defeat. She regained her spirit and left town to make it as a movie star in Hollywood. With Erica departed from his life, Tom's friendship with Brooke grew into something more. But their budding relationship ran into a roadblock when Erica, having failed in Hollywood, returned to Pine Valley. She used a variety of ploys to work her way back into Tom's life and into his bed. She promised to turn over a new leaf, but her new resolve didn't last. The allure of fame beckoned once again in the person of cosmetics magnate Brandon Kingsley. Brandon offered Erica a top modeling job with Sensuelle Cosmetics. Fearing Tom wouldn't approve of her budding new career, Erica lied about her frequent trips to New York. When he discovered her deception, Tom called a halt to their marriage once and for all and headed to the Caribbean for a divorce. He went ahead with plans to marry Brooke despite Erica's machinations to keep them apart.

To liven up her humdrum life, Devon McFadden began a torrid but short-lived affair with that callous cad, Sean Cudahy.

Tom Cudahy's wayward brother Sean arrived in Pine Valley and seduced Ellen Shepherd's plain-Jane daughter, Devon McFadden. Neither marriage to the kind-but-dull Wally nor motherhood could satisfy Devon. She easily became infatuated with the smooth-talking Sean, and they began a sizzling, secret affair. While Devon wasn't proud of the sordid affair she carried out in hourly-rate motel rooms, she was having the time of her life. For Sean, the thrill was short-lived. Once Devon became the pursuer, he lost interest. Sean had his eye on sexy nurse Sybil Thorne and set out to seduce her. Devon did her best to compete with Sean's dazzling new girlfriend. She wondered if a sophisticated new hairstyle or different makeup could win Sean back, but nothing worked. Devon always ended up feeling unattractive and insecure, and Sean did nothing to counter Devon's lack of self-esteem, often citing Sybil's sexy attributes. Unable to compete, Devon turned to the bottle for comfort. Wally had had enough and told his mother-in-law, Ellen, that he was filing for divorce. She told him he was acting rashly, and he reluctantly agreed to support Devon through her alcoholism. Regardless, the marriage was doomed.

On a happier note, Cliff and Nina were reunited when Janice Rollins admitted she had lied to Nina about Cliff's fathering her baby. Cliff asked Nina to marry him, but Nina was reluctant. Marriage to Cliff or any man meant facing another overbearing problem. Then Palmer struck again, convincing Nina she had been responsible for the long-ago death of her mother Daisy in childbirth. Nina confided her fears to the family housekeeper, Myra Murdoch, who knew of a way to assuage Nina's guilt. While Palmer was away on a business trip, Myra arranged a seance to call Daisy from the dead.

Smoke filled the air as Myra chanted Daisy's name, and an ethereal figure appeared at the top of the staircase: the ghost of Daisy Cortlandt, who had returned for a fleeting moment to put her daughter's mind at ease.

In reality, not only was Myra Daisy's mother, but Daisy was very much alive. Banished years earlier by her husband Palmer after embarrassing him with an extramarital affair, Daisy returned to Pine Valley in 1980. She took on the secret identity of Monique Jonvil and began an affair with the devilish Sean Cudahy. At the same time, Sean set out to work his charms on Daisy's daughter Nina. They grew close when both were held hostage during a robbery at the Pine Valley Bank.

In Cortlandt Manor, housekeeper Myra Murdoch and young Nina Cortlandt held a spooky seance to summon up the spirit of the not-so-late Daisy Cortlandt.

Still, nothing could keep Nina and Cliff apart. Their love grew stronger as the year passed. Palmer attempted yet another scheme to separate them when he falsely informed Nina she was going blind because of a condition related to her illness called diabetic retinopathy. What Nina didn't know was that a new non-invasive surgical technique, using a laser beam, could abate her condition. Palmer conveniently neglected to tell his daughter that there was hope for her condition. He wondered aloud how Nina could ever be a real wife to Cliff with such a handicap. He knew Nina wouldn't want to tie Cliff down to an invalid.

Palmer's manipulative words sunk in. Nina coldly returned her engagement ring to Cliff, who was so distraught at losing her that he turned for comfort to Sybil Thorne. Cliff was ripe for seduction and Sybil knew how to stir a man's passion. They made love.

In time, Nina learned that treatment for her eye problem was possible. With Palmer by her side, she traveled to Baltimore's Wilmer Eye Institute and underwent a successful procedure to prevent blindness. Happily, Nina reconciled with Cliff, and they planned a fall wedding. But the seeds of doom had been planted. Sybil Thorne was pregnant.

The last thing Sybil wanted, of course, was to be a mother. She had no use for babies and considered an abortion. Palmer knew that wouldn't do. In his effort to stop his daughter's impending marriage, he paid the young nurse to keep her child.

After marrying Nina in a beautiful outdoor ceremony on the grounds of Cortlandt Manor, guilt-ridden Cliff knew he couldn't keep his impending fatherhood a secret for long. When he finally broke the news to Nina, she became hysterical. Spurred on by Palmer, she left Cliff and returned home to Cortlandt Manor. The marriage was over for now, but their love, though denied by both of them, survived.

Kelly Cole was convicted and sentenced to death for the murder of her manager, Eddie Dorrance. Linc Tyler's painstaking investigation

Issues and Answers
Diabetes

When Nina Cortlandt developed diabetic retinopathy in 1980, All My Children went on location to the Wilmer Opthalmological Institute in Baltimore, Maryland, where Nina underwent successful laser surgery to correct her condiction. Thousands of Americans learned about the breakthrough medical procedure through this story, and like Nina, underwent successful surgeries themselves.

The Complete Stories

On Location

Taylor Miller (Nina) and James Mitchell (Palmer) had fun playing croquet between scenes taped at the Waveny Mansion—the estate that serves as Cortlandt Manor—in New Canaan, Connecticut.

revealed that the real killer was Claudette Montgomery, who, while trying to flee, was critically injured in a car crash. As her life slipped away, Lincoln begged Claudette to confess. With her last breaths, she explained how she had caught Eddie skimming money off the books at The Chateau. Eddie had picked up a gun to kill her, but when he turned his back for a moment, she lunged for the gun and grabbed it. Every word of her deathbed confession was captured on tape. Both Eddie and his killer, Claudette Montgomery, were dead. Kelly was free—free to marry Linc.

Billy Clyde Tuggle escaped from prison, drugged and raped his wife Estelle, and later planned to bury her alive in a cemetery with her new love, Benny Sago. Chuck Tyler heroically overpowered Billy Clyde and rescued his dear friends. Benny presented Estelle with an engagement ring, but their happiness was marred when she learned she was pregnant with Billy Clyde's child. Benny persuaded her to marry him anyway. She accepted and they agreed to tell everyone he was the father.

Donna Tyler failed in her efforts to buy a black-market baby. Frustrated by her inability to give Chuck a child, she left him. Falling under the spell of Palmer Cortlandt, Donna was manipulated into moving in with him at Cortlandt Manor—and obtaining a speedy Caribbean divorce from Chuck. Wealthy snob Palmer and ex-hooker Donna were an unlikely combination.

The new year brought fresh hope to many in Pine Valley. Tom Cudahy's annulment of his marriage to Erica went through, freeing him to marry Brooke. Erica was enjoying her exciting new life in New York City, and Palmer was relishing the opportunity to transform his new wife Donna into a woman of the world.

For others, 1981 was a year filled with anguish and sorrow. Paul Martin grieved with the Tylers when their beloved Anne was killed by a bomb planted in Paul's car. Brooke made the horrifying discovery that the woman she believed to be her mother, Peg English, was actually "Cobra," the leader of an international drug cartel.

While at Cortlandt Manor, painfully estranged from her beloved Cliff, Nina was absolutely miserable. She found herself forever running into Sybil Thorne, who never missed a chance to gloat over Cliff and her impending motherhood. It pained Nina to see the man she loved, but she masked her pain with anger. At times, she refused even to acknowledge Cliff's presence. Nina's trusted friend Monique Jonvil knew Nina still cared for Cliff because Nina had told her so. Monique also knew Nina and Cliff belonged together, but wasn't sure how to bring about a reconciliation.

With the help of Nina's friend Betsy Kennicott, Monique managed to convince Nina that Sybil didn't want to keep her baby, only acting as if she wanted it to trap Cliff into marrying her. If Cliff returned to Nina, Sybil might be forced to give up her baby for adoption. Persuaded by their argument and guided by her deep feelings for Cliff, Nina agreed to give him another chance. Monique and Betsy were wrong about Sybil. Encouraged by Sean—who had his own designs on Nina—Sybil had other ideas. She decided to keep her baby, determined to get Cliff back. Sean would help if Sybil promised to keep his name out of it. Sean had begun working as right-hand man to Palmer Cortlandt. While searching his boss's personal files, Sean made an amazing discovery. He found several checks made out to Daisy Cortlandt in 1975. He wondered aloud to Monique how this was possible since Daisy had been dead for years. Greatly alarmed, Monique—who was, in fact, Daisy—encouraged Sean to keep quiet.

Cliff and Nina, meanwhile, celebrated their reconciliation with a dinner party. They wanted all of Pine Valley to know they were back together. Their public profile as a happy couple so infuriated Sybil that she stormed over to their house, went into labor, and delivered baby Bobby in Cliff and Nina's living room. With Nina by his side, Cliff delivered his own son.

Sybil took her newborn baby home to her dreary boarding house, where motherhood proved difficult. When the baby's incessant cries drove the other boarders to complain, Sybil's landlord threatened to evict her.

Nina offered to help, asking Sybil to let her adopt the child, but Sybil wouldn't even consider it. She needed a savior and found one in Palmer Cortlandt. He wrote Sybil check after check, promising to continue supporting her only on the condition that she agree to help him and Sean break up Cliff and Nina. Sybil joined in the scheme. Her first mission was to order Nina to get a divorce.

Sybil threatened to give Bobby away to strangers if Nina didn't comply. Nina felt she had no choice and told Cliff she wanted out of their

Brooke made the horrifying discovery that the woman she believed to be her mother, Peg English, was actually Cobra, the leader of an international drug cartel.

The Complete Stories

At Dr. Cliff Warner's trial for the murder of Sybil Thorne, Monique Jonvil delivered stunning testimony in which she revealed the real murderer's identity.

During Cliff's murder trial, Nina listened in horror as Monique Jonvil testified that she was Nina's long-lost mother.

marriage. But this time he refused to believe her. He demanded to know who put her up to it. Nina admitted Sybil was the culprit, and an enraged Cliff swore he would kill her. Cliff headed to Sybil's apartment, where he found her dying from a gunshot wound. Within days, Cliff Warner was arrested for the murder of Sybil Thorne.

Cliff's hopes looked dim as he stood trial for the crime. It didn't help his chances for acquittal when Sybil, just before dying, called out Cliff's name. It also didn't help that Erica Kane had overheard Sybil demanding that Cliff see her the night of her murder.

What did help was Monique Jonvil's coming forward to confess she knew the murderer: Sean Cudahy. In her testimony, Monique admitted the startling truth that she was Nina Cortlandt's mother. Nina stood up in total incredulity and slowly approached the witness stand where Daisy sat, delivering her fateful testimony. Nina wouldn't believe Daisy was her mother, and when Daisy begged her for forgiveness, Nina fainted.

Meanwhile, Sean was experiencing the shock of prison life. Frightened by his new surroundings in the Pine Valley jail, he confessed to the crime, insisting to his brother Tom that Sybil's death had been an accident. He admitted Palmer Cortlandt was behind it all. Sean had only gone to Sybil's to put the fear of God into her. Sean hadn't planned to kill her, but things got out of hand. Sean would have plenty of time to think about his foolish actions. Convicted of murder, he was sentenced to serve three-to-five years in the state prison. Palmer paid for his misdeeds in another way when Nina refused to see him. She couldn't believe he had lied to her all that time.

As Nina left her father's life, so did his new wife, Donna. With his world collapsing around him, a shamed Palmer went on a drinking binge that landed him in the sleaziest part of Center City and made him ripe for a mugging. He suffered a complete loss of memory when he was hit over the head. Needing a job, an amnesiac Palmer Cortlandt, one of the world's wealthiest men, went to work as a busboy at Foxy's, a Center City bar. It would be months before he recovered both from the injury and the shame. When Palmer did return to Cortlandt Manor, he was determined to win back the heart of his first love, Daisy.

All was not well at the Martins. Ruth had grown increasingly jealous over Joe's concern for a battered wife named Leora Sanders. Ruth was still grieving over the death of her son Phil. His decision to take on a top-secret government mission had proved fatal. His plane exploded and he was killed, leaving Tara to raise their young son Charlie alone. Ruth was less than thrilled when Tara took up with school psychologist Jim Jefferson so soon after Phil's death. Ruth reluctantly attended their wedding and was saddened when Tara took Charlie and moved to Portland with her new husband.

Then there was Tad. The Martins' problems were complicated by the behavior of their teenage son, whose pot smoking habit had turned him into a bitter young man—and a thief. Tad bought his drugs with money he stole from Gran's sugar bowl. Young Tad was heartbroken over the breakup with his girlfriend, Suzanne. Despondent and under the influence, he smashed up the Martin family station wagon. When the pressure of life at home proved too much to handle, he ran away.

If Tad had stayed in Pine Valley only a few months longer, he would have met his real mother and his long-lost sister. In the summer of 1981, Opal Gardner, an outrageously wacky woman, turned up on the Martin doorstep with her sweet and innocent teenage daughter, Jenny. Opal feigned a heart condition and pushed her daughter into taking a job at Foxy's bar in Center City.

While at Foxy's, Jenny met Jesse Hubbard, a streetwise black kid, nephew of Dr. Frank Grant and his wife, Nancy. Jenny and Jesse struck up an instant friendship as they compared details of their young but eventful lives. Jesse, who had dropped out of school, agreed to re-enroll when Jenny offered to help him with his homework. They leaned on and stood by each other, especially after Jesse nearly burned down his Uncle Frank's house when he carelessly left a cigarette burning in an ashtray.

And then there was Greg Nelson, the son of one of Pine Valley's leading families. Greg was a clean-cut, upstanding young man who was instantly captivated by Jenny, a girl from the other side of town. Greg's fascination with Jenny bothered Liza Colby, a purebred snob Greg had known all his life. When Greg fell in love with Jenny, Liza was furious.

Life couldn't have been sweeter for Pine Valley's princess, Erica Kane. At the end of her cross-country promotional tour for Sensuelle, she joined her new love Brandon Kingsley for a weekend tryst at his Nassau condominium. Their joyous trip was cut short when Brandon was called back to the States. He told Erica there was a business emergency, but he was lying.

The emergency turned out to be a wife, Sara, a daughter, Pamela, and a never-seen son, Roger. Brandon had a complicated life he hadn't bothered to tell Erica about. Even when she found out about it, Erica was still determined to marry her man. That is, as soon as he agreed to divorce his wife. But Sara had no plans to give up her position as Mrs. Brandon Kingsley. She made no bones about what she thought of Erica's sordid affair with her husband. And Brandon had no intention of divorcing his wife as Erica thought. He decided to string Erica along as long as he could.

But competition for Erica entered the picture—both romantically and professionally. Kent Bogard, a handsome young millionaire, and his father, Lars, tantalized Erica with an exciting offer to leave Sensuelle Cosmetics to become the spokeswoman for a new line of cosmetics—named after her.

Issues and Answers
Domestic Violence

In this 1981 story spotlighting the issue of domestic abuse, Curt Sanders emotionally and physically abused his wife Leora, who eventually sought help from Dr. Joe Martin.

In 1982, there was trouble for Pine Valley's young lovers, Greg and Jenny, and its name was Liza Colby. Liza seized every opportunity to make Jenny feel unworthy of Greg. But even her vicious mind games couldn't keep Greg and Jenny apart. In those first exciting months together, Jenny and Greg shared their innermost feelings and secrets. Greg listened sympathetically to Jenny's troubles with her mother, Opal. Jenny was embarrassed by her mother when she barged in on them. She didn't think Greg's mother would ever be so smothering. But Greg knew otherwise.

Enid Nelson was beside herself, stricken by the mere thought that Greg would date a girl who was so clearly beneath him. Enid felt she had to do something to nip the romance in the bud. When Greg gave Jenny his class ring, Enid joined Liza to stop this romance. Together, she and Liza manipulated the impressionable young Jenny into believing she must break up with Greg—for his own good. Heartbroken, Jenny wrote Greg a letter.

Jenny's friends—and her mother Opal—couldn't understand why she broke up with Greg when they had seemed so happy. Fabricating an excuse, Jenny told Opal she ended their relationship in order to pursue her modeling career and went back to work at Foxy's to make money for her upcoming trip to New York. Jenny's friend, Angie Hubbard, knew better. She knew Jenny loved Greg, and she told him so. Before long, Greg and Jenny were back together, much to Enid and Liza's disdain. Liza vowed to make Jenny pay. And pay Jenny did, when both Liza and she vied for the coveted title of Miss Junior Pine Valley. It appeared Jenny had won the crown, but when the votes were counted, Liza was declared the winner. Jenny came in a close second. Opal refused to accept the results. She knew Jenny had won and suspected foul play. She was right. Unknown to anyone, Liza's friend Amanda had deliberately miscounted the judges' votes. Opal got to the bottom of things when she polled each of them individually and learned that the results were fixed. Thanks to Opal's efforts, Phoebe Wallingford declared Jenny Gardner the new Miss Junior Pine Valley.

Stewing over her failure, Liza faced embarrassment in the halls of Pine Valley High School. As usual, her enemy Jesse Hubbard let her have it. Liza couldn't wait to exact revenge on Jenny. She picked the night of the high school prom to destroy Jenny's life with the evil truth that her father, Ray Gardner, wasn't dead, as Jenny had told Greg, but was in jail. Jenny begged Liza not to tell Greg about her father, but Liza didn't feel right about keeping the sordid truth from her oldest and dearest friend. Jenny pleaded that Greg wouldn't understand.

In that moment, Liza stunned Jenny with an incredible secret: her father, Ray Gardner, had been locked away for raping Ruth Martin. Jenny didn't believe her at first, but Liza pulled out clippings that detailed the rape. Liza felt Greg needed to know the whole disgusting story about Jenny's father.

In shock, Jenny paid a visit to her father in jail and was so upset by the reality of what he had done and by the despicable nature of her family that she fled immediately for New York.

Meanwhile, Erica was stunned to learn that Kent Bogard had purchased Sensuelle Cosmetics. This meant that both she and Brandon were employees of the Bogard family. That arrangement didn't last long. When Brandon learned Kent had given Erica an expensive fur coat, he returned it to Kent himself—then quit, turning to his wife Sara for com-

Chuck Tyler and his new girlfriend, Melanie Sawyer, hit the slopes while vacationing in Switzerland.

Trapped by an avalanche, Chuck and Donna barely escaped with their lives in these action-packed scenes taped in Grindenwald, Switzerland in 1982.

fort. When Erica found out about Brandon's renewed interest in his wife, she broke off her engagement to him and headed for Milan on a promotional tour. Kent Bogard accompanied her on this fateful European jaunt. Erica and Kent made love in Milan, and Erica arranged for Brandon to find out about it. Upon her return to New York, she begged Brandon's forgiveness. She also pleaded for him not to tell Kent of their reunion for fear she'd lose her job.

The battle for Erica's hand exploded at a New York restaurant when Brandon and Kent came to blows. Defeated in business, Brandon accepted a job in Hong Kong and tried to persuade Erica to come with him. Torn between her career and her love life, she made her decision when Lars Bogard offered her a starring role in his new movie. Erica was finally going to become a Hollywood legend. Though unmistakably beautiful, she was no actress, and was demoted to a supporting role in the movie. At the same time, a mysterious and mousy woman named Silver Kane arrived on Erica's doorstep, claiming to be her half-sister. Busy with her many pursuits, Erica allowed Silver to stay on with her as her assistant.

Brandon finally had enough of Erica, split from her for good and reconciled with Sara. At the same time, Lars broke the news to Erica that she'd been cut out of the film entirely. Devastated, she disappeared from Pine Valley—and when she resurfaced, Erica learned she was about to be replaced as "An American Beauty." She wouldn't allow it and quickly ordered a press conference, where Erica triumphantly announced her

Greg Nelson was often forced to step between those warring enemies, Jesse Hubbard and Liza Colby.

return. That forced Lars to keep Erica on. She wasn't as successful in her attempts to win back Kent, who rejected her. Erica's sister, Silver, had better luck with him. As time went on, she dropped her mousy exterior and grew more beautiful before Kent's eyes. Silver set out to land him, all the while convincing Erica she was indispensable to her.

While honeymooning in Switzerland, Palmer and Donna were surprised to run into Chuck and his new girlfriend, Melanie Sawyer. They planned a ski trip together, but when Melanie sprained her ankle, the three members of this love triangle hit the slopes with their guide. A sudden storm engulfed the mountain, trapping them, and Palmer's life was in dire danger when he fell off a cliff, landing precariously on the ledge below. Chuck and Donna could only watch helplessly as a helicopter, not seeing them, rescued Palmer. Fearing for their lives, they took shelter in a cave, where they huddled together for warmth. Without food or heat, Chuck and Donna feared they wouldn't last the night. But they made love and survived.

Back home, Nina used part of her trust fund to solve a business problem at Cortlandt Electronics. Impressed by his daughter's business acumen, Palmer asked Nina to attend a board meeting with him so she could learn more about the company's inner workings. This meeting led to others, and Cliff grew annoyed when his wife wasn't at home as much as he liked. As time went on, their arguments over her newfound business interest grew worse. Cliff accused Nina of becoming consumed with her new career and failing to spend enough time caring for their son Bobby.

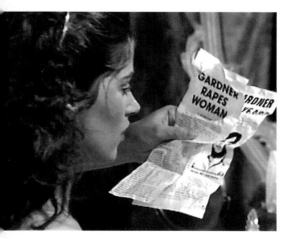

Liza Colby shocked Jenny Gardner with proof that her father, Ray Gardner, was a convicted rapist.

At Cortlandt Manor, Donna was thrilled to learn she was pregnant. She gushed the news that she was carrying Palmer's child to anyone who would listen. Unfortunately, Myra and Daisy were listening all too well. They knew the truth: Palmer was sterile and the women figured the baby must be Chuck Tyler's. Palmer suspected the awful truth, too, but put a brave face on the situation. He hoped to convince everyone he was the real father. Privately, he met with a fertility expert who told him there was no way he could have fathered a child. Palmer was devastated but recovered. Purely to allay Myra and Daisy's suspicions, he endowed the unborn child with a $20-million trust fund.

As the months passed, Palmer grew progressively more disgusted by Donna's pregnancy. To distract himself, he resumed his old folly of breaking up Cliff and Nina. Just to be meddlesome, he arranged a research grant for Cliff, thinking the extra work would monopolize Cliff's time and further antagonize his already strained relations with Nina.

Cliff's research project kept him away from home as Palmer planned. Nina soon found herself enjoying the company of co-worker Steve Jacobi. Things had deteriorated so much between Nina and Cliff that she had to beg him to attend their own party, a Labor Day weekend affair hosted by Palmer in honor of their anniversary. The party was doomed from the beginning, starting with the presence of Ray Gardner. Ray had deviously arranged an early parole and persuaded Daisy to give him a job working at the party where the Martins would be guests.

Fortunately, both Ray's plan to kidnap Joey Martin and Palmer's attempt to kill Chuck were foiled at the picnic. Now married to young Carrie Sanders, Chuck had learned the truth about Donna's pregnancy when he came across an old medical file belonging to Palmer, and the two men arrived at an uneasy truce over the child's paternity. Donna would soon give birth to Palmer John Cortlandt and, much to Palmer's disgust, she asked Chuck and Carrie to be god-parents.

At the same picnic, Nina and Cliff fought incessantly and Steve Jacobi seized the opportunity to surprise Nina with a kiss. Even though the Warners made up, Nina couldn't stop thinking of Steve. When Palmer arranged for Nina and Steve to take a business trip together, Nina insisted she didn't want to go but secretly fantasized about succumbing to Steve. Nothing happened. But when she came home, Nina fantasized about Steve while making love to Cliff.

Soon thereafter, a giant storm hit Pine Valley and the two coworkers were stranded alone together at Cortlandt Manor. In front of a roaring fireplace, they eyed each other and finally gave in to their passion. Nina vowed that it would never happen again, though her attraction to Steve continued to grow more intense. Even Cliff noticed a difference in her but attributed it to all her hard work.

Although Ellen told Mark she wanted a baby, she still had doubts about having a child so late in life. Ellen refused to tell even her closest friends about their plans for parenthood and grew reluctant to make love with her husband. The tension increased when Mark was refused tenure at Pine Valley University, where he had been teaching music. Crushed by his failures, Mark confided his woes to student Pamela Kingsley, Brandon's beautiful, college-age daughter.

Jesse and Jenny forged an unbreakable bond during their sweltering summer in New York.

Growing more despondent with his failure to find work, Mark Dalton fell more deeply in lust with Pamela Kingsley. Things were looking up when a New York producer took an interest in a new play Mark had written. After the play's rousing success, Pam and Mark celebrated by making love for the first time. Days later, they met again, and the torrid affair flourished behind Ellen's back. When Ellen surprised them at a picnic together, Mark panicked. He reassured Ellen that Pamela's crush was harmless. Realizing the consequence of his actions, Mark broke off the affair. Feeling rejected and desperate, Pam overdosed on pills. She recovered, but not before Ellen learned the shocking news of her husband's infidelity. Ellen confronted Mark about the affair. When he admitted to it, she moved to New York, saying they needed a temporary separation.

After running away to New York City, Jenny was lucky to find a landlady as friendly and caring as Mrs. Gonzalez.

New York was the place to be for *All My Children* during the summer of 1982. While Jenny tried to make ends meet in the Big Apple, she told Opal she was in California. She felt friendless and forsaken in the big, cold-hearted city, but not for long. Jesse Hubbard was on his way. After learning that Liza had made threats against Jenny, Jesse confronted Liza. When she slapped him, he reacted by pushing her down and running away. Ripping her own clothes, Liza cried rape, and Jesse, in a panic, fled to New York.

Jesse arrived just in time to rescue Jenny from being forced to participate in a porno film. She finally got a respectable job working as a receptionist at a fashion house, where she bore the humiliation of mod-

The Complete Stories

when Jenny Gardner's face appeared before them. Humiliated, Jenny bolted from the theater, pursued by Greg, who was trying to explain that he understood. Running to get away from him, she escaped onto a catwalk high above the auditorium. Greg risked his life to save her, but in the course of his heroics, lost his balance and fell from the ledge. Lying immobilized on the floor, he was alive, but Greg knew something was terribly wrong.

The students looked on in shock as naked, undulating bodies appeared on the movie screen. Then the audience erupted in screams when Jenny Gardner's face appeared on the screen before them.

Greg had suffered severe injuries to his spine and soon learned he was paralyzed from the waist down. As time went on with no improvement, Greg broke off with Jenny to spare her the pain of living with a cripple. In time, he slowly began to regain the use of his legs but, spurred on by his mother Enid, kept the news of his possible recovery a secret from Jenny. Besides, he wanted to wait until he could stand up and take her in his arms. With determination, he started months of grueling physical therapy.

It seemed everyone but Donna knew Chuck Tyler was her baby's father. When Daisy told Phoebe the truth of little Palmer John's paternity, Phoebe ran to Donna with the news. Donna moved out of Palmer's home the same day. Coming home to an empty house, Palmer became irrational and confronted Donna. He threatened her physically and swore he would ruin Phoebe. In the aftermath of her discovery, Donna was furious that Chuck had kept the truth from her. Donna was also furious when she discovered he also knew about Palmer's affair with Daisy and kept it from her in an act of vengeance. Donna forbade Chuck from seeing their son. With this drastic action, Chuck realized how much John and Donna meant to him. When his wife Carrie left him, the non-traditional family grew closer.

Silver finally revealed a shocking secret to Erica when she admitted to having an affair with Kent Bogard. Furious with her "lover," Erica confronted Kent at The Founders' Day Ball and carried their argument into Kent's hotel room. In a struggle, the gun Erica had given Kent for his birthday discharged, and Kent slumped to the floor dead. Silver, who had witnessed the accidental shooting, lied to the police. She claimed Erica had murdered Kent in cold blood. After her arrest, Erica was released into Mona's custody. When Erica learned she had no chance for an insanity plea, she ran, pausing only long enough to disguise herself as a nun in order to attend Kent's memorial service. Never one to miss an opportunity, Silver turned to Lars and began pressuring him to make her the next American Beauty.

When a fugitive Erica found out Nick Davis was back in town, she arranged a secret meeting with him in his room at the Valley Inn. Brooke, now a journalist, spotted Erica on the way there, and struck a deal with her. In exchange for an exclusive interview, Brooke would keep Erica's secret. When the landlady overheard Erica's version of the story, she turned her in. Erica was arrested and jailed until her trial.

The plot thickened when Silver was told not to leave Pine Valley, since she was the star witness against Erica. When Tad Martin saw Silver's picture in the *Bulletin*, he immediately knew something was amiss. He recognized Silver as Connie Wilkes, a grifter Tad had met in California. Once Tad identified Silver as an impostor, Erica was cleared of all charges. Connie was extradited to California, where she ended up in prison. But Erica paid a heavy price. Because of all the notoriety, Lars refused to re-sign her as An American Beauty.

A fugitive from justice after being charged with the murder of her lover Kent Bogard, Erica donned a nun's habit to sneak into his memorial service.

Erica was down, but far from finished. She was about to embark on a whole new career. Retiring from modeling, she formed her own cosmetics company, Enchantment, designed to put Sensuelle out of business. She was in business again and gloried in her comeback.

When Jesse and Angie sneaked away to a motel room to consummate their relationship, Angie was so uncomfortable they decided instead to marry in order to make things legal. Together, they journeyed across the state line and tied the knot at a simple ceremony with a justice of the peace presiding. When they got home, Jesse and Angie both realized the enormity of what they had done and decided to keep the marriage to themselves. Soon after, Angie received the devastating news that she was pregnant. Given her stormy union with Jesse and her volatile relationship with her parents, Angie kept her condition a closely guarded secret.

After confiding the truth about her pregnancy to her mother, Pat Baxter, Angie went to Jesse to see how he felt about children. When Jesse said he couldn't even think about it for a few years, Angie decided a divorce was the best answer to her dilemma and flew to Haiti for quick legal action.

Meanwhile, Daisy had began an affair with Lars Bogard. Palmer vowed to win Daisy back by proving himself the more powerful of the two. In a drunken rage, Palmer headed over to Daisy's with a shotgun, hoping to scare Lars off. Instead, he tripped on a doorstop and accidentally shot himself in the head. This miraculously minor injury stopped Palmer only momentarily from continuing his fight to win Daisy back.

Without revealing their plans to anyone, Angie Baxter and Jesse Hubbard drove across the state line to be married by a justice of the peace.

Nina, with her strict, traditional upbringing, felt uncomfortable living with Steve without the benefit of marriage, but he told her he wasn't ready for that kind of commitment yet. Palmer even tried to bribe him into marriage, but to no avail. Meanwhile, Cliff and Devon were finding they had a lot in common, both being single parents, and when she got a job in the hospital, their friendship grew even closer. One day, Devon's daughter Bonnie almost choked. Cliff saved her by administering the Heimlich maneuver. As he was teaching Devon the same life-saving technique, the session ended in a kiss, and they finally revealed their feelings toward each other.

Despite Cliff's love for Devon, Nina was still in his heart. During a fierce argument with her, Cliff's anger turned to passion and they ended up in bed together. Nina felt she had to tell Steve, who was hardly shaken. So Nina decided to leave him and go home to Cortlandt Manor. When Cliff told Nina they had made a mistake, she was devastated. After a time, Cliff realized he would never love Devon the way she loved him and told her he wanted to cool it for a while. Devastated, Devon, who was an alcoholic, almost took a drink. But she found support from her new friend, child psychologist Lynn Carson. Lynn was gay, a fact she revealed to Devon.

Tad's pursuit of Liza Colby paid off when she finally fell for his charms. Tad began modeling along with his sister Jenny. When he was caught sleeping with a model in Erica's apartment, his career was finished. Tad retreated to Pine Valley while Jenny stayed on in New York. Through her agent, modeling mogul Olga Swenson, Jenny met Tony Barclay, a strikingly handsome male model who was destined to be her partner in work and love. Or so it appeared. In truth, Jenny and Tony's love affair was engineered by Olga purely for business and public relations reasons. It worked so well, Olga suggested they publicize a phony engagement to the press.

Back home in Pine Valley, Tad took a less-than-glamorous job at the Glamorama. Liza Colby's mother, the sex-starved Marian, so enjoyed Tad's shampoos that she suggested they meet again after hours. Before long, Tad was sleeping with both Liza and her mother. When Liza finally discovered her mother was the other woman in Tad's life, she went on a self-destructive rampage.

Erica's new business was going so well, she eagerly began work on her autobiography, *Raising Kane*. She was shocked that the ghostwriter, Michael Roy, had never heard of her but nevertheless found herself attracted to him when they spontaneously kissed after an argument.

Events turned tragic that summer in Pine Valley, when the whole town mourned the death of an innocent child. Chuck was called to the hospital on an emergency and brought Palmer John to The Chateau, where Donna was singing. When a fire broke out, the baby died from smoke inhalation. Donna, unable to accept her son's death, became delusional, believing a rag doll was her son. She ran away to stay with her hooker friend, Candy.

Myrtle told Greg that Jenny and Tony's engagement was a trumped-up publicity stunt, but Jenny insisted it was genuine. Greg finally went to

Jenny and admitted he never blamed Jenny for his accident. Jenny almost revealed the truth to Greg, but Tony arrived home before she could. When Greg left, Jenny told Tony the wedding was off and sent a letter to Greg declaring her love. Greg's mother intercepted the letter and hid it from Greg in his art history book.

Mark continued his downhill spiral, finding himself unable to compose a single note of music without snorting cocaine. Then Ellen suffered a miscarriage, and Mark was so depressed he went on a dangerous binge. When Ellen found out, she started divorce proceedings, despite Mark's promise that he would get help. Even after his rehabilitation, Ellen insisted he stay away from her. He was further rejected when he was turned down for a teaching job at the university.

When Angie first held her newborn son in her arms, she realized she couldn't give him up. But her scheming father Les Baxter was so persuasive he eventually convinced her to sign the adoption papers. When Jesse learned about the baby, he rushed right to the hospital, but was too late. His son had already been given to the adoptive parents. Angie and Jesse began a desperate search for their son. They ended up kidnapping the baby and escaped to Sea City, where they were married again by a justice of the peace. To their shock, they discovered they were wanted by the FBI for kidnapping.

Devon was growing increasingly possessive of her friend, Dr. Lynn Carson. Devon told Lynn how important she was to her. When Lynn's ex-lover called and wanted to see her, Devon felt so jealous, she was convinced she must be gay too. Devon told Lynn she wanted to be her lover. Lynn was stunned and flattered, but she turned her down, knowing Devon would always be straight.

Issues and Answers

Homosexuality

In 1983, Devon McFadden was drawn to Dr. Lynn Carson, daytime's first admitted lesbian character. The doctor/patient relationship grew complicated when a confused Devon declared her feelings for Lynn. The doctor proved to be an understanding friend as she gently helped Devon realize she was heterosexual.

1984

After Jenny's jet-ski exploded, Tad Martin helped Greg Nelson carry his wife to shore. Sadly, she died from her injuries.

Fully recovered from his paralysis, Greg Nelson believed he had lost Jenny forever—until the day he found the letter from Jenny his mother had hidden. Greg was barely able to contain himself as he read the letter and realized she still loved him. He wasted no time going to Jenny, who was to marry Tony that same day. Greg raced to the church, hoping and praying he could stop the ceremony in time. The heads of the stunned wedding guests spun toward the rear of the church, where Greg Nelson stood wild-eyed in the doorway, calling Jenny's name. He charged up the aisle and punched out Tony, demanding to speak with the bride. Greg told a startled Jenny that his mother, Amanda and Tony had kept Jenny's letter from him. When he finally read it, he knew that Jenny still loved him. Greg wanted her to know he felt the same way. He had never stopped loving Jenny.

With this incredible misunderstanding out in the open, Jenny and Greg could finally be together. To the strains of their special song, Irving Berlin's "Always," Jenny and Greg married on Valentine's Day 1984, and began to plan on having a baby. Then Tony came to Pine Valley, determined to win Jenny back. He began an obsessive quest. When Tony confided in his sister, she urged him to give up the fight. She didn't know that Tony plotted to kill Greg during the summer while he and Jenny and Tad were enjoying a midday retreat at a nearby lake. Tony hooked a bomb to the engine of the jet ski Greg had been eager to ride. Tragedy struck when Jenny decided to ride the jet ski first. She was mortally injured in the explosion, and within hours she was gone.

A shattered Greg thought he was hallucinating when he saw a woman who looked almost exactly like Jenny hanging around his wife's grave. Everyone in town was haunted by this Jenny look-a-like named Sheila. Greg would eventually ask her to marry him. But Myrtle persuaded Sheila to leave town. She knew Greg was still in love with his dead wife, Jenny.

Meanwhile, Erica was happily in love and engaged to Mike Roy until a new man arrived on the scene who would have a profound impact upon her life.

With a fierce determination to leave behind memories of his poverty in West Virginia, Adam Chandler came to Pine Valley in the fall of 1984 and became instantly obsessed by the beautiful and alluring Erica Kane. Adam was producer of the forthcoming movie *Raising Kane*, based on Erica's autobiography, which she had written with Mike. According to Erica, she was the only person who could play "Erica Kane." She saw a chance to become a Hollywood legend at last. But first she had to land the role. Mike cautioned Erica that she was a model, not an actress. An insulted Erica argued that as a model she was always acting, creating images. Adam Chandler would be performing cinematic murder if he assigned this role to any other actress.

With steely confidence, Erica finagled a screen test. Flying to Hollywood, she played herself in a dramatization of the moment she had killed Kent Bogard. Unimpressed, Adam hired another actress, Danielle, to play Erica Kane. Erica drugged Danielle's coffee during the shooting so she might take over the role herself. Adam finally gave in and cast Erica in the lead.

Meanwhile, Adam secretly plotted to become Erica Kane's husband. To do so, he had to get Mike Roy out of the picture. Knowing Mike enjoyed writing and that his special interest was Tibet, Adam arranged to have him sent there on a book-writing assignment. When Mike and Erica argued about his leaving, Adam was delighted. With his competition gone, Adam charged full throttle to claim his prize. Adam saw to it that Erica never knew he was behind Mike's departure. On an angry rebound, Erica married Adam and moved into the Chandler mansion—where strange things were beginning to happen.

Ellen's granddaughter, Bonnie McFadden, began to talk about her imaginary friend, Willy, whom she met at the Chandler estate. A worried Ellen started dating Adam's nephew Ross in an effort to uncover what was going on within the walls of the Chandler estate. Meanwhile, Erica began hearing eerie noises coming from the west wing. Adam was keeping a closely guarded secret. When Erica learned the truth, she was horrified. Adam had an identical twin brother named Stuart. He was Adam's mirror image, but it was clear something wasn't right about Stuart.

One day, Stuart escaped the west wing and joined a tour of the neighboring Cortlandt manor. Wielding a knife at Palmer, Stuart publicly declared Palmer's true identity.

Palmer Cortlandt was born Pete Cooney, the Chandlers' lifelong enemy. Decades earlier, Pete had gotten their sister Lottie pregnant back in their hometown of Pigeon Hollow, West Virginia. Before Pete knew Lottie was pregnant, he was sent off to war. Lottie thought that he had deserted her and suffering from a broken heart, she took her own life. She left behind Pete's legacy: a son, Ross Chandler. To this day, the Chandlers had carried a vendetta against Pete Cooney, the man who rose above his humble beginnings and changed his name to Palmer Cortlandt.

Cliff Warner's troubles continued after his divorce from Nina when his wild, flame-haired sister Linda came to town with her low-life boyfriend, Chris. When Chris was shot in a robbery, Linda desperately tried to convince her brother to remove the bullet but not report the crime. Cliff knew he would be in breach of ethics, but he gave in to the

Gone, But Not Forgotten
Jenny Gardner

Jenny Gardner was the sweetest, most innocent and certainly one of the most beautiful characters to light up our afternoons. When Jenny and her beloved Greg finally overcame life's obstacles and married, no two young people had a brighter future. Their life together proved sweet but oh-so short, when Jenny was tragically killed just months after their wedding.

The Complete Stories

desperation in his sister's eyes. That proved to be a disastrous mistake for young Doctor Warner. When the authorities discovered he had aided and abetted the criminals, Cliff's medical license was suspended. Without his beloved medical career to keep him occupied, Cliff floundered. He held a variety of non-medical jobs before starting work as a medical consultant for a local TV station. Liza Colby, who worked at the same station, grew very close to Cliff.

Edna Thornton constantly belittled her teen-age daughter Dottie, insisting that the girl was too fat and unattractive to get a date.

Meanwhile, Nina became mesmerized by the phony healing abilities of a con artist from Locust Street named Zach Grayson. Donna recognized Zach from her days on the street and didn't trust him. But Liza's mother, Marion Colby, did and began an affair with Zach.

Cleared of kidnapping their own child, Jesse and Angie Hubbard settled into married life with their infant son, Frankie. Jesse soon found that supporting a family was more difficult than he had imagined. Along with Greg and Jenny, the Hubbards had jointly decided to buy a restaurant/club called The Steam Pit. Jesse went to a loan shark named Murray for his part of the purchase money. Murray tormented Jesse for payment of the loan, and eventually he took over The Steam Pit. Later it was destroyed by an explosion.

Palmer took a major hit when the IRS froze his assets and charged him with income tax evasion. Palmer's financial woes were not his fault. He had been foiled from the grave by Lars Bogard. Lars had paid Cortlandt Electronics VP Lois Klingensmith to spy on Palmer and to fix his books. Now Lars was dead, Lois was missing and Palmer was penniless. Palmer had to shut down Cortlandt Electronics. He was forced to take a menial job as front man for Adam Chandler, who wanted to build a controversial gambling mall in Pine Valley. Brooke English thwarted Adam's "get-even-richer" plans when she spearheaded a grassroots movement that eventually passed a referendum outlawing gambling in Pine Valley.

A pregnant Brooke left Tom after he and Erica had gotten drunk and slept together the night before Erica married Adam. Tom tried to prove Brooke was an unfit mother before she even had the baby. Meanwhile, Brooke and Mark had grown close. Mark was with her the night she gave birth to her and Tom's daughter, Laura.

Tad was being secretly paid by Edna, Dottie's mother, to take Dottie out, only Dottie really fell for him. Phoebe had taken under her wing a young college student named Hillary, who was Langley's daughter by a former wife. Tad fell in love with Hillary and rejected Dottie. To hang onto him, Dottie threw away her birth control pills and got pregnant. She tried to force Tad to marry her, but he was in love with Hillary. When Hillary learned of Dottie's pregnancy, she encouraged Tad to do the right thing, although Tad only wanted Hillary. Tad did marry Dottie, who proceeded to miscarry, a fact she kept from Tad. Meanwhile, Tad's friend, Bob Georgia, fell in love with Hillary.

By now, Palmer had regained his fortune when the Cortlandt Electronics corporate VP, Lois Klingensmith, was apprehended. With Lois behind bars, the government unfroze Palmer's assets. Ellen and Ross got married at Cortlandt Manor. Ross's hateful former wife Cynthia Preston attended the wedding and at Palmer's invitation, moved into Cortlandt Manor with her son, Andrew.

To test his wife Erica's affections, Adam faked his own death. Erica realized she was still in love with Mike Roy, and after Adam's "death," got re-engaged to him. When Adam showed up alive, Erica was furious. Adam told her that if she wanted a divorce, she must choose between his fortune and her love for Mike. She chose Mike.

On her death bed, Betty Wilson revealed to her daughter Hillary that Langley Wallingford (a.k.a. Leslie Wilson) was her natural father.

83

Almost everyone in Pine Valley, it seemed, had a reason to kill Zach Grayson, the hustler and con artist who ingratiated himself with, and proceeded to blackmail, anyone who crossed his path. Zach drugged Nina, propped her unconscious body beside him in bed, and got Cliff's bad-seed sister Linda to snap blackmail photos. Then he tried to sell the incriminating images to a furious Cliff. Daisy even slept with Zach in an attempt to recover the damaging photos. Palmer tried to pay Zach off in exchange for the pictures. Zach also took blackmail pictures of Palmer's new wife Cynthia while she was having a one-night stand with her ex-husband Ross, who was currently married to Ellen.

Desperate to stop Zach, Cynthia finally asked Ross to hire a hitman and do away with the blackmailer. Ross refused—but someone did kill Zach Grayson. Ross found Zach dead one night in his apartment, a hysterical Daisy holding a bloody knife over Zach's body. She swore she didn't kill him, but Daisy was arrested and brought to trial.

Meanwhile, Tad suffered through his marriage to Dottie, all the while loving Hillary, who had turned for comfort to Tad's best friend, Bob Georgia. When Tad finally discovered Dottie wasn't pregnant, he raced to Hillary, hoping beyond hope they could resume their relationship. But Tad was too late. She was already engaged to Bob Georgia. Hillary felt she had to go through with the wedding because Bob was suffering from a terminal illness and had only a year to live. Hillary was determined to fill Bob's waning days with happiness.

Tad understood Hillary's reasons for marrying Bob and spent every precious moment with her in the weeks before the wedding. They shared their feelings and confessed their love for each other. Phoebe,

On Location

In a 1985 storyline involving freedom of the press, journalist Brooke English was jailed for failing to reveal a source. The drama was heightened by realistic scenes taped in an actual prison. *All My Children* was the first and only daytime drama to receive permission to bring its cameras to Sing Sing, the New York State correctional facility at Ossining.

worried Hillary would fall again for Tad, insisted that her step-daughter marry Bob right away. Longing for Tad but duty-bound, Hillary fulfilled her obligation and married Bob, with a melancholy Tad serving as best man. Afterward, on a long walk to ponder his future, Tad stepped right into a new adventure. On the road, he hitched a ride with a gorgeous blonde stranger named Mickey Barlowe who turned out to be working for a call-girl ring operator. Kristie, a hooker neighbor of Tad's, stole from the ring operator a computer disk full of valuable client addresses and planted it on Tad. Mickey's boss, Barton Crane, desperately wanted to recover the disk and would do anything to get it, so Tad went on the run. Unknown to anyone, Tad's little brother Joey had innocently stowed the disk in his toy chest after finding it in the pocket of one of Tad's suits. Once the disk was found, Tad was out of danger.

Brooke English and Mark Dalton look on in despair after Mike Roy was shot while investigating a scandal involving corruption in the legal system. Mike died from his wound.

Meanwhile, Bob Georgia had made an amazing discovery. His disease had gone into remission; he wasn't going to die. Realizing this good news could mean the end of his marriage, Bob didn't tell Hillary. But Alfred Vanderpoole, Pine Valley's resident nerd, discovered the benign state of Bob's disease and mentioned to Hillary, who promptly sued her husband for divorce. Finally, Tad and Hillary were free to become man and wife.

Erica, in love with Mike, now a journalism professor at Pine Valley University, continued to be harassed by an obsessed Adam. TV anchorwoman Brooke English was sent to jail for not revealing a source in a municipal scandal she exposed. After getting out, Brooke went to a party with her fiancé Mark. There, a henchman of the corrupt judge involved in the scandal tried to shoot them. Mike took the bullet instead, and Erica swore their long-delayed wedding vows over Mike's body just as he died.

Erica left to scatter Mike's ashes in Tibet, where she learned Mike had once saved a fellow monk's life. Erica told Kantu, head of the monk's order, that she didn't want to live anymore without Mike. Kantu served Erica some tea, and she fell into a deep sleep. In Erica's dream, Mike came to her, urging her to return to Pine Valley, something wonderful awaited her. Upon her return home, Erica took a job as editor of *Tempo* magazine. She met a handsome man named Jeremy who came to do some art work for the magazine. Erica didn't know Jeremy had been sent there from Tibet or that he was the monk Mike had saved. She and Jeremy were instantly attracted and fell in love, but he was reluctant to consummate their relationship because he had sworn a vow of celibacy.

An aspiring singer named Yvonne Caldwell, with whom Jesse sang duets, became romantically interested in her partner. Jesse's half-brother Eugene then conspired with her to break up Jesse and Angie. They

The Complete Stories

Issues and Answers
Sexual Harassment

In 1985, Dr. John Voight tried to take advantage of intern Angie Baxter by intimating that he would give her higher grades if she'd have an affair with him. After considerable anguish caused by her dilemma, Angie reported the sexual harassment to hospital superiors and Doctor Voight was fired.

Gone, But Not Forgotten
Kate Martin

KAY CAMPBELL
1905-1985

Kay Campbell was the second actress to play Kate Martin, but in the hearts and minds of *All My Children* viewers, she will always be our "Grandma Kate." Who will ever forget Kate serving up a warm batch of cookies to her friends Mona and Myrtle, or doling out sensible advice to her wayward grandson, Tad? She was the heart and soul of Pine Valley—a warm, wonderful friend who is still greatly missed by those who loved her. Kay Campbell died in 1985.

nearly succeeded when Yvonne lured Jesse into her bed and made sure that Angie discovered the short-lived liaison. Angie eventually forgave Jesse for his indiscretion, but not before she became embroiled in a potentially scandalous situation of her own.

By 1985, Angie Hubbard was attending medical school and was deeply committed to finishing at the top of her class. One of her professors, Dr. John Voight, a married man, tried to take advantage of Angie by suggesting she could improve her grades and her standing in class by having an affair with him. Anguished by her dilemma, Angie reported his sexual harassment to hospital superiors, and Voight was fired. Jesse and Angie resolved their marital problems. When Yvonne and Eugene left town, the couple reveled in a temporary interlude of peace.

Tragedy struck Pine Valley in 1985 when Joe Martin's mother, Grandma Kate, died in her sleep. She was mourned by everyone and eulogized by her son, Joe. "Let us not mourn Kate Martin's death but celebrate her life, just as she would want us to," Joe counseled Kate's friends and loved ones who gathered to pay their respects. "Celebrate her warmth and understanding, her wisdom and counsel, her kindness and generosity, her patience and forbearance, her great strength of character and her wonderful sense of humor. Yes, celebrate even her apple pies, her pot roast and her Sunday morning coffee cake. All these gifts she gave to us with such an abundant outpouring of love that they can enrich us as long as we walk the earth."

Daisy Cortlandt was convicted and sent to prison for Zach Grayson's murder. Fortunately, her unjust imprisonment didn't last long. Soon after Daisy's incarceration, Donna Beck Tyler began having strange nightmares and started to sleepwalk. When Donna's fiancé Benny found blackmail photos of Cynthia and Ross in Donna's closet, he suspected Donna knew more about Zach's murder than she was able to recall. Donna agreed to take truth serum and, under its influence, remembered she had been at Zach's apartment the night of the murder. She vividly recalled seeing a pocketbook with the initial W or possibly an M on it—a pocketbook she had once seen during a social visit to the Wallingfords. Donna remembered the pocketbook belonged to Marion Colby and declared her the murderer. Liza's mother had been sleeping with Zach and confessed to the crime. Marion claimed the murder was self-defense but was still sent to prison. She was released in record time for providing unspoken "favors" to the warden.

Finally over Chuck Tyler, Donna was looking forward to her wedding to Benny. She planned every last detail of the ceremony. Not even Donna could have anticipated the astonishing event that would mar her long-awaited day. A distressed and deeply disturbed Nina Cortlandt Warner—mistakenly believing Donna was responsible for her mother Daisy's unhappiness—secretly carried a gun into the wedding and tried to shoot Donna. Fortunately, Nina missed, but she was sent to a mental hospital, where she regressed into a teenager. Nina completely forgot her marriages to Cliff. When

Palmer tried to exploit the situation to keep Nina and Cliff apart for good, once again he failed.

Palmer was embroiled in a romantic game of his own. After a whirlwind courtship, he married the manipulative Cynthia Preston, who only wanted two things from her reign as Mrs. Palmer Cortlandt: money and power. Cynthia turned Palmer's life upside down. Daisy—who lived nearby in the Cortlandt carriage house—was amused at the upheaval in Palmer's life. She saw through Cynthia's charade and in time so did Palmer, who grew increasingly disenchanted with his new wife. But he did grow to love her son Andrew and legally adopted him, finally gaining a son to carry on the Cortlandt name.

Unfortunately, the Preston/Cortlandt union was short-lived. Seeing the error of his choice, Palmer divorced Cynthia and tried desperately to win back Daisy's love. As she was the only woman Palmer ever truly loved, he vowed to make himself worthy of Daisy if she would just give him another chance.

Brooke and Mark grew apart as she became so busy tending to her career and her daughter Laura she had little time to spend with her husband. While trying to mend her troubled relationship with Mark, Brooke was courted by charming newcomer Gilles St. Clair, who made his living as a professional daredevil. For fun and profit, Gilles performed amazing feats—like scaling the world's tallest buildings. Brooke became infatuated with her fabulous Frenchman, falling into a relationship with him when Mark left to play piano on a cruise ship. Mark told Brooke he didn't know when—or if—he'd ever return to Pine Valley.

To escape his frustrating romance with Erica, Jeremy made a trip to his father's home in Canada. His father Alex was married to a much younger woman named Natalie, a beautiful blonde full of life and passion. Erica invited Alex and Jeremy to come and live in her house in Pine Valley.

In time, Erica was heartbroken to discover that the mysterious woman who had shattered Jeremy's heart in the past was none other than Natalie, who still loved Jeremy. She wanted Jeremy back at any cost, even though she was married to Jeremy's father. And Natalie had an insidious plan to free her from Alex. Aware that he was suffering from heart trouble, Natalie figured she could seduce Alex to his death.

To Erica's immense relief, Kantu the Tibetan monk leader released Jeremy from his vow of celibacy. For the first time Jeremy felt free to be with the woman he loved without the burden of the overwhelming sense of guilt that had plagued him for months. But there was more trouble on the horizon for the lovers. Though married to Jeremy's father, Natalie had eyes only for Jeremy. The last woman she wanted to have him was Erica. To make matters worse, Natalie learned she was pregnant—with Alex's child.

In her new role as editor-in-chief of *Tempo*, Erica visited Canada to interview celebrated author R. L. Peyton. Alex Hunter accompanied her. He was the last man Erica expected to make a pass at her, but Alex did, despite his married state. Disgusted by his gall, Erica rebuffed him, escaping in his Land Rover. Driving through the most rural part of Canada, Erica was suddenly trapped by a rocky landslide. She managed to escape serious injury and make her way to Peyton's cabin, but with the phone lines down, she couldn't establish contact with the outside world. Alex, too, was missing and presumed dead. Jeremy and Natalie joined a fruitless search for their loved ones.

Erica and her date, Alexander Hunter, attended a gala party at the Nexus nightclub in New York. Though she spent the night on the town with him, the man Erica loved was his son Jeremy.

While Jeremy grieved, Natalie used the situation to her advantage. She got him drunk and slipped into bed beside his sleeping body. The next morning, she convinced him that they had made love. Though Jeremy had no memory of the encounter, he was forced to believe his seemingly sincere stepmother.

Jeremy rejoiced when Erica was found alive. Alex also survived the Canadian landslide and returned to Pine Valley, but within weeks, his life would come to an abrupt end. During a fox hunt, Alex fell off his horse and died. When it was discovered that the foot strap of his saddle had been cut, the authorities and Natalie cried foul play. She tried to blackmail Erica with phony evidence that Jeremy committed the murder. But Jeremy was proven innocent when the killer was revealed as young Andrew Cortlandt. Andrew had attempted to sabotage Ross Chandler's mount, but at the last minute, Alex and Ross switched horses. Alex, with his weakened heart, fell to his death.

With Alex Hunter's demise, the pregnant Natalie pursued Jeremy with renewed fervor. He was engaged by now to Erica, but Natalie surprised him with news she was pregnant with his baby. Jeremy was stunned and felt compelled to marry her, leaving Erica in the lurch. Before long, Erica and Jeremy had rekindled their love affair. When Natalie discovered them in their secret hide-away making love, she went after Erica with a gun.

Jeremy arrived on the scene just as the disabled elevator they were in gave way and was about to plunge downward. Jeremy could save only one woman at a time and was torn about who to rescue first. Because of her pregnancy, Jeremy pulled Natalie up first, but returned too late to save Erica. Fortunately, Tom Cudahy was able to grab Erica before the elevator collapsed. Natalie may have won that round, but Erica, as usual, had the last word. Erica revealed that Natalie's marriage to Jeremy was a fraud. They were married by an actor Erica had hired to play a minister.

Recovering from the mental illness that had forced her to be institutionalized, Nina Cortlandt Warner became infatuated with a most unlikely man, Benny Sago. Nina and Benny were a source of strength for each other. Benny, whose marriage to Donna had grown strained with time, was drawn to Nina's innocence and warmth. Though Nina swore she loved Benny, he was reluctant to give his heart to the rich young heiress. Benny remained loyal to his marriage and told Nina nothing could come of their mutual admiration. Dejected by Benny's rejection, Nina joined Daisy and departed on a long cruise.

Meanwhile, the enchanting Dr. Amy Stone became interested in Cliff. With Nina gone, he soon feel in love with Dr. Stone. When Nina returned, Amy overheard her saying she still loved Cliff. To dissuade everyone from that idea, Nina began to date Matt Connelly. Cliff and Amy decided to spend a weekend on Martha's Vineyard—but so did Nina. After Amy's arrival was delayed, Cliff and Nina met accidentally on the beach and shared a romantic afternoon filled with laughs, tears and joy. As they were going their separate ways, both Nina and Cliff refused to admit that they were still very much in love. When Amy and Cliff announced their engagement plans, Nina stoically congratulated them. And when Nina broke up with Matt, Matt angrily confronted Cliff. He called Cliff on his feelings for Nina and forced him to see they still loved each

After escaping from her nearly-deranged husband Adam, Erica Kane sought refuge with her hero, Jeremy Hunter, in these romantic scenes tinged with danger, taped on location in rustic Canada.

other. Matt's words hit home. Realizing the depth of his feelings, Cliff couldn't bear to go through with his marriage to a woman he didn't love. He gently broke the news to Amy.

Deeply upset, Amy ran out in the street and was struck down by a drunken driver. As she clung to life, Dr. Joe Martin called on Pine Valley Hospital's most skilled surgeon to save her life: Cliff Warner. Amy's injuries were too massive. Her death devastated Cliff. Nina stood by and helped Cliff pick up the pieces of his shattered life. After reuniting in Maine, Cliff and Nina became engaged to marry for the third time. Soon after their spectacular black and white wedding at New York's Tavern on the Green, Cliff departed for a special medical mission in Hong Kong, promising to be back soon.

This was the year Tad Martin seemed finally to have gotten his act together. Though Phoebe Tyler Wallingford still had her doubts about his worthiness to marry her stepdaughter Hillary, she reluctantly tended to the arrangements for their Valentine's Day wedding. She even set up young Tad with a respectable job at the Pine Valley Bank. Life was good for Tad Martin, but not for long. On Valentine's Day, the guests gathered at the church for Tad and Hillary's wedding. With everyone in attendance and the bridal party in place, the question still remained: Where

On Location

All My Children's producers ventured to Connecticut for this 1986 scene in which Hillary Wilson, wearing her wedding dress, ran out into the street and was run down by a car driven by Edna Thornton.

was the groom? Phoebe grew impatient and declared Tad the same irresponsible scoundrel he'd always been. Hillary was determined to prove Phoebe wrong. She took off through the snow-covered streets of Pine Valley in search of her groom. Without looking, she stepped into the path of a car driven by Edna Thornton Sago and her daughter, Dottie. Barely escaping injury, Hillary passed out in the middle of the street. Tad's absence wasn't his fault. That morning, robbers had ransacked the bank, locking him and Robin McCall in the vault. When the calamity was cleared up, Tad and Hillary were finally married in a simple ceremony at the Wallingford Mansion.

In 1986, Pine Valley mourned the passing of Dr. Charles Tyler, who had devoted the last years of his life to charitable work and, of course, to his loving wife Mona. Greg Nelson left town, and a newcomer arrived. She was Julie Rand, a spunky young girl who was adopted by newlyweds Ross Chandler and Ellen Dalton.

On a flight south, longtime rivals Erica Kane and Brooke English were hijacked by a band of kidnappers. Jeremy hired fellow ex-mercenary Matt Connelly to save them, though Jeremy wound up saving them himself—and declaring his love for Erica. While stranded on a private island together, Jeremy delivered Natalie's son, Timothy.

Still nursing his obsession with Erica, Adam Chandler rigged a paternity test to prove that Jeremy was the father of Natalie's baby. The deception was soon discovered and Natalie was forced to confess that Alex was the father. Although Jeremy settled an impressive sum on Natalie, she went to work as a nurse for Palmer who was paralyzed after being shot by a thug hired by Adam. Natalie's presence at Cortlandt Manor was just the situation that the competitive Adam relished. He paid Natalie to spy on Palmer.

Erica had a secret, too. Unknown to anyone, she was hiding her brother Mark in the attic of her home. Mark, who had spiraled downward since the failure of his marriage to Ellen, was now a drug addict. To complicate matters, he had been having an affair with a married woman whose jealous husband, Earl Mitchell, came gunning for him. Jeremy was arrested for killing Earl and was sent to jail, where he was severely beaten. This incident petrified Erica, who was desperate to get him out.

Erica made plans to marry Jeremy in prison, secretly scheming to break him out of jail during the ceremony. She even got Matt to fly a helicopter over the prison at the time. As the minister began the ceremony, Erica suddenly faked a faint and in the ensuing confusion, waved Jeremy to follow her to the prison roof where Matt waited in his chopper to whisk them away to free-

Gone, But Not Forgotten
Dr. Charles Tyler

As the Chief of Staff of Pine Valley Hospital, the kindly Dr. Charles Tyler served up medical advice with a homespun flavor that belied his upper-crust upbringing. Dr. Tyler deserved sainthood for putting up with the ravings of his haughty wife, Phoebe, whom he eventually divorced. Charles's last years were happy ones, spent in peace with his devoted wife, Mona. Actor Hugh Franklin, an original cast member, played the role with grace and style, and a warm, welcoming smile. He passed away in 1986.

dom. Jeremy refused to escape, citing the consequences. He chose to remain behind and was freed when Mark Dalton was charged with—and eventually cleared of—Earl Mitchell's death. Erica, furious and unforgiving, departed from Jeremy's life forever.

Tad and Hillary moved into a Pine Valley apartment and were immediately unsettled by the arrival of a beautiful young singer, Skye Patterson. She was later revealed to be Adam Chandler's long-lost daughter. She seductively tempted Tad and infuriated Hillary with her brazen flirtations. But she wasn't the first sexy young woman to drive a wedge between the newly married Martins. Tad became attracted to Robin McCall, his former bank vault-mate.

Robin's brother, a slick young con-man named Wade Matthews, arrived in Pine Valley and set his sights on the wealthy Phoebe Tyler Wallingford. Wade succeeded in splitting up Phoebe and Langley. He lured the former Mrs. Wallingford to the Caribbean, where, in a drunken stupor, she became his wife. Back in Pine Valley, he and his girlfriend Shelley plotted to poison Phoebe, but the plan backfired when Shelley tumbled down a staircase to her death. Phoebe was jailed for pushing her, and Wade started selling off her possessions. She soon discovered his treachery after her release from behind bars. When Wade was caught red-handed, he proceeded to drug Phoebe and left her to die. But she survived and Wade was apprehended as he tried to make his way out of town dressed as a woman. When Hillary found out Tad had known of Wade's scam all along, she exploded, demanding a divorce. With his life in shambles, Tad broke the news to his mother, Ruth, that he had decided to leave Pine Valley. He confided that he needed a fresh start and conceded that his father may have been right; that it was time Tad grew up. With a loving hug, Tad was gone.

On Location

A rooftop high above New York's Westchester County's Wingdale hospital provided the setting for suspense in 1986 when Erica Kane concocted a scheme to spring Jeremy Hunter from prison on their wedding day. Erica's elaborate plan failed when Jeremy refused to go along with a daring helicopter escape.

Nina was overjoyed to get the news that her husband Cliff, who had been working in Hong Kong for months, was on his way home. Before reaching the United States, Doctor Warner stopped in a war-torn South American country to deliver emergency supplies. Knowing he was undertaking a dangerous mission, Cliff took every precaution to insure his safety. He promised Nina he'd be home within days. But when the day of Cliff's return came and went, Nina grew alarmed.

Soon the words Nina dreaded came: Cliff had been shot and killed by rebel forces. Nina held back her grief, refusing to accept that the impossible had happened. She couldn't accept it. Nina took off for South America to see for herself. She was not alone for long. Matt Connelly, a former mercenary soldier, joined her on her fruitless search.

A devastated Nina returned home to Pine Valley, then retreated to Martha's Vineyard to be alone with her memories of Cliff. Matt followed Nina to the beach house to offer comfort, where he was met with a barrage of anger. Nina demanded to be left alone. But Matt wasn't going anywhere. Nina warmed to Matt after he refused to adhere to her demands, and when he finally announced he was leaving, Nina urged him to stay. In Matt's comforting arms, Nina at last broke down, releasing her grief. Clinging to each other, they made passionate love. The next morning, she stunned Matt by asking him to marry her. Perhaps not even Nina realized how much her conservative, traditional background still influenced her.

After a painstaking investigation, Brooke English discovered that her real mother was Jane Dobrin, a homeless woman.

To the utter surprise of her family, Nina returned to Pine Valley as Mrs. Matt Connelly. But plagued by memories of Cliff, Nina was never able to give herself fully to Matt, and their marriage suffered because of it. Then she learned Cliff was alive. He had not been killed by the rebel forces, but was held prisoner for several months. Cliff and Nina enjoyed a romantic reunion, reaffirming their love with a night of lovemaking. Yet she couldn't bring herself to reveal that she had married Matt. When Cliff learned the truth, he stormed away from her in a rage.

Jesse and Angie Hubbard's turbulent marriage took another dramatic turn when Jesse's old flame Yvonne Caldwell turned up in town nine months pregnant, declaring that he was the father of her child. Jesse held to the truth that he'd never slept with her—there was no way he was the baby's father. Seeing the error of her ways, Yvonne called Angie and admitted the truth before going into labor and giving birth. Yvonne planned to give up her infant to a baby-selling ring.

Jesse went undercover to find the leader of this heinous organization, discovering that "Mr. Big" was none other than his father-in-law, Les Baxter. Jesse stumbled upon Les's secret life at a time when his father-in-law was blackmailing senatorial candidate Travis Montgomery. Les claimed Travis was the father of Yvonne's child. Travis feared that this information, preposterously untrue, if leaked, could cripple his candidacy. Without telling Angie, Jesse followed Travis to his meeting with "Mr. Big," hoping to catch him in a bribe. The plan went awry when Les spotted his son-in-law. Angie arrived on the scene in time to witness her husband holding a gun on her father. When Angie's scream distracted Jesse, Les kicked the gun out of his hand. A struggle ensued and Les fell down a stairwell, plunging to his death. Jesse received a commendation for his heroic efforts, but the reward was bittersweet. Angered by her husband's deception, Angie left him.

Though his problems with the law were over, Mark Dalton's cocaine abuse escalated. Erica was blind to her brother's drug problem until the day she found him secluded in his attic hideaway, high as a kite. Feeling deceived, she insisted Mark get help. Summoning Mark's friends Brooke English, Jeff Martin and his former wife Ellen, Erica spearheaded an "intervention" on Mark. Alone in a room, Mark's loved ones pointed out all his lies and deceits, swearing they wouldn't have anything more to do with him unless he sought professional help.

Mark was unmoved by their efforts at first. But abandoned by those whose love he cherished, Mark quickly came to see the error of his ways. He checked himself into a rehabilitation center and was finally able to come to grips with his problem.

While in recovery, Mark was mortified to learn that Fred Parker, one of his drug-taking cronies, had died of AIDS. Fearing he may have contracted the AIDS virus, a worried Mark took an HIV test, which fortunately proved negative.

Fred Parker's widow, Cindy, a lovely, kind young woman in desperate need of a place to stay, soon arrived in Pine Valley with her young son Scott in tow. Cindy accepted Angie's gracious offer to live in her house, and within days of her arrival, became friends with her son's art teacher, the kindly Stuart Chandler.

Ross Chandler continued to play with fire by carrying on a torrid affair with Palmer's private nurse, Natalie Hunter. He felt neglected by his wife Ellen, who was devoting her time and energy to helping her ex-husband Mark recover from his addiction. Ross became obsessed with his fair-haired paramour, but their affair remained secret—until the January day Jeremy Hunter stumbled upon the lovers in the throes of a passionate kiss. Jeremy agreed to keep silent, but it wasn't long before others learned of the affair taking place behind closed doors at Cortlandt Manor. In March, Ross's adopted daughter Julie witnessed her father and Natalie in a clinch and recorded what she saw in her diary. When Adam Chandler found and read her entry, he used it to threaten his nephew. The walls were closing in on Ross. His life grew more complicated when Palmer proposed marriage to Natalie. Feeling she would never possess Ross completely, Natalie accepted Palmer's offer and became his wife.

Though he still ached for Natalie, Ross tried to resume his marriage to Ellen, but their union unraveled that September when he murmured Natalie's name in his sleep. Ellen listened in stunned horror, then packed her bags and left him.

His personal life in ruins, an enraged Ross angrily moved through the huge mansion, entered Natalie's room, and raped her. Hearing Natalie's screams, Julie fled Cortlandt Manor in tears, boarding a train out of town.

Family Crisis Intervention Therapy

When music teacher Mark Dalton became addicted to cocaine and refused to seek help, his friends and family intervened in 1987. Guided by family therapists, those closest to Mark—his ex-wife, sister Erica and friend Brooke—confronted him about his problem. With therapy, Mark eventually came to grips with his illness.

Mark Dalton's family intervention

Erica:
Mark, it's okay. It's all right, Mark, it's all out in the open now, it's okay, all the lies, all the deceptions, it's out. And now we can start dealing with it.

Mark:
I don't know if I'll ever get out of this Erica. I feel like I'm up to my...

Ellen:
Mark, listen to me, you have taken the first step, the first step, Mark. Look around you, you're not alone. These people are just like you, and look, they're fighting, they're fighting to get over it, to make their lives better. They're not giving up, Mark. And we won't let you either, do you understand? We love you too much for that, we do!

Witnessing the rape was a devastating blow for young Julie Chandler, an innocent girl in love with her teenage sweetheart, Charlie Brent. In 1987, Julie was overjoyed when she came to know her natural mother, Elizabeth Carlyle, who made the surprising confession that Mark Dalton was Julie's father. Elizabeth harbored another explosive secret. The reason she had given Julie up for adoption was that she had been a prostitute. Earlier on the night of Natalie's rape, Julie confronted her mother, who was forced to admit this devastating secret.

Still reeling from these disturbing events, Julie fled to New York, where she met Creed Kelly, who claimed to be her friend. In reality, he was a sworn enemy of Julie's natural mother, Elizabeth, and he was determined to get back at her by seducing Julie. Creed wasn't alone in his scheme to ingratiate himself with Julie. Assisting him was his nephew, Nico Kelly, a darkly handsome young man who appeared, at least on the surface, to be as cold and ruthless as Uncle Creed. But Julie came to see that beneath his frosty exterior, Nico had a heart of gold.

Back in Pine Valley, Julie's lonely beau, Charlie, was ripe for seduction at the hands of Cecily Davidson, Phoebe's feisty god-daughter. As the weeks passed, Julie found herself both attracted and frightened by her protector, Creed. Her suspicions were warranted. When Creed tried to seduce her, Julie screamed and ran into the bathroom, where she found her mother Elizabeth, bound and gagged. Creed's plan to rape Julie in front of her mother was thwarted by his nephew, Nico, who raced in, overpowered his uncle and stopped him. Creed fled, and Julie apologized to Nico for misjudging him. He was later apprehended and imprisoned for his role in Creed's scheme, but by that point, he and Julie were very much in love.

In November, all eyes were on the Pine Valley courthouse where Ross Chandler stood trial for the rape of Natalie Hunter Cortlandt. Natalie had a difficult time proving her case because she had no witnesses or corroborating evidence. It was her word against Ross's. He coolly told the jury that Natalie seduced him on that fateful night. While the jury deliberated, Julie returned and confronted Ross. She forced him to acknowledge that what took place that night was not seduction—it was rape.

As the judge was about to announce the verdict, Ross raced in to the packed courtroom and announced he was guilty of raping Natalie. Ross was sentenced to prison where he underwent intense therapy. There he came to grips with his deeply rooted reasons for taking his anger out on Natalie.

Erica found herself increasingly attracted to suave businessman and aspiring politician Travis Montgomery. But she soon found herself butting heads with Travis's ex-wife, chic business whiz Barbara Montgomery. While campaigning for the Senate, Travis was shot. It turned out the bullet—which barely grazed him—was actually intended for Erica. The chief suspect became Adam's vengeful sister-in-law Joanna, who eventually kidnapped Erica. Before Joanna could inflict any harm on her captive, Travis rescued her, and their problems appeared to be over until Joanna claimed she knew nothing about the shooting. Erica hoped Travis would propose to her, but he was too caught up in his many business and political interests. Marriage was the farthest thing from his mind. His attitude changed dramatically when Erica

In December 1987, Dr. Angie Hubbard broke the news to a devastated Cindy that she had contracted the AIDS virus.

became pregnant with his child. Erica intended to keep the news secret from Travis for fear it would destroy his campaign. But Barbara blurted it out to him, and Travis asked Erica to marry him.

While planning her wedding, Erica met and became intrigued with Travis's brother, Jackson Montgomery. He was an unscrupulous attorney who helped Travis win the race for Senate but ultimately brought about his brother's political demise by mismanaging Travis's campaign funds. Newly elected, Travis chose to resign before the truth came out.

Complicating matters for Erica was the revelation that Noelle Keaton, a young woman suffering from amnesia, was actually her long-lost sister, Silver. While helping Noelle unlock the secret of her past, Jeremy Hunter fell in love with her. Erica joined in the quest, which took them to Cobbler's Island in Canada, where they encountered Silver's mother, Goldie Kane. Goldie's hatred of Erica was ignited when Eric Kane's will designated her daughter Silver as the sole owner of the island—but only in the event of Erica's death. Erica was stunned to discover that Goldie had hypnotized Silver to carry out Erica's murder. By the end, it was Goldie who pulled the trigger, shooting the pregnant Erica in the abdomen. Travis had arrived on the island earlier and married Erica in their own private ceremony. He rushed his wife back to Pine Valley, where emergency surgery was performed to remove the bullet that put the life of her unborn child in danger.

Back on Cobbler's Island, Goldie Kane's life appeared to come to an end when, in a struggle with Silver, Goldie fell off a boat and disappeared into the sea. Traumatized by these tragic events, Silver returned to Pine Valley with Jeremy and began treatment at Oak Haven Sanitarium with psychiatrist Dr. Damon Lazarre. Jeremy was wary of Dr. Lazarre, and his suspicions were confirmed when the doctor turned out to be the head of a mysterious cult. The manipulative Dr. Lazarre was discovered to be Silver's husband and was the force behind Goldie's plan to kill Erica. The storyline culminated on a bridge where Lazarre, his secret exposed, was about to push Erica and Silver to their deaths. But Jeremy raced heroically to their rescue, and after a struggle, Lazarre fell to his own death.

At year's end, Angie broke the sorrowful news to Cindy Parker that she had contracted the AIDS virus from her late, drug-using husband, Fred. The news at first shocked her friends, but they remained devoted to her.

Jesse's fear of AIDS December 1987

Jesse:

I know that you can't catch AIDS by living in the same house with somebody. And whether you have it or not,
I don't want you to move.

Cindy:

You told Angie...

Jesse:

I know what I told Angie, and I'm sorry you overheard that. I was wrong, and when I'm wrong, boy am I wrong. The point is you and Scotty are practically family.... I want you to know that you have a place with us if you need. I'm just sorry I shot my mouth off before I knew what I was talking about. Forgive me?

Cindy:

Thank you.

The Complete Stories

One memorable winter afternoon in February 1988, Erica Kane gave birth to a healthy baby girl, no small feat for Erica. Late in her pregnancy, she developed a searing pain in her head, causing her to collapse in her apartment. She was rushed to Pine Valley Hospital and diagnosed with toxemia. Joe Martin told Travis if it wasn't treated, Erica

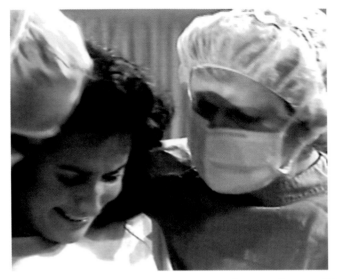

could have a stroke, resulting in the possible death of Erica and her baby. Travis tended to her every need and gave her a wedding ring, promising to place it on her finger no matter what happened. Weakened by her condition, Erica lapsed into unconsciousness. In her dream state, Erica imagined she was on a movie sound stage. There, she encountered all the men she had ever loved and lost, including her father, Eric Kane. Erica returned to reality and went into labor. With Travis by her side, she safely delivered her baby. She named her daughter Bianca, and the child became the darling of Pine Valley.

Ellen and Ross's marriage, destroyed by his affair and subsequent rape of Natalie, ended in divorce, but Ellen refused to give in to depression. Mark was waiting in the wings and they soon discovered love is sweeter the second time around. They married in hopes of a happy home life with Mark's natural daughter, Julie. But Julie wasn't so willing to accept Mark as her father. Having broken up for good with Charlie Brent, who returned to Stanford University, Julie turned her romantic attentions to Nico Kelly. Nico had recently been released from

prison and placed on probation. By year's end, Julie and Nico had married, facing the future together. Returning to Pine Valley as man and wife, they were blissfully unaware that their marriage was invalid because the small-town mayor who officiated their simple ceremony was not authorized to perform weddings.

The romantic triangle of Cliff, Nina and Matt grew more complicated when Nina became pregnant. Nina had slept with both men and realized that either man could be the father of her unborn child. Believing she truly loved Matt, the pregnant Nina sadly divorced Cliff and left town with her new man.

Angie broke the sorrowful news to Cindy that she had contracted the AIDS virus. At this point, Cindy was romantically involved with Stuart Chandler, who vowed to stand by the woman he loved. The rest of Pine Valley was not as understanding. Cindy was harassed and nearly killed in a fire set by a vigilante group who wanted the young AIDS victim to leave town. Cindy would have died in the fire if not for the heroic efforts of Adam Chandler's daughter, Skye, who was now married to Tom Cudahy. Skye raced into the burning fire and rescued Cindy. Having inhaled the noxious smoke, Skye passed out and fell into a long coma. Tom discovered his wife had been one of the AIDS-fearing vigilantes. He was shocked when he learned it was Skye who had arranged the fire, only to have second thoughts at the last moment.

With Skye in a coma, Tom turned to Barbara Montgomery for comfort. Before long, romance blossomed between them. Skye finally woke from her three-month-long coma on Stuart and Cindy's wedding day. She lurked in the background and watched as they exchanged their vows. But something more caught her eye. The impact of seeing Tom with Barbara Montgomery sent Skye back into a coma. Only this time, it was a lie. Skye had devised a plan to keep Tom by her side, and it worked. He promised not to desert her, not knowing whether she could hear him or not. She was determined not to lose Tom to Barbara, even after she miraculously recovered a few weeks later. Feigning paralysis, Skye's scheme to keep Tom was failing. Tom had fallen deeply in love with his mistress. But that didn't stop Skye. In desperation, she kidnapped Barbara at gun point and threatened to kill her. She might have done it if Sean Cudahy hadn't alerted his brother to her actions. Arriving on the scene, Tom pleaded with his deranged wife to hand over the gun. A defeated Skye surrendered it and was carted

off to jail where she slipped into a catatonic state and was taken to Oak Haven Sanitarium.

With that crisis behind him, Tom looked forward to happiness with Barbara. He never guessed that within a few short months, he would suffer the greatest loss of his life. Barbara was baby-sitting Tom and Brooke's daughter Laura one night. Engrossed in her work, Barbara didn't realize the gravity of her decision to let Laura play with a friend who lived across the street. As the little girl crossed the street, she was run down and killed by a passing car. The driver, police officer Josh Waleski, had just come from a party and was driving drunk. Numb with grief, Tom and Brooke donated Laura's organs so others might live.

The Complete Stories

Issues and Answers

Drunk Driving

In 1988, Brooke and Tom's young daughter, Laura Cudahy, died at the hands of a drunk driver when she ran into the street and was killed by an oncoming car. The driver was an intoxicated Josh Waleski, a Pine Valley police officer who had just come from a departmental party. This emotionally charged story demonstrated that even nice people can kill when they drink and drive.

Haunted by the memories of her last moments with Laura, Barbara worried that this tragedy would destroy any hope she had with Tom.

Having served his time in prison for killing Sybil Thorne, Tom's wayward brother Sean resurfaced in Pine Valley determined to start anew. Sean assured Tom he had changed, but it wasn't long before his money-grubbing ways took over. He had set his romantic sights on Cecily Davidson, whose attractive trust fund made Sean salivate. Cecily's meddling mother Bitsy stubbornly insisted that a former convict wouldn't make a suitable husband for her daughter, but Cecily agreed to marry Sean. She didn't know that Bitsy wanted Sean for herself. Bitsy even had the gall to suggest Sean dump Cecily and run away with her, an offer Sean needed time to consider.

Defying Adam, Stuart and Cindy married in a beautifully tender ceremony and exchanged personal vows. Soon after, Cindy's weakening condition kept her in and out of Pine Valley Hospital. Stuart supported her while she bravely fought off the infections that ravaged her frail body. She tried to maintain as normal a life as possible for her family, considering the circumstances.

Now that their lives were free of the tumult that plagued their first year together, Jeremy and Silver tried unsuccessfully to resume their courtship. She soon became obsessed with the idea that Jeremy was still attracted to Natalie. Though she claimed she was through with men, having just divorced Palmer, it was clear Natalie still had eyes for her first love, Jeremy.

Erica encouraged Silver to toughen up if she expected to keep Jeremy and Natalie apart. Erica warned that Silver was dealing with a vulture, and Silver took her sister's words to heart. Clad in black, she broke into Natalie's house pretending to be a rapist. Repeated attempts to unnerve Natalie were all in vain. She was too late. Jeremy and Natalie had fallen in love.

Jeremy confessed his feelings to Silver, sadly delivering the news that they must break up. Angry and distraught, Silver confronted Natalie in her apartment. Natalie carried a gun because she feared the rapist was on the premises and was shocked to learn it was Silver Kane who had stalked her. Deranged with anger, Silver blasted Natalie for stealing Jeremy and lunged for her gun. A struggle ensued and the pistol went off. Silver fell to the floor dead. In a panic, Natalie hid Silver's corpse, but she couldn't keep the death from Palmer, who happened upon the scene, then placed a call to his lawyer. He calmly told Walter he and Natalie were ending divorce proceedings. Palmer took care of all the arrangements, making it appear that Silver had left town. With Natalie's help, he dumped the body in a pond on his vast estate and blackmailed Natalie into becoming his wife again.

When Silver's body surfaced weeks later, it looked as if Natalie would be charged with murder. Fortunately for Natalie, the telephone answering machine in her apartment had accidentally recorded the encounter with Silver. The tape, which Palmer had stolen, exonerated Natalie. The charges against her were dropped, but Palmer was arrested for obstruction of justice and sentenced to serve one-to-three years in prison. Using

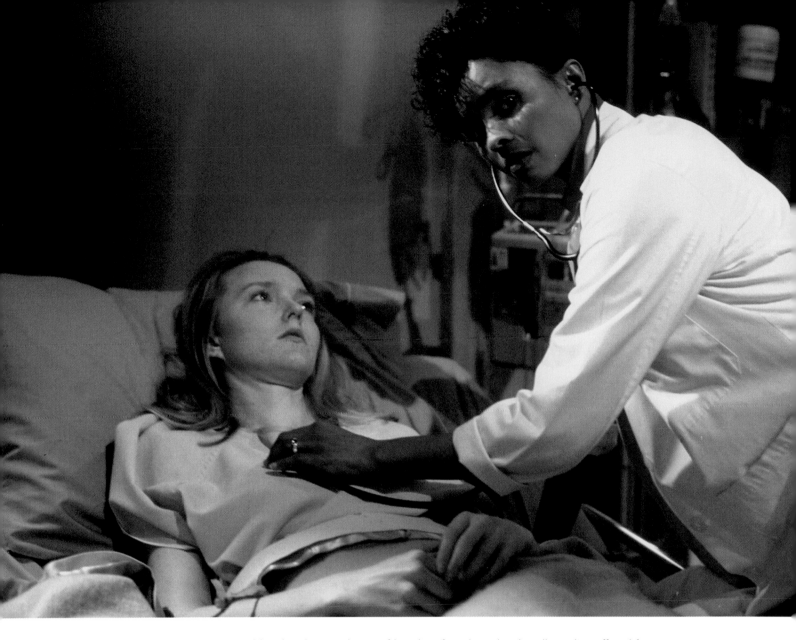

At Pine Valley Hospital, Dr. Angie Hubbard took special care of her dear friend Cindy Chandler, who suffered from AIDS.

his power and money to its full advantage, he enjoyed special privileges at the prison work farm.

The cloud of scandal that hovered over Natalie finally lifted in the autumn of 1988 when she married Jeremy Hunter, whom she had loved for so long. After a year fraught with adultery, rape, murder and blackmail, she looked forward to a happy future with Jeremy. While walking down the aisle, Natalie didn't notice that Palmer Cortlandt, who was on furlough from jail, was in attendance. Palmer's plan to stop the wedding was thwarted when he suddenly took ill and retreated to the vestibule where he collapsed. A mystery

Issues and Answers

AIDS

In 1988, Stuart Chandler fell in love with Cindy Parker, a young woman who became infected with the AIDS virus from her drug-addicted husband. Despite a challenge from his brother Adam, Stuart married Cindy and they demonstrated tremendous courage in the face of this terrible disease. When some misguided Pine Valley residents, among them Stuart's niece Skye Chandler, attempted to drive Cindy out of town they stood together. Upon her death, Cindy's friends and family designed a cloth square to contribute to the national AIDS quilt.

woman named Marissa Rampal came upon the stricken Palmer and rushed him to Pine Valley Hospital, where it a near-fatal heart attack was diagnosed.

Marissa had been secretly tracking Jeremy's every move. She turned out to be a former flame Jeremy had believed was dead. He was understandably stunned to see her alive. She surprised him again with the news that they had a son. The following week, David Rampal, a strong and handsome teenager, arrived in Pine Valley. Meeting his father for the first time, a distant David was reluctant to accept Jeremy. Jeremy came to love the boy nonetheless and worked to earn his affection and admiration while David harbored a secret dream that his parents would reunite.

Angie and Jesse reconciled, but their happy time together was brief. Jesse, now a police officer, was gunned down by a bullet meant for a slick criminal character he was pursuing. Angie was devastated and many years would pass before she could think romantically about anyone.

Angie pleaded for her husband Jesse not to die. Sadly, Jesse passed away moments later.

Dixie Cooney and her brother Will left Pigeon Hollow in search of their late rich uncle, Pete Cooney. Pete had long since changed his name to Palmer Cortlandt and hired Dixie as a maid for Cortlandt Manor, not knowing she was his niece.

Erica, Travis and Bianca appeared to finally have it all, but Travis was too proud to admit to Erica that his financial empire was crumbling. With help from Travis's envious brother Jack, Adam Chandler led a hostile takeover attempt of Travis's company. Travis managed to survive Adam's bid, but the ordeal left him in severe financial straits. To pay off his massive debts, Travis concocted a phony kidnapping plot in which his insurance company would pay $15 million for his safe return. When the plot backfired, Steven Andrews, the man Travis hired to execute the scheme, was hell bent on revenge and snatched Bianca, demanding the $15 million for himself.

Travis was able to get Bianca back, but lost his wife in the process. Erica couldn't believe he could sink to such extremes. She took Bianca and secretly fled to Sea City in hopes of a fresh start, without lies and deceits. To keep her husband from finding her, she changed her name to "Sally" and applied for a waitressing job at Al Darby's diner. Erica took a room at Jean's boardinghouse, where in an astonishing coincidence, her fellow houseguest was none other than Steven Andrews, now using the name Dave Gillis. Unaware he was Travis's former partner in crime, Erica struck up a friendship with the handsome and seemingly kind gentleman. Before long, they were lovers, and Dave begged Erica to run away with him to the Riviera. They might have been successful in their attempt to flee the country if Travis hadn't raced to Sea City and stopped them. In a fight to the death, Andrews was shot and killed. Travis suffered a severe head injury and Erica, stunned by this incredible turn of events, realized she still cared for him. Calling off the divorce, she was determined to make a new start with her husband. But before leaving Sea City, Travis was mugged and beaten, leaving him disoriented. When Erica found him, he had no idea who she was.

Gone, But Not Forgotten
Jesse Hubbard

Jesse Hubbard had several strikes against him. Born in the ghetto, Jesse managed to rise above his humble beginnings to become one of Pine Valley's leading citizens, and a loving husband and father to Angie and Frankie. As a police officer, Jesse served the people of Pine Valley, only to tragically lose his life in the line of duty.

1989

With Nina gone from his life, Cliff was drawn to Angie Hubbard, still grieving over the untimely loss of her beloved Jesse. She also found herself sharing time with the mysterious Remington, who was revealed to be a former FBI agent. Angie's budding relationship with Remy bothered Cliff more than he let on. He realized he was falling in love with her. Mounting an offensive, Cliff suggested to Angie that she see him exclusively and she agreed. After Cliff and Angie got engaged and began to plan their wedding, Nina returned to Pine Valley. It wasn't her intention to break up Cliff and Angie. She came back seeking Cliff's expert medical opinion because her son, Michael, was gravely ill. In the process of saving Michael's life, Cliff and Nina discovered what they always suspected, that Michael was Cliff's son, not Matt's. The revelation shattered Nina's marriage to Matt, but it brought Nina and Cliff together again.

In a heartfelt moment, Nina admitted to Angie that she still loved Cliff. Nina's mother Daisy, who had recently returned to Pine Valley, helped Cliff realize he was lying to himself by denying his love for Nina. Giving Cliff up wasn't easy for Angie, but she knew Cliff and Nina were destined to be together. In a beautiful garden ceremony at Cortlandt Manor, they married for the fourth time, leaving to start a new life in Denver. Palmer was doubly devastated. Not only was he losing his daughter, but after the wedding, Daisy turned down his proposal of marriage and departed for France, leaving him alone once again.

For the fourth time, Cliff and Nina Warner got married, this time with their son Bobby and Nina's father Palmer looking on.

Meanwhile, Adam had Brooke, but their marriage suffered when she was unable to give him the son he wanted so desperately. Pretending he wanted to adopt a child was easy for Adam, but producing his own blood heir required a strategy. Adam had one—and her name was Dixie Cooney. In 1989, Dixie left Cortlandt Manor and her Uncle Palmer to work for his long-time nemesis and neighbor, Adam Chandler. She was hired as the nanny for Brooke's daughter Laura. After the child was killed by the drunk driver, Dixie stayed on as a servant in Adam's employ. Dixie was beautiful and, unlike Brooke, fertile. She was also falling hopelessly in love with Adam Chandler. Adam swept Dixie off her feet and slept with her in the Chandler boathouse. His plan had worked: Dixie became pregnant, and Adam secretly plotted to adopt her baby when it was born. Brooke would never know it was his. But when her baby boy was born, Dixie refused to give him up. She demanded Adam make a choice between her and Brooke. Adam told Dixie she was his choice. Brooke overheard the entire exchange and was disgusted. She packed her bags and went to Pine Valley's hot-shot attorney, Jackson Montgomery, who helped her win half of Adam's fortune. Scrambling to secure his legacy, Adam promised to marry Dixie.

Tad Martin was one person who refused to accept Adam's actions at face value. After being dumped by Barbara Montgomery, who had since split with Tom, the resilient Tad found himself falling in love with Dixie. He knew she cared for him but there was a problem with her husband, Adam Chandler.

In the second part of his sinister plan, Adam attempted to drive Dixie insane and get her to commit herself to Laurel Hill, a mental institution.

If his plan was successful, Adam Junior would be solely Adam's. Fortunately, Tad realized what Adam was up to and helped Dixie escape from the hospital. Armed with a Caribbean divorce, Dixie married Tad. Before the bride and groom departed in a hail of rice and good wishes, Dixie tossed her bouquet, which was grabbed by Tad's recently returned mother, Opal Gardner Purdy.

In February 1989, Cindy Chandler lost her valiant fight with AIDS. Stuart Chandler dedicated a panel to the AIDS quilt in her memory and promised to raise her son Scott with love and care. In the weeks before her death, Cindy reconciled with her twin sister Karen who was as wild and irresponsible as Cindy was sweet and sincere. Karen Parker's stay in Pine Valley was brief. In August, she kidnapped Dixie and Adam's baby. With a million dollar ransom in hand, she was nabbed by Tad as she tried to flee the country.

Having lost much of his memory, Travis alienated himself from Erica and took up with his former wife Barbara. When he discovered he had a life-threatening brain tumor, Travis left town to have an operation, telling his loved ones that he was going through a mid-life crisis. What Travis didn't know at the time was that Barbara was pregnant with his child. Labeling Travis irresponsible for leaving so suddenly, Tom Cudahy encouraged Barbara to tell everyone Tom was the father of her baby. Overwhelmed by Tom's selflessness, Barbara accepted his proposal of marriage and continued to keep her pregnancy a secret from Travis. Midway through their wedding ceremony, Barbara went into labor. The scene shifted to Pine Valley Hospital where, between contractions, the ceremony continued. Seconds after marrying Tom, Barbara Montgomery Cudahy gave birth to an angelic baby girl named Molly.

By the time their relationship had cooled considerably, Julie and Nico made the startling discovery that their marriage was invalid. When a pregnant Julie lost their baby, the marriage crumbled. Julie left for Washington and, out of the blue, Nico married Cecily Davidson. There was a reason for this unlikely union. Cecily was set to marry Sean Cudahy, but just before their wedding she overheard Sean and her mother Bitsy engaged in seductive conversation. Cecily was furious but decided to wait until the wedding ceremony to unleash her wrath. When she did, Sean and Cecily were finished. Cecily was determined to get sweet revenge against her mother. She turned to Nico Kelly for help, informing him that if he married her, she would instantly come into her trust fund and they'd both be rich. This was strictly a business arrangement. In fact, Nico and Cecily were incompatible. After a quarrelsome honeymoon in New York, they started married life together in separate rooms.

No matter how much they tried to deny it, this odd couple was falling in love and before long were sharing the same bed. Nico and Cecily soon realized they were made for each other and flew to Hawaii for a romantic second wedding. Upon their return, they decided to leave Pine Valley for good.

Gone, But Not Forgotten
Cindy Parker

She lived life to the fullest. And faced death with courage. The mother of a young son, Cindy Parker contracted AIDS from her husband, Fred, whose intravenous drug use led to his own death from the dreaded disease. At the heart of Cindy's story was her very special love for shy and gentle Stuart Chandler and her precious son Scott. As viewers, we watched Cindy run the gamut of heart-wrenching emotions, fears and frustrations as she fought the fatal illness which finally took her life in 1989.

A very pregnant Barbara Montgomery went into labor during her wedding to Tom Cudahy. Moments after the pair tied the knot, she gave birth to her daughter, Molly.

The Complete Stories

Viewers were thrilled when Nico Kelly and Cecily Davidson finally tied the knot.

Right up to the last minute, Bitsy Davidson tried in earnest to convince Cecily that she should cancel her wedding to ex-con Sean Cudahy.

Jeremy's newfound son, David, discovered his true love when he met Palmer's sweet and naive niece, Melanie, who had arrived in Pine Valley from West Virginia in the winter of 1989. Meeting in the Cortlandt stables, David and "Lanie," as she was called, marveled at their common experiences. It was clear to everyone these two kids brought out the best in each other, which disturbed Uncle Palmer. Then tragedy struck when David's mother, Marissa, who was in cahoots with Palmer to break up Jeremy and Natalie, fell down a flight of stairs after a frenzied altercation with Natalie. David arrived on the scene in time to witness the horror. Overwhelmed with bitterness, he turned away from his father and Lanie. Lanie soon found a sympathetic ear in Trask Bodine, a poor but handsome student she was tutoring at Pine Valley University.

Erica's only dream was to have her father's love. Eric Kane, the noted movie director and infamous philanderer, had left his wife and daughter when Erica was only nine. Mona, who was always there for Erica, was never as important to her as the father who wasn't. Though years had passed, Erica was most reminded of her father when she took young Bianca to the circus and visited Barney the clown. Erica suspected Barney was her father, and when the circus left town, she set out to find him and investigate further. Erica joined the circus in Texas in order to get close to him. When Erica confronted Barney, he admitted being her father. After an emotional reunion, Eric explained he had faked his death for financial reasons. Erica welcomed him back into her life, her home and even her company, giving him a five percent share of Enchantment. But Eric sold his stock to Erica's worst enemy, Natalie Hunter, betraying his daughter once more before he walked out of her life again. By now Erica had embarked on a new romantic trail with Travis's brother, Jack.

To cap off the year, Adam held an elaborate masked ball at the Chandler Mansion. This elegant soiree was designed to herald the lord of the manor's most triumphant career achievement. Little did he know that behind one of the many masks lurked Palmer Cortlandt, about to darken his brightest hour. Palmer revealed to the assembled guests that his own recent business exploits had culminated in ownership of Adam Chandler, lock, stock and barrel. Palmer's shocking declaration led to Adam's professional demise and a lengthy stay at Pine Valley Hospital. Adam recovered from a massive stroke while he ruminated over his sudden downfall.

On Location

In 1989, *All My Children* aired a romantic springtime adventure featuring young lovers David and Melanie, taped on location in the spectacular Blue Ridge Mountains of North Carolina.

"It's the profoundest celebration anyone has ever hosted!" proclaimed Adam Chandler of his masked ball in 1989. The party guests wore extraordinary one-of-a-kind masks to this lavish celebration.

The Complete Stories

Erica's involvement with the dashing Jackson Montgomery deepened in early 1990. Accepting his proposal of marriage, she told Jack she couldn't set a wedding date because of Bianca. While Erica wanted to marry Jack, Bianca desperately wanted her mommy and daddy together; so did Travis. Jack and Erica proceeded with their wedding plans until Bianca, returning from a trip to Disneyworld with her father, fell deathly ill with Reye's Syndrome. As her daughter's life hung in the balance, Erica retreated to the hospital chapel where she made a bargain with God to spare her daughter. It was the first time in Erica's life that someone else's life meant more to her than her own.

Bianca recovered, and her ordeal brought Erica and Travis close together again. Not wanting to hurt Bianca, Erica came up with a plan to date the Montgomery brothers on alternate nights. Plagued by jealousy and back-stabbing, the three-way arrangement not surprisingly proved an utter failure. A frustrated Jack gave Erica an ultimatum. She had to make a definite choice. After a month of deliberation, she broke the news to Jack that they were through and she couldn't marry him. While an elated Travis planned a small wedding with Erica, Jack drowned his sorrows in a raucous evening with his pals, Tad and Brooke.

The fight was far from over. Jack wasn't about to give up entirely on the woman he loved. On Erica's wedding day, he appeared at the church with plans to whisk her off to Paris. Erica spotted him as she walked down the aisle and stopped the proceedings. She ushered him into the church vestibule where she bid him a tender farewell before marrying Travis a second time.

On Travis and Erica's second wedding day, Jackson showed up to make one last effort to persuade her to run away with him. Gently declining the offer, she went through with the ill-fated wedding to Jack's brother.

Blond and beautiful Ceara Connor came to town in search of a prestigious job and a man of means. She found both in Pine Valley. While living with her Aunt Myrtle Fargate, Ceara was hired as chief fund-raiser for Pine Valley University. There she met David Rampal. That David was much younger didn't faze Ceara. That he was rich did. David's father, Jeremy, considered Ceara a golddigger and schemed to break them up by seducing Ceara and making her fall in love with him.

Opal Gardner Purdy declared to anyone who would listen that she intended to marry Palmer Cortlandt in 1990. He had everything she was looking for. But Palmer wanted no part of Opal. He even paid Sean Cudahy to date Opal and do whatever it took to get her out of his hair. Opal dated and eventually became engaged to Palmer's old prison pal, Stan, better known as "Mr. U.," but it was Palmer she pined for.

Palmer's gloom vanished when his ex-wife, Daisy, popped back into Pine Valley. Although she put off Palmer's advances, declaring they were never meant to be together, Daisy couldn't help noticing the chemistry between him and his zany friend, Opal. Ever the matchmaker, Daisy set out to transform Opal's tackiness into sophisticated style. She helped create a woman more fit for an urbane gentleman like Palmer. Daisy's efforts paid off when a glamorous Opal made a grand entrance at the

University Ball, catching the eye of her intended. Palmer saw a different Opal and asked her for a dance. A satisfied Daisy glided out of town, her job well done. In November, Opal became the latest in a long, long line of Mrs. Palmer Cortlandts, but determined to be the last.

Another exasperating romance was taking place between the newly rich Natalie Hunter and gruff detective Trevor Dillon, who had been a friend and fellow mercenary with Jeremy. Having inherited a small fortune from an aging millionaire she nursed prior to his death, Natalie could have had any man she wanted. Somehow that man always seemed to be Trevor. Despite their obvious dislike for each other, some crisis always landed them back together. Trevor did everything in his power to be around Natalie. He even commandeered a boat with Natalie aboard and got them both shipwrecked on a deserted island where they battled the elements and each other.

While their game of cat and mouse continued back in Pine Valley, Adam Chandler proved a formidable contender for Natalie's affections. He was the antithesis of Trevor: suave, slick and wealthy. Natalie didn't love Adam, but she married him anyway because she was angry at Trevor. The latter raced to stop the wedding but arrived seconds too late.

Donna Tyler remedied one of the biggest mistakes in her life when she reunited with her first love, Dr. Chuck Tyler, who had returned for a visit to Pine Valley and decided to stay. Donna's life was far from peaceful due to the reappearance of the contemptible Billy Clyde Tuggle. He slithered back into Pine Valley and befriended his daughter Emily Ann, who had been adopted years earlier by Donna and her soon-to-be ex-husband, Benny. Donna panicked when she learned that Emily Ann's boss at the new Cyclops disco, "John Henry Rockefeller," was actually Billy Clyde.

As Emily Ann grew up, Donna had shielded her precious daughter from the knowledge that this vile creature was her natural father. Emily Ann was also blissfully unaware that both Donna and Estelle, Emily Ann's natural mother, had been prostitutes. Throughout 1990, these secrets would be revealed to poor Emily Ann, whose world came crashing down as she comprehended the horrifying tale of her parentage. Billy Clyde broke into Emily Ann's Willow Lake hideaway one night and declared he was her father. Traumatized by the sordid truth of her heritage, Emily Ann ran off and married her boyfriend, Joey Martin. That marriage got off to a shaky start when Emily Ann, racked by nightmares, spurned Joey's romantic advances. Less than two months after her ill-fated wedding, the troubled Emily Ann wanted out. Joey signed annulment papers, but they were promptly torn up when Emily Ann discovered she was pregnant. She lost the child, but the unhappy marriage continued.

Dixie Martin soon became the object of Billy Clyde's affections. In 1990, Tad and Dixie got off to a stormy start when Tad expressed his desire to move out of Pine Valley to start a new life away from Dixie's demanding Uncle Palmer. But Dixie wasn't ready to leave their home.

Palmer did his best to break up Tad and Dixie. Paying Loretta Rutherford to claim she slept with Tad worked like a charm and convinced Dixie her husband was a hopeless philanderer. When Tad received divorce papers, he soothed his pain by sleeping with Brooke, with whom he was working closely on a story about kickbacks in the construction industry. Dixie made a new friend in Billy Clyde Tuggle, who offered a sympathetic ear to her sorrows and secretly fantasized about Dixie as his "southern bride-to-be." When detective Trevor Dillon warned him to leave Pine Valley, Billy Clyde chloroformed Dixie and dragged her away to an

An obsessed Billy Clyde unleashed his pent-up wrath when he abducted and nearly raped Dixie Martin. Fortunately, Tad saved the day.

Issues and Answers

Bone Marrow Transplants

Little Molly Cudahy desperately needed a matching bone-marrow transplant to combat leukemia in 1990. First Lady Barbara Bush took time out of her busy schedule to appear in a public service message on behalf of the National Bone Marrow Registry.

isolated cabin. Searching for her frantically, Tad found her just in the nick of time, just as Billy Clyde was about to rape her. Trevor and officer Derek Frye arrived on the scene, and after a tense standoff, Billy Clyde burst out of the cabin, spraying bullets everywhere. Seriously wounded, Derek was whisked back to Pine Valley Hospital. As Billy Clyde escaped, Tad rushed into the cabin to get Dixie, and she collapsed into his arms.

Billy Clyde's reign of terror came to an end two months later. Having reconciled with his true love Dixie, Tad promised to keep her safe forever. When Billy Clyde learned of their Christmas wedding, he sprang into action, luring Tad to a railroad yard where Billy Clyde had rigged a bomb. On the railroad bridge on the outskirts of Pine Valley, Tad and Billy Clyde met for a final showdown.

While they struggled, the bomb exploded, plunging both men into the icy, raging waters. Billy Clyde's lifeless body was recovered, but Trevor could find no sign of Tad. Trevor was faced with the difficult task of telling Dixie her husband was presumed dead. However, Tad was indeed alive and had lost his memory. Accepting a ride from a truck driver, he was headed for California. Dixie grieved and so did Brooke, who was pregnant with Tad's child.

Tom and Barbara's happy home life was torn apart by the discovery that Barbara's daughter, Molly, suffered from leukemia. She needed a bone marrow transplant to stay alive. Desperately needing to find a match, Barbara was forced to tell Travis that Molly was his daughter. Feeling left out, Tom stood by as Barbara and Travis pledged to do anything to save Molly. When a donor could not be found, they came up with a plan to conceive a second child of their own in order to provide a bone marrow donor for Molly. In a hotel room, Barbara and Travis secretly made love.

Many lives changed when Barbara and Travis's secret rendezvous was discovered. The strain of her pregnancy proved too much for the alcoholic Tom Cudahy, and he fell off the wagon. He asked his wife for a divorce. Erica, too, announced to Travis that their marriage was over. For Bianca's sake, they stayed together in name only and waited for the right moment to break the news to their daughter. After some soul-searching, Erica told Jack she loved him and wanted him. They soon began an affair.

Everyone wondered who was poisoning Palmer when it was discovered someone was putting drops of CRS-17, an experimental mind-altering drug, in his juice. For weeks, his strange mental lapses were the talk of Cortlandt Manor. The situation took a dangerous turn when he wandered onto the thin ice of the Cortlandt pond, fell in, and was rescued by Charlie Brent. Opal had practically forced the poisoned health drink down her husband's throat, and Palmer wondered if she was the culprit. To make matters worse, a vial of CRS-17 had fallen out of her coat. Will Cortlandt was also under suspicion. He was the nephew who was thought to be seeking an easy road to the top of the Cortlandt corporate ladder. It turned out that Palmer's right-hand man, Stan Ulatowski, "Mr. U," was the guilty party. He had sought revenge when Palmer stole his fiancée, Opal, away from him. Stan eluded capture when, trapped in a plane by officers Derek Frye and Mimi Reed, he jumped out the door, presumably to his death. His body was never recovered.

By this time, Opal and Palmer had separated. He had been wrong to suspect she was poisoning him and begged her forgiveness, but Opal wouldn't relent. Not, that is, until Daisy pretended to want Palmer back, then Opal forgot how furious she had been and happily reunited with her "Love Bug."

Clean-cut, all-American Craig Lawson came to town to console Tad's widow, Dixie, and investigate the supposed death of her husband and his best friend, Tad Martin. No one in Pine Valley had ever heard mention of Craig Lawson, but the seemingly sincere Lawson wove a believable tale that he had become best buddies with Tad when he moved to California following his divorce from Hillary. Craig proved to be a source of strength for Dixie. He was her hero. In a valiant act, Craig saved Dixie from a gunman who was about to kill her after realizing she had witnessed the murder of a clerk in a store robbery.

Dixie's brother Will was determined to one day inherit their Uncle Palmer's corporation, Cortlandt Electronics. Seeing Craig as a competitor, Will tried to oust the newcomer from the company by any means he could. That included sabotaging Craig's work, hiring a private investigator to unearth his past and, finally, fixing the books to make it appear Craig had stolen $20,000 from the company. Will's last vengeful act backfired when Palmer fired him and renounced him as his nephew. Defeated, Will took a job with Erica Kane at Enchantment Cosmetics.

In the meantime, Craig eloped with Dixie to nearby Elk Green, but his plan to bilk Tad's rich widow was derailed when his ex-fiancée, Gloria Marsh, came to town and took a job at Pine Valley Hospital. She caught wind of Lawson's scheme and blackmailed him into resuming their old affair. Brooke English stumbled upon Craig and Gloria kissing and threatened to tell Dixie the truth about her two-timing husband. Instead, Craig promised to tell Dixie himself. Grabbing some cash and jewelry from the Cortlandt safe, he left a good-bye note to his new wife on the way out. Dixie never discovered her husband's betrayal. Realizing how much his leaving would hurt Dixie, Craig rushed back home before she could find his farewell letter. Craig begged Brooke not to tell Dixie, and she agreed to keep silent on one condition: that he end his fling with Gloria.

As the year wore on, Jackson Montgomery grew more and more impatient with Erica's ongoing sham of a marriage to his brother Travis. Erica stalled Jack for time, insisting she only needed time to prepare Bianca. Jack's fury reached its peak when Bianca innocently blurted out that her "mommy and daddy" were sleeping in the same bed. Erica couldn't

explain this away, at least not to Jack's satisfaction. When Bianca saw Erica kiss her Uncle Jack, she angrily set fire to her "Jack doll." As the blaze spread, Erica frantically raced into Bianca's bedroom and was overcome with smoke. Travis came to the rescue, saving the Montgomery women from harm. Bianca told her daddy about the kiss, and when Travis caught Erica and Jack in bed together, his arrangement with Erica ended.

Travis sued for sole custody of Bianca. During the hearing, Erica lied that she and Jack had only slept together that one time and begged Jack

After a car accident in which Brooke nearly lost her life, Trevor Dillon arrested his niece Hayley when she admitted that she had been driving the offending vehicle. In truth, it was Hayley's drunken mother Arlene who drove the car that crashed into Brooke's car.

to testify similarly. She knew she would lose custody of her child if it was revealed she and Jack had been having an on-going affair. As an officer of the court, Jack could not bring himself to commit perjury, and in confessing the truth, he exposed Erica as a liar under oath. After a bitter custody battle, Erica lost custody of her precious Bianca. Travis took their daughter away to his new home in Seattle. In time, Travis married Barbara and she gave birth to their new daughter, whose bone marrow saved little Molly's life.

On Location

All My Children headed south to the Disney/MGM studios at in Orlando, Florida to tape this terrifying car crash. Disney/MGM's production expertise was employed to produce an intricate scene in which a car driven by a drunken Arlene Vaughan, traveling with her daughter Hayley, careened into poor pregnant Brooke English and Jackson Montgomery, seen here moments after the crash.

Acrimoniously dumped by Erica for being honest, Jack found solace with Brooke English. By now, Brooke had given birth to Jamie, her son by Tad. She had nearly lost the child in a violent collision with a car driven by alcoholic Arlene Vaughan. Although her daughter Hayley was only a passenger in the car, Hayley pretended she was driving, knowing that her mother's license had already been revoked for driving while intoxicated.

In defeat, Erica turned her attentions to Charlie Brent, the son of her former husband Phil, and the grandson of her former lover, Nick. All grown up and recently returned to Pine Valley from Stanford, Charlie had abandoned his plans to become a doctor. After deflowering and subsequently dumping Melanie Cortlandt, Charlie became the new spokesman for Enchantment Cosmetics: "The Man of Enchantment." In the process, he enchanted Erica and alarmed his grandmother, Ruth.

On Location

Erica Kane and Charlie Brent shared an afternoon interlude filled with fun and romance in this 1991 excursion on the lake in New York's Central Park.

Three generations of her men had fallen victim to Erica's allure, and Ruth was beside herself. Erica's mother, Mona, teamed up with Ruth to protest this May/December affair, but Charlie and Erica ignored their pleas and planned to marry. Charlie's grandfather, Nick, arrived in town and attempted to sway Erica before she took the plunge. Cornered at a Martin family dinner, Nick challenged her intentions. He cited Erica's history with men and brought to light her constant dissatisfaction with each new conquest. When she couldn't say she loved Charlie, she had the grace to call off the wedding and give Charlie a gentle send-off.

Ruth was relieved her grandson had been spared the wrath of Erica Kane but was once again troubled when her youngest son Joey's marriage disintegrated. His bride Emily Ann had gone insane and in her demented jealousy tried to kill Mary and Dan's sweet sister, Katie Kennicott, who had recently arrived in Pine Valley.

Determined to keep the mercenary Ceara Connor from marrying his son David, Jeremy Hunter continued his seduction scheme to break them up by romancing Ceara until she gave in to his charms. When she finally did, it was clear that during his seduction of Ceara, Jeremy had fallen in love with her. David was incensed to learn of his father's scheme but came to accept Ceara and Jeremy's love. David eventually found his way back to Lanie. They married before leaving Pine Valley.

For Ceara, her problems were only beginning. As the oldest of seven children from a poor, blue-collar family, Ceara Connor had been sexually abused by her father when she was just nine years old. When George Connor showed up in Pine Valley and tried to molest her again, her long-buried nightmares resurfaced, and she shot and killed him in self-defense. Suffering a mild breakdown, the guilt-ridden Ceara went into therapy with Dr. Anna Tolan. With the help of an incest-support group, she slowly came to grips with her father's horrible act. On New Year's

The Complete Stories

Issues and Answers

Sexual Abuse

All My Children *frankly dramatized the effects that child abuse can have on its victims as they grow into adults. In this 1991 story, Ceara Connor was a troubled woman who unearthed repressed memories and came to see that she had been sexually abused by her father.*

Eve, one year to the day after their first loveless kiss, Jeremy and Ceara were married.

Having divorced Natalie and realizing that he'd lost Brooke forever, Adam was haunted by thoughts of his 1984 marriage to Erica. He determined to get her back. She was the only woman he ever truly considered his equal. But Erica wanted no part of her ex until he told her the horrible news that they were never divorced. A horrified Erica listened as Adam explained how he'd sent Stuart to impersonate him in order to get their quickie Caribbean divorce all those years ago. Adam claimed that they were still married, her precious Bianca was illegitimate and warned that if Erica didn't marry him again in a public ceremony, he would share his little secret with the *National Intruder*, and Erica could never win her custody appeal. She had no choice and agreed to the marriage. In a masterful maneuver to outwit Adam, she hired a phony minister to preside at their ceremony.

Hayley Vaughan had blown into Pine Valley like a hurricane. Having run away from her alcoholic mother, she lived with her Uncle Trevor, who called her "Tinkerbell," and she referred to him as "Uncle Porkchop." Hayley caused quite a stir when she made an outrageous claim on the front page of the *National Intruder* that she was Adam Chandler's illegitimate daughter. Hayley didn't know that her terrible lie was, in fact, true.

On a mission to drag her daughter back to Chicago, Arlene Dillon Vaughan was astounded to encounter Adam Chandler, her long-ago lover and Hayley's real father. The news was a terrible blow to the resentful Hayley who had always believed that the recently-deceased Harry Vaughan was her father. In time, Hayley came to love her newfound daddy. When Hayley did finally manage to show up for school, she met sweet, straight-arrow Brian Bodine, the younger brother of Trask, and love blossomed.

In 1991, Pine Valley was visited by Janet Green, Natalie's overweight, down-and-out sister. Growing up in the shadow of her beautiful blond sister had turned frumpy Janet into a resentful woman who wanted everything that belonged to her sister, including Natalie's new fiancé Trevor. Janet set out to seduce him, failing miserably at every attempt. Still determined Natalie would not win again, Janet transformed herself into a clone of her glamorous sister. After perfecting her imitation of Natalie in secret, Janet set her plan in motion. She threw Natalie into a well on the grounds of Dimitri Marick's sprawling estate and proceeded to live Natalie's life with her fiancé. Natalie's desperate cries for help went unanswered as Janet "From Another Planet" was leading Trevor to the altar.

A thunderstorm raged on "Natalie" and Trevor's wedding day. The gloom of this dreary occasion foreshadowed the events to come. As the real Natalie languished in her dank prison, Janet married Trevor and found her way into his bed. Weeks passed and Natalie became delirious. When handsome Dimitri Marick peered into the well and discovered her, she was overcome with gratitude. Only when he took her back to his mansion, Wildwind, and nursed her through horrible bouts of claustrophobia and nightmares, did it finally dawn on Natalie that she was free. Janet's masquerade had come to an end, but not before she kidnapped Hayley and shot young Brian.

Officers Derek Frye and Mimi Reed helped bring this crisis to an end. Only a few knew that Derek and Mimi's partnership extended beyond working hours. Dating a fellow officer was strictly against the rules, and for months Derek and Mimi managed to contain their mutual attraction. When they finally gave in to their passion, Mimi suffered the consequences and was suspended from the force.

Back at Wildwind, Natalie was torn between her savior Dimitri and Trevor, who had been so easily duped by Janet. Dimitri became enamored of Natalie, fantasizing that she was the personification of his wife, Angelique, who had been hospitalized in a deep coma for the past fifteen years. But Trevor ardently persisted and nearly succeeded in winning Natalie back when Janet summoned him to her prison cell with news she was pregnant. Trevor threatened to kill Janet and lunged for her throat. But the damage had been done. Trevor was the father of her baby.

Natalie spent many torturous weeks at the bottom of a well, courtesy of her crazed sister, Janet.

In near seclusion at Wildwind, Natalie tried to bury the painful memories of 1991. With Dimitri's tender guidance, she vowed to put the past behind her. Throwing the cigar band Trevor had once given her as a wedding ring into a roaring fire was the first step to accepting her new life as the soon-to-be Mrs. Dimitri Marick. But Dimitri's past would soon rear its ugly head.

Dimitri's wife, Angelique, was said to have died in Vienna after spending fifteen years in a hopeless coma, but Jackson Montgomery was suspicious. He told Brooke he had strong reason to believe Angelique was alive. Dimitri's housekeeper and mother-in-law, the eerie, menacing Helga, had been behaving strangely ever since Dimitri and Natalie announced their engagement. Jack's suspicions were confirmed the night of Natalie and Dimitri's engagement party. At the stroke of midnight, Dimitri raised his glass in a toast to his new bride. Helga then announced that his bride was already present and wheeled in Angelique Marick. Dimitri gasped and a dark hush fell over the ball as he identified his wife. Natalie was stunned and raced out of Wildwind, landing curled up in a ball outside Trevor's front door. After a night of bitter reflection, she was certain of only one thing, she was through with Dimitri. But Natalie didn't return to Trevor's open arms. She was still recovering from Janet's imprisonment and insisted she could never accept her sister's child as her own.

Angelique Marick's sudden comeback was nothing short of a medical miracle. Dimitri took his wife back to Wildwind and hired Gloria Marsh as her private nurse. Gloria was still suffering the onus of a severely tarnished reputation as a result of her involvement with Craig Lawson in the betrayal of her supposed best friend Dixie. By hiring her, Dimitri placed a trust in Gloria that helped her slowly regain her lost self-respect. Dimitri made no promises to Angelique that the two of them would ever resume their marriage. Even so, Helga held out hope that her daughter would someday regain her rightful place as mistress of the manor.

Terrence Frye, the teenage son of attorney Livia Frye, wasn't looking for trouble when he applied for an after-school job at Tom Cudahy's health club. But it came looking for him because Terrence's skin was black. Two young white men, Rod and Jay, taunted Terrence with racial slurs. When he turned the other cheek, that only angered the ruffians, who were looking for a fight. Terrence wasn't about to give them one. After hours one night, they returned and savagely beat him into a coma. Terrence's uncle, police officer Derek Frye, made it his personal mission

While working at Tom Cudahy's Health Club, Terrence Frye became a victim of racial violence when he was beaten into a coma by two angry white patrons, who eventually went to prison for the crime.

to make the offenders pay for their crime. When he tracked down and handcuffed Jay, he was finally able to let out his rage: "You have no idea how many people, black and white, love my nephew. You just don't think of things like that, do you? Because his skin is darker than yours! You're better than him, you want to believe that! But you're not fit to look at him. You're not fit to clean his shoes!"

At the ensuing trial, the two white youths were brought to justice. Terrence made a full recovery, though Pine Valley would never again be the same innocent town after racism had reared its hateful head.

Erica Kane reluctantly began 1992 as the old/new Mrs. Adam Chandler. She surprised Adam by becoming the perfect wife, but her "happy homemaker" mode was only a sham, part of her plan to drive Adam mad with kindness. She realized he was obsessed with control, that he had to be in charge of everything. Erica's first deed was to launch a redecorating frenzy, turning the manly Chandler mansion into a softer, more womanly estate, better suited to the likes of Erica Kane. By doing so, she proceeded to make her husband miserable.

On the work front, Erica rallied her forces in an attempt to stop Dimitri Marick's hostile take-over of Enchantment. Determined to seize control of Erica's company, Dimitri appeared in a face-to-face meeting on television's "Market Street Week." Afterwards, the pair met privately and argued, but the chemistry between them couldn't be denied. The fight turned to passion when Dimitri pulled his rival into a kiss. Erica responded and a new romance was born.

Hayley and Brian's own troubled romance soon went awry. Young, impressionable and a bit stubborn like Hayley, Brian wanted to prove his love and to make love. He proposed marriage, but she gently turned him down, maintaining she still wasn't ready for that kind of commitment. Brian was furious.

Brian figured Adam was behind Hayley's refusal and was sick of his constant interference in her life. Brian poured out his heart to his new friend, An Li, a beautiful Chinese girl who had come to America with her mother, a maid at Cortlandt Manor. Indeed, Adam didn't want to see Hayley marry Brian and did everything in his power to keep them apart. Knowing Hayley was jealous of Brian's growing friendship with An Li, Adam revealed to An Li that she could get the green card she so desperately needed by marrying a U.S. citizen. In desperation, An Li turned to Brian for help, and he obliged.

Shocked by the news of Brian's marriage, Hayley threw herself into the arms of the despicable Will Cortlandt, who had grown into a bitter and violent man. His violence was released on Gloria Marsh when he brutally raped her after picking her up in a bar. This only compounded the problems of this already emotionally unstable woman.

In a shameful attempt to get his hands on her trust fund, Will worked his "charms" on Hayley. Turning to alcohol to drown her sorrows, she made a fateful choice. A drunken Hayley, heartbroken over Brian, eloped with Will. Brian found his new wife An Li a convenient source of comfort, and he slept with her, getting her pregnant.

Issues and Answers

Racism

All My Children highlighted the evils of racial prejudice when in 1992 Terrence Frye, a young black teenager, was harassed and beaten into a coma by two white peers at the Pine Valley Health Club. In a subsequent storyline, Taylor Cannon Barnes, a black female police cadet, used makeup and a wig to masquerade as white in order to infiltrate Deconstruction, a racist group headquartered at Pine Valley University.

Mimi Reed looked on as Derek Frye unleashed his rage on one of the two white hoodlums who attacked his nephew Terrence.

Having transformed himself into the most hated man in Pine Valley, Will Cortlandt was destined to die. When Hayley refused to sleep with him, Will grew bitter and angry. One fateful night, Hayley finally promised to consummate their marriage, but flashes of her true love, Brian, prevented Hayley from giving in to Will's advances. His anger flared as she pulled away, and Hayley barricaded herself in the bedroom, making a frantic call to Brian. When An Li answered the phone, Hayley pleaded with her to get Brian over there. An Li promised to give him the message, and she did, but much later. When Brian finally pulled Hayley's message out of his jealous wife, he raced to save Hayley. Adam Chandler happened upon the scene at Will's apartment and couldn't believe his eyes. There stood Brian Bodine with a crowbar in his hands. At Brian's feet lay Will Cortlandt, bludgeoned to death.

Among those interested in who killed Will Cortlandt was Pulitzer Prize-winning journalist Edmund Grey, a top-notch investigative reporter who arrived in Pine Valley to cover the case. Many who wondered about the murderer were suspects themselves. Fifteen citizens of Pine Valley were considered to have likely motives to kill Will Cortlandt.

After reconciling with Hayley, Brian was arrested by Derek and Mimi. He bravely stood trial for the crime, hoping for the best. There seemed to be a conviction near when on May 11, the real killer was revealed to be Janet Green. She had slipped out of the hospital room where she was awaiting the birth of her baby and, disguised in Trevor's raincoat, killed Will. In her twisted mind, Janet believed that by killing Will, she would be enabling Trevor to spend more time with her and their baby and less time protecting his niece Hayley from Will Cortlandt's abuse.

In a final, desperate act, Janet kidnapped her sister Natalie and took her for a train ride she'd never forget. Janet was going into labor as they stopped off in the middle of nowhere. She took Natalie at gun point to a remote cabin where she planned to kill her. When Natalie tried to escape, Janet shot her sister in the leg. Before Janet could pull the trigger again, she was overcome by a contraction and dropped the gun. Natalie picked it up and ran. Realizing she was about to deliver, Janet begged her sister not to leave her alone.

In a gallant show of compassion, Natalie returned and delivered her sister's daughter, innocent Amanda Dillon. Janet went

Livia Frye defended a grim Brian Bodine when he stood trial for Will Cortlandt's murder.

to jail soon after, and Natalie returned to Pine Valley where she married Trevor and began a new life with him and baby Amanda.

Late in 1992, Erica finally managed to work her way free from Adam's marital grasp. Hayley helped Adam see that no matter what extreme measures he took, he would never win Erica's love. Reluctantly, Adam

116

granted Erica the divorce she so desperately desired. Although she was free at last, Erica steadfastly refused to begin an affair with Dimitri. She had no desire to take second place again and refused to be the "other woman." Dimitri forced her to admit she wanted him and promised her they would have it all. But Erica had grown wiser through the years and would not succumb to the promises and charms of an already married man. Despite her resolve, the fates conspired to bring Erica and Dimitri together on a stormy night as she was driving from Pine Valley to New York. The fierce winds and torrential rains forced her to take shelter in a nearby hunting lodge, where she came upon Dimitri. Feeling vulnerable, Erica confided in Dimitri that she never wanted to lose him, and with a single kiss, she fell in love all over again. They made passionate love and Dimitri declared that his life was with her. He promised to inform Angelique that their marriage was over. But when the time came, Dimitri fell short of his word and couldn't bring himself to leave his still-ailing wife.

A newcomer brought terror with him to the town of Pine Valley in the spring of 1992. Carter Jones was handsome, smooth and smart. But not smart enough to stay away from his ex-wife, assistant district attorney Galen Henderson. Carter had just been released from prison after serving time for spousal abuse. He immediately began stalking Galen, careful to stay on the right side of the law while he acted out his revenge.

After a prank phone call warning her he was back, Galen was gripped by fear and turned to Trevor Dillon, who vowed to hunt him down. He kept a watchful eye on Carter's every move hoping to catch him in the act. But Jones wouldn't be stopped. In a heartless act of vengeance, Carter set fire to Trevor's house while Natalie was trapped inside. Trevor rushed into the burning house and dragged her to safety. Natalie was blinded by the furious blaze and doctors at Pine Valley Hospital diagnosed that she might never see again. Carter was furious that his vengeful plan had failed and felt guilty that an innocent woman had become his unwitting victim. He disguised himself as a kindly hospital orderly named Kyle and befriended an unsuspecting Natalie. Ultimately, Carter became obsessed with Natalie and when he realized she had figured out his true identity, he kidnapped her. Trevor raced to Natalie's rescue for a second time. He confronted Carter aboard his houseboat hideaway, but Carter fell overboard and escaped only to surface again in Corinth, a sister town to Pine Valley, where his reign of terror continued until he was finally captured and imprisoned.

Trevor Dillon heroically rescued his wife Natalie from their house after it exploded and burned. Natalie was blinded by the blaze.

Back in Pine Valley, reporter Edmund Grey was making Pine Valley his home while wooing fellow journalist Brooke English. Edmund was no stranger to the town, having grown up at Wildwind where his parents Alf and Flora Gresham had been servants to lord of the manor Hugo Marick. No one but the brooding Helga knew Edmund was actually Hugo's bastard son. In a desperate attempt to insure that Angelique remained mistress of the manor, Helga burned the codicil of Hugo's will in which he admitted Edmund's true parentage, leaving him Wildwind. Unknown to Helga, Edmund had caught a glimpse of the document before it was destroyed, but when he returned to its hiding place, the will was gone.

Although Edmund and Dimitri were brothers, neither felt an ounce of brotherly love. Dimitri refused to admit Edmund was his blood brother, which further damaged an already tenuous bond. When Dimitri gave in and allowed Edmund to exhume Hugo's body for DNA testing, the crypt was empty. Edmund accused Dimitri and Erica of masterminding the farce and took off on a search for the truth. His mission took Grey around the world to Budapest, where he tracked every move of Erica and Dimitri, who had days earlier rediscovered their love in the beautiful Hungarian city.

Waiting for an opportune moment, Edmund kidnapped Erica, holding her hostage in a wine cellar below Vadzel, the Marick ancestral home. Hoping to make Dimitri honor Hugo's missing will seemed simple enough, but Dimitri refused to give in to his brother's demands. Erica was released by her captor, and she returned to Dimitri only to witness the sight of him holding Angelique in his arms. Feeling betrayed, Erica returned to Edmund and agreed to become his accomplice. She was certain that together they could secure everything they wanted from Dimitri. Erica was right. Dimitri finally relented and gave in to Edmund's demands. But the crisis was far from over when Helga found Erica and locked her in a crypt. Chilled by the ghoulish surroundings, Erica discovered she was sharing the crypt with Hugo's missing corpse.

The Marick brothers teamed up to confront Helga, finally cornering her atop an ancient stone wall. Before falling to her death, Helga admitted to burning the will and proclaimed the truth that Edmund was Dimitri's brother. Edmund's search was over, but Erica's life seemed doomed. When the men found her in the crypt, she was in a catatonic state of shock, but physically would recover.

At year's end, Tad Martin returned to Pine Valley with a new identity. Two years earlier, he had wandered into a Napa Valley

On Location

The beauty and charm of Budapest provided the backdrop for a 1992 storyline that brought Erica and Dimitri together to confront their "destiny on the Danube."

vineyard, not knowing who he was. The vineyard's owner, Nola Orsini, felt in her heart that the mysterious stranger was her long-lost son, Ted. "Ted" returned to Pine Valley on business, his head searing with pain, and began to experience brief flashes of his past.

On Christmas Eve, with a snowstorm paralyzing the East Coast, Opal Cortlandt went into labor. She and Palmer had named the child their "miracle baby" since Palmer thought he was sterile. With the roads blocked by snow drifts, Palmer realized he would have to deliver the child himself. With Joe Martin instructing him by phone, Palmer brought their darling son Peter into the world. Opal was furious and insulted when at first Palmer doubted the baby's paternity. But paternity testing confirmed the baby was indeed his.

As friends and family gathered at the Dillon house to sing carols and celebrate the season, no one noticed that Natalie, blind for months, was standing transfixed in front of the newly trimmed tree. As carolers sang "Hark, The Herald Angels Sing," Natalie was overwhelmed when the angel atop the tree slowly came into focus. A Christmas miracle had occurred. Natalie could see again.

On Christmas Eve, Trevor looked on in confused wonder as a blind Natalie miraculously regained her sight.

Upon returning from Hungary, Erica faked amnesia in an effort to hold on to Dimitri. Aboard a train, Erica kept up her charade as she gleefully allowed Dimitri to court her in style. But Erica's romantic scheme backfired when Edmund arrived on board and revealed her phony ploy to keep Dimitri. Dimitri was so furious, he stormed out of Erica's life. But Dimitri and Erica were still very much in love and, with Edmund's help, they were able to settle their differences. On March 18th, Dimitri slipped a ring on Erica's finger and asked her to be his wife.

A whole new chapter in Erica's ever-changing life began when she opened her door to a bedraggled young woman named Kendall Hart. Kendall claimed to have idolized Erica Kane all her life, and Erica hired the young woman as her personal assistant. But Kendall had a secret reason for showing up at Erica's doorstep. Her landlady Myrtle Fargate was dumbfounded when Kendall showed her the adoption papers she had found, stating that her birth mother was none other than Erica Kane.

Mistreatment of the elderly

*Pulitzer Prize-winning jour-
nalist Edmund Grey exposed
abuses against the elderly in
1993 when he discovered
that Peggy Moody, the
woman who raised him at
Wildwind, was being mis-
treated at a local nursing
home. Edmund's investiga-
tion proved that Peggy was
being fed pills by the staff to
keep her quiet, making her a
victim of "chemical
restraint," the official term
for overmedication.*

Journalist Edmund Grey exposed a
nursing-home scandal when he discovered that his old family friend,
Peggy Moody, was being overmed-
icated to keep her quiet.

Erica's mother, Mona, was alarmed when she noticed a birthmark on Kendall's neck during Erica and Dimitri's engagement party. Mona became convinced the oddly shaped mark could mean only one thing and confessed to Nick Davis a long-buried family secret. On a trip to visit her father Eric in California, a fourteen-year-old Erica had been raped and become pregnant. After Erica gave birth, she put the baby up for adoption without ever seeing her and proceeded to block the entire nightmare from her consciousness. But Mona had held her infant granddaughter, and when she saw the same birthmark on Kendall Hart that she had seen on that baby all those years ago, she knew the young woman standing before her was Erica's daughter. When Erica's precious Bianca was hurt in a riding accident, a jealous Kendall blurted out the truth that she too was Erica's daughter. Erica told Dimitri the whole story and invited Kendall to move in with them.

Gloria Marsh was still on the mend after the traumatizing events of previous years and had a staunch supporter in Stuart Chandler. Their spe-cial friendship, constantly challenged by Adam, grew into love on Stuart's part, and he proposed. Gloria accepted, feeling Stuart's faith in her was enough to keep them together. But she was wrong. Stuart didn't captivate her the way Adam did, and she wasn't in love with Stuart. Realizing the mistake she would be making, she broke off her engagement to Stuart, and after a brief and tempestuous courtship, married his brother.

Jackson Montgomery met and fell in love with a beautiful mystery woman named Laurel Banning, who worked at the community center where Natalie was a fund-raiser. The two women became good friends, but Trevor was wary of Laurel. His detective's intuition told him there was more than met the eye where this newcomer was concerned. Natalie resented Trevor's mistrust of her friend, and they quarreled. Natalie and Laurel continued working together to raise funds for the community center, where one of the chief benefactors was Adam Chandler. With his help, Natalie came to the realization that her sup-posed friend Laurel was trying to embezzle one million dollars from the organization. Jack was also shocked when he found several fake I.D.s belonging to Laurel in a motel room. It was revealed that Laurel's real name was Carla Benton. As it turned out, Trevor was right to mistrust Laurel, but it took a tragic turn of events to resolve the situation.

On Erica and Dimitri's wedding day, Adam and Natalie drove to the church together to confront Laurel and have her apprehended. The pair never arrived because on the way, they got into a terrible accident, while the impact of the collision threw Adam from the vehicle, Natalie remained slumped behind the wheel. Both victims were rushed to Pine Valley Hospital, but only Adam survived. Adam suffered paralysis in both his legs, but Natalie's severe head injuries forced doctors to put her on life-support systems. Trevor knew by the doctor's foreboding looks that there was no hope. He was forced to make the agonizing decision to let his beloved "doll" die in peace, donating her organs to save others' lives.

Trevor and Natalie's son Timmy were devastated. Trevor blamed Laurel for his wife's death and was determined to make her pay for her crimes. His vengeance was halted when he found a letter Natalie had written to him before her death. In it, she apologized for berating him about his mistrust of Laurel and explained the reason Laurel had stolen the money: She was using the embezzled funds to keep her autistic daughter Lily at a special school. After hearing Laurel's story, Trevor decided not to press charges.

Trevor bid a final farewell to his comatose wife, Natalie, who had been fatally injured in a car accident.

Timmy fell into depression after his mother's death and developed a drug problem, smoking marijuana to numb his pain. When Timmy was caught with a joint, he blamed his new pal Jamal, who had become a foster son to Tom and Livia Cudahy. Jamal was backed by Tom and Livia when he denied the accusation. He was resolutely against drugs because his mother had been an IV drug user and had died of AIDS. But Trevor chose to believe Timmy and ignore the problem. Timmy's drug use escalated until one day, while on a bad LSD trip, he was almost hit by a car. Luckily, Laurel heroically pushed Timmy out of the path of the oncoming car. A grateful Trevor forgave Laurel and finally woke up to his son's addiction.

Laurel's abusive ex-husband Denny showed up in town demanding money from Laurel, who grew furious when he claimed he wasn't Lily's father. When Denny attacked her, Laurel grabbed a bookend and made a fatal imprint in her ex-husband's head. Jack arrived on the scene to find Laurel standing over Denny's lifeless body. She begged him not to tell the authorities. To prevent Laurel from running away or turning herself in, Jack made an unlawful decision. With Laurel's help, he wrapped the corpse in a rug and dumped it into a mine shaft on Dimitri's property. Eventually, a secret witness to the crime came forward and testified that Laurel had acted in self-defense. For his role in covering up Laurel's crime, Jack's license to practice law was suspended.

Confined to a wheelchair, Adam feared he would never be able to make love with his beautiful bride again. He brought in handsome but ruthless businessman Alec McIntyre to run Chandler Enterprises while he dealt with his personal circumstances. Alec's ambition had no bounds. He wanted everything that was Adam's—including his wife Gloria. While Alec was lusting after Gloria, she was harboring her own fantasies about him.

Issues and Answers

Autism

In 1993, Jackson Montgomery's lady love, Laurel Banning, embezzled money from her friends in order to keep her seven-year-old autistic daughter Lily in a school that specialized in assisting children with her enigmatic condition. Laurel had been told by misinformed doctors that her daughter's condition was her fault. The story proved therapeutic for many viewers by showing that even good people will do desperate things out of guilt.

One night, when Alec and Gloria were snowed in at Adam's ski lodge, they gave in to their mutual attraction. An enraptured but worried Gloria would make love to Alec on one condition: he must leave town right away. Driven by his desire to have her, Alec promised he would. To Gloria's dismay, he reneged on his promise.

With Brooke's help, Tad regained his memory and after narrowly missing her for months, was reunited with Dixie. She thought she was hallucinating when she first heard his familiar voice and saw his face, but Tad assured her he was real. They enjoyed a tearful reunion, but their momentary joy wasn't enough to bring them back together. Too much had happened in the years Tad was gone. He was distressed to learn Dixie had been married twice during his absence. After her disastrous marriage to Craig Lawson, and haunted by the ghost of her evil dead brother Will, Dixie had fallen into a deep depression that bordered on psychosis. Adam had sought custody of their son, Adam Junior, during this time. Concerned for her mental state and the welfare of her son, Brian Bodine grew close to Dixie and helped in her recovery. Shortly before Tad's return, they were married. The news that Brooke English had borne Tad a child from their brief relationship threw both Tad and Dixie. Though their love was strong, this was too much to bear. Desperately wanting to be a good father, Tad married Brooke. Dixie divorced Brian and began a friendship with the newly arrived Ted Orsini, who bore more than a striking resemblance to Tad.

At the same time, Dixie entered into a secret affair with Tad. Despite their lengthy separation, they could never deny their unmistakable

Stalked by the evil Ted Orsini, Dixie and Tad faced danger together in the Canadian wilderness.

mutual attraction. Tad began lying to Brooke about his whereabouts so he could spend time with Dixie. Brooke knew something was wrong with her marriage when Tad uncharacteristically abstained from sex, successfully resisting all her efforts to seduce him.

By now, Ted Orsini's feelings for Dixie had developed into an obsession. Desperate wanting to eliminate his competition, Ted lured Tad to a remote part of Canada under the guise of a friendly hunting trip. Dixie rushed north of the border when she realized Ted's motives and managed to talk him out of killing both her and Tad.

Meanwhile, Edmund Grey was devastated when his true love Brooke married Tad. After foiling a senior citizen real estate scam, during which Edmund saved Brooke from sinking in quicksand located on the property in question, he declared his love for her. Even after Edmund told her about Dixie and Tad's affair, Brooke chose to stay with her husband. While still carrying a torch for Brooke, Edmund became engaged to the beautiful Dr. Maria Santos.

The rugged beauty of the Canadian wilderness set the scene for high adventure when *All My Children* took its cameras to Owen Sound, Ontario to tape scenes involving Tad, Dixie and Tad's vengeful lookalike Ted Orsini. One of the highlights of this thrill-packed remote was a daring water rescue of Tad by his true love, Dixie.

Rookie cop Taylor Cannon went undercover as a white woman named Diana to bust "Deconstruction," an underground racist group on the campus of Pine Valley University. When Tom and Livia's house was bombed by the group, Taylor was seriously hurt.

Officer Mimi Reed, Taylor's rival for the love of Derek Frye, was romantically involved with both Derek and Lucas Barnes, Taylor's adoptive father. When Mimi became pregnant, she wasn't sure which was the father.

Kendall Hart had become obsessed with finding her biological father. Erica, who had blocked the horrible rape from her mind, realized while watching an old film directed by her father that her rapist was one-time matinee idol Richard Fields. Erica forbade Kendall to look for her father, but just like her mother, once Kendall set her mind on something, nothing would stop her.

Kendall managed to con Dimitri into helping her locate Richard Fields, now sickly and pallid and living in a nursing home. When Erica learned of Kendall's continued pursuit, she told Dimitri her daughter had to leave their home. Dimitri challenged her decision, so Erica asked him for a divorce and moved out of Wildwind. After Kendall spent a night with Dimitri's Hungarian ward, medical student Anton Lang, she ran to Erica and told her Dimitri had raped her. An enraged Erica confronted her estranged husband. Hallucinating about the night Richard Fields raped her, Erica grabbed a letter opener and, in a moment of madness, plunged it into Dimitri's chest. Dimitri slumped to the floor, gasping in pain and disbelief that his own wife had stabbed him.

𝕰𝖆𝖗𝖑𝖞 𝖎𝖓 1994, Brooke was faced with a life-threatening crisis when she became pregnant by her new husband, Tad. She was diagnosed with a tubal pregnancy which if not treated could prove fatal. Unable to face the inevitable loss of her child, Brooke ran away. She did her best to ignore the throbbing pains in her abdomen when she boarded a bus with her son Jamie and left Pine Valley. An anguished Tad persuaded the police to issue an all-points bulletin on Brooke and anxiously awaited word on her whereabouts. When Brooke realized she was being pursued, she left the bus and sought refuge in an abandoned farmhouse. Knowing Tad was still in love with Dixie kept her from calling him. Instead, she contacted the one man she could trust: Edmund Grey.

On Location

In February 1994, the cast went on the road to nearby Garden City, New York for the very special winter wedding of Edmund Grey and Dr. Maria Santos. The historic Cathedral of the Incarnation, built in 1885, provided the setting for some exquisite exterior footage.

It was Tad who showed up at the farmhouse door, begging Brooke to come home and have the surgery that would save her life but end the life of her unborn child. But Edmund was the only one she would listen to. He helped Brooke understand that she needed to go back to Pine Valley and have the operation. Returning, Brooke stoically suffered the loss of her child and the end of her marriage.

Edmund's fiancée Maria Santos was extremely jealous of his devotion to Brooke. But just days after these troubling events with Brooke, Maria was able to realize her dream of marrying Edmund in a beautiful church ceremony. On their honeymoon in Hungary, they discovered the private letters of a housemaid named Corvina, older sister of Dimitri's ward, Anton Lang. They learned Corvina was not Anton's sister, but his mother. Even more shocking, Anton had been fathered by a drunken Dimitri Marick, who could not remember the night many years ago when Corvina had seduced him.

When Corvina came to Pine Valley and confessed the truth of Anton's paternity to Dimitri, he swore to keep the secret. After learning this news, Dimitri grew protective of his son and became hell-bent on keeping Anton out of the clutches of troublemaker Kendall Hart. Edmund Grey suspected Kendall was up to something when she started spending so much time with a stranger named Del Henry. Edmund wondered if they were having an affair. Kendall was indeed up to something, but it wasn't an affair. She had teamed up with the handsome blond writer to collaborate on a scandalous, tell-all book about the life and loves of her mother, Erica Kane.

Del Henry proved to be a man of mystery. His intense fascination with Dixie worried Tad, who mistakenly suspected Del was romantically interested in his wife-to-be. Alone with Dixie in the Cortlandt Manor gazebo, Del revealed at least part of his secret. He was Seabone Hunkle's son—which made him Dixie's brother.

Del left out one vital bit of information in his heartfelt confession to Dixie. He had come to Pine Valley in dire need of a kidney transplant, and only a close relative could provide the matching tissue necessary to keep him alive. Dixie was his only hope for survival. In time, she grew sympathetic to Del's plight, but Tad did not. He knew that his wife wanted to have children, and when he learned the risks involved for a woman with one kidney having a child, he urged Dixie not to submit to Del's request.

Maria was wary of Del for different reasons. They had been lovers eight years earlier while attending college in Texas. Del had charmed Maria but deserted her when she brought up marriage. Heartbroken after he left her, Maria soon discovered she was pregnant with his child.

Erica anxiously awaited the day she could defend herself in court against attempted murder charges for her attack on Dimitri. Her trial would become the media event of the year. Taking the stand in her own defense, Erica claimed she loved Dimitri Marick and proceeded to relive every last detail of that fateful night. She hadn't meant to stab Dimitri and leave him to die. Only after she got to the hospital did she realize she had critically wounded Dimitri, not Richard Fields. Where her mother had painstakingly told the truth, Kendall Hart blatantly lied through her teeth, swearing under oath that Dimitri's seduction of her daughter had so enraged Erica that she stabbed him. This was only the beginning of Kendall's madness.

In early 1994, she brought her newfound father Richard Fields to Pine Valley. Kendall showered the frail and elderly man with attention and devotion, but in time came to see his true colors when he tried to molest Kendall's younger sister, Bianca. Seeing the error of her ways, Kendall recanted her damaging testimony. When Kendall was sent to jail for committing perjury on the witness stand, her mother was set free.

Richard Fields never lived to see the outcome of the trial. Mona saw to that. She had told Joe Martin peace would come only with Richard Field's death. On a blustery March evening, Mona Kane went to the Pine Cone Motel and paid an unexpected visit to Fields in his seedy room. Brandishing a knife, Mona told Fields it was his turn to die. He taunted Mona, daring her to stab him. Mona backed down under his smug facade, admitting she couldn't kill him. But when she reached for the phone, threatening to call the police, Fields demanded she hang up and, clutching his chest, collapsed to the floor. Mona assumed he was "acting" and ignored his pleas for help, leaving her daughter's rapist to die.

Sadly, this courageous act was one of Mona's last. Later in the year, Erica discovered her mother had died peacefully in her sleep. Erica was devastated but stoic as she made arrangements for Mona's funeral. Though they had frustrated each other endlessly, the love between them had endured until the end. Erica had lost her champion, her defender, and as Mona's casket was lowered into its final resting place, the pain finally hit her. Consumed by overwhelming grief, Erica reached for the casket and begged her mother not to leave her. It was a chilling, emotional moment that few in Pine Valley would ever forget.

Meanwhile, in jail, Kendall Hart encountered a most unusual fellow prisoner named Janet Green, mother to Trevor's daughter Amanda and sister of the late Natalie. Janet had consented to radical new cosmetic

Dr. Maria Santos, now happily married to Edmund Grey, worried when her ex-boyfriend Del Henry showed up in Pine Valley.

Gone, But Not Forgotten
Mona Kane

"Oh, Erica—how could you?" Those immortal words, uttered in exasperation time and time again by Mona Kane Tyler, will never be heard again. Actress Frances Heflin, an original cast member, passed away in June 1994. Fittingly, *All My Children* chose not to re-cast the pivotal role, and two months after her real-life death, the character of Mona passed away in her sleep. Mona's legacy lives on in her sweet granddaughter, Bianca.

This is your life, Janet Green! Swathed in bandages, Janet journeyed on a dreamy fantasy in which her loathsome life came back to haunt her!

surgery which would either give her an entirely new face or leave her horribly disfigured.

After waiting several agonizing weeks, Janet braced herself as the doctors removed her bandages. When she gazed upon the results, she was delighted. Janet had a new lease on life. Released from prison, she returned to Pine Valley. Using the name "Jane Cox," she wormed her way back into the lives of her former lover Trevor and their beloved daughter Amanda. The only resident who recognized Jane as Janet was her old nemesis, Timmy's friend and protector, Harold the dog. Janet acted quickly to dispose of Harold, drugging and shipping him off to California in the back of a moving van.

Embarking on his new law career, Trevor Dillon represented Tom and Livia Cudahy's foster son Jamal during a most unusual custody case. In a story inspired by a real-life teenager who divorced his birth parents, young Jamal Wilson announced in no uncertain terms that he did not want to live with his natural father, Alec McIntyre. He went to court to divorce his father. As the judge was about to announce his decision, Alec stood up and addressed the court. Tired of fighting and wishing only love for his son, Alec relinquished his parental rights officially and permanently.

In early 1994, Mimi Reed gave birth to a baby daughter, Danielle, still uncertain whether the father was architect Lucas Barnes or fellow police officer Derek Frye. Before she knew the answer, Mimi agreed to marry the man she loved, Derek. He promised to be a father to Danielle regardless of the test results. Before the tests could be administered, Danielle was kidnapped. At first, it appeared that an embittered Lucas had taken the child. But the culprit turned out to be Grace Keefer, who sought revenge after Mimi had shot and killed her son Tony during a robbery attempt the year before.

Upon Danielle's return, tests revealed Derek was indeed the father, and before long, he and Mimi were married.

In time, Kendall Hart came to the stunning realization that Pine Valley newcomer Jane Cox was actually her old prison partner, Janet. As a tornado approached Pine Valley, Janet confronted Kendall in the Chandler boathouse, begging her to keep her secret. When fierce winds blew in the boathouse window, a ceiling beam collapsed, trapping Kendall. She cried out to Janet who wasn't sure saving Kendall was a good idea since everyone wanted her dead. Dimitri arrived on the scene in time to save Kendall, but not before Janet elicited a solemn promise from Kendall to keep quiet about her identity.

Pine Valley's terrible tornado claimed several victims in its short but devastating sweep through the Valley. Inside the Chandler ballroom, a chandelier came crashing down on Julia Santos, shards of glass slicing and scarring her beautiful young face. Deeply depressed by her disfiguring injury, she ran away, finding shelter with the streetwise and sensitive Noah Keefer. Julia was further traumatized when she was raped by a drug dealer.

During the tornado, Joe and Ruth Martin watched in horror as their ceiling came crashing down on Tad. Hovering between life and death, he had a remarkable near-death experience in which he encountered his deceased loved ones: Jenny, Jesse, Nola—and his hated father, Ray Gardner.

The tornado arrived the same night Gloria Chandler sprang a surprise upon her husband Adam during their lavish remarriage in the Chandler ballroom. With a minister presiding, the assembled guests listened as Adam professed his love to Gloria. When it was her turn to speak, she announced she wouldn't marry Adam Chandler if he were the last man on earth. Gloria's incredible declaration came moments after she had discovered Adam had faked his own kidnapping in order to test her loyalty. He wanted to see for himself that Gloria truly loved him, not Alec McIntyre.

Gloria had been frantic with worry while Adam was missing and was unaware he was right under her nose the entire time, posing as his twin brother Stuart. When Gloria learned the truth, she insisted their wedding go on as scheduled in order that she might reject and expose him in front of everyone. With the shock his life, Adam landed in jail. And it came as a blow to Gloria to discover that she was pregnant with Adam's child.

After her face was horribly scarred, Julia Santos found comfort and reassurance in her friendship with streetwise Noah Keefer.

Custody Battles

In a 1994 story inspired by Gregory K., the real-life teenager who divorced his natural parents, All My Children *told the tale of a bitter and highly unusual custody battle. The parties involved were Jamal, Alec McIntyre, biological father of the African-American youngster and Jamal's foster parents, Tom and Livia Cudahy. Jamal announced that he did not want to live with Alec, and he went to court to, in effect, divorce his dad. The courtroom story explored a child's right to challenge long-established parental rights, which Alec eventually relinquished, prompting the judge to grant full custody of Jamal to the Cudahys.*

Chapter 2

THE FAMILIES

he backbone of Pine Valley has always been the family. Whether it be the Martins or Tylers, Cortlandts or Chandlers, *All My Children* has consistently provided its audience with well-defined and thoroughly orchestrated family drama. Each character is linked to a "family" of others by blood, marriage or friendship through carefully interwoven stories.

When *All My Children* premiered in 1970, three families were introduced. Dr. Joe Martin was a widower with three children when he left California to live with his mother Kate. He married Ruth Brent, whose son Phil had fallen in love with Joe's daughter Tara. Ruth and Joe adopted Tad Gardner and later had a son, Joey. Through marriage several times over, the Martins were tied to the blue-blood Tylers, who mixed in more exclusive circles than the Martins, a point Phoebe Tyler made repeatedly. The Martin/Tyler couplings didn't challenge her standards as much as the Kane women did. Phoebe's husband Charles fell in love with and eventually left Phoebe for his secretary, Mona Kane. Mona's daughter Erica worried Phoebe whenever she pursued the Tyler men. But when Erica became her partner in crime, Phoebe dropped her snobbish air.

In its second decade, *All My Children* introduced two more families. Strict patriarch Palmer Cortlandt brought his daughter Nina and her grandmother Myra. Nina's mother followed, as did a legion of nieces and nephews. An old rival of Palmer's made Pine Valley his home in 1984. Adam Chandler entered the scene under a cloud of mystery, bringing with him his twin brother Stuart and nephew Ross, followed by daughters and sons, nieces and nephews of the next generation.

Into the show's third decade stepped Dimitri Marick. He learned he was to share his vast family fortune with his half-brother, Edmund Grey. The Maricks have discovered their tie to various family members since arriving in Pine Valley, and a son he had no idea existed.

These pillars of the town of Pine Valley continue to wreak happiness and havoc on each other's lives. And we can always expect that there will be new arrivals into the Valley to make life evermore interesting for its inhabitants. And for the viewers.

Palmer Cortlandt ruled his family with an iron hand. He dominated his diabetic daughter Nina, keeping the teenager sheltered from the world, especially young men—until an attack of appendicitis put her in the hospital, where she met and fell in love with Dr. Cliff Warner. From the leather chair in his library, he hatched scheme after scheme to keep Cliff and Nina apart.

The Martin Family

Forbidden love: Widower Dr. Joe Martin worked side by side with married nurse Ruth Brent (above) at Pine Valley Hospital since *All My Children* premiered in the winter of 1970. Their relationship remained strictly business until Ruth's husband Ted Brent was killed. Doctor and nurse fell in love and married in a simple ceremony at the Martin home

Dr. Joe Martin was a widower with three children when he met nurse Ruth Brent at Pine Valley Hospital. As their work at the hospital brought them closer, they couldn't bring themselves to admit their feelings for each other because Ruth was still very much married to Ted Brent, a demanding, working-class man who made Ruth's life miserable when he became convinced that Ruth was having an affair with the handsome doctor

At home, Ruth and Ted held a closely guarded secret: Their son Phillip (who had fallen in love with Joe Martin's daughter, Tara) was actually her nephew! Only a select few knew that Phillip Brent was actually the illegitimate child of Ruth's sister, Amy, and her long-ago lover, Nick Davis.

When Ted died in a car accident, Joe comforted Ruth, and their love blossomed. Joe's children and kindly mother, Kate, welcomed Ruth into their family and home. Today, the Martins and their extended family remain a cornerstone of Pine Valley.

Kate, Ruth and Joe enjoyed many a warm summer evening sharing conversation on the porch of Kate's comfortable and cozy home.

The Tyler and Martin clans united for the first time when Anne Tyler, on the rebound from her disastrous marriage to Nick Davis, accepted Paul Martin's proposal.

In 1973, Joe and Ruth took an abused and abandoned young boy, Tad Gardner, into their home and instantly fell in love with the precocious lad. Tad had many problems, though, and grew up to become a rebellious teenager who smoked marijuana, wrecked the family station wagon and ran away from home to escape the disciplinary rules imposed by his parents.

Joe, Tara, Kate and Tara's beau, Phil Brent gather in 1971. Joe's calm demeanor provided a steadying influence for the Martins during these rocky early days.

The Families

After his tumultuous marriage to the flamboyant Erica Kane, Joe's son Jeff Martin discovered love with sweet and simple Mary Kennicott.

Just before her Christmas 1976 wedding day to Phil, bride-to-be, Tara received some words of wisdom from grandma Kate (above).

For many years, Tara concealed the fact that her son Charlie was actually the son of her first love, Phil Brent. Everyone, including young Charlie, believed that Chuck Tyler (whom Tara married when Phil was presumed dead in Vietnam) was the boy's natural father. In 1979 the family posed for a portrait: Tara, Philip and son Charlie (above).

In July 1994, a tornado tore through Pine Valley, leveling the Martin house and nearly killing Tad, who was crushed by the rubble. Joe and Ruth worked feverishly to free their beloved son from the debris (below).

Tara had a special bond with her wise and compassionate father, Joe.

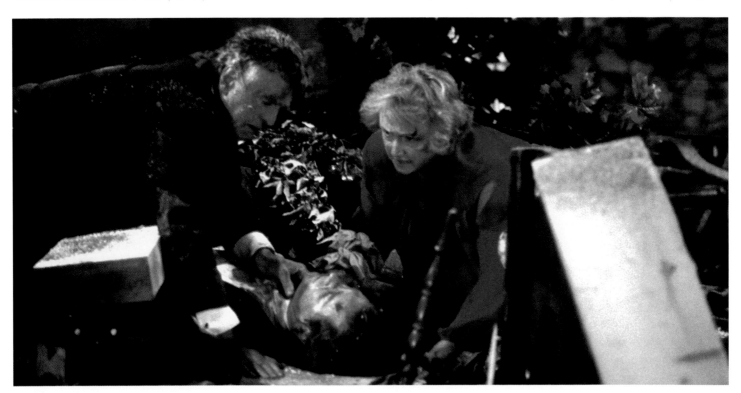

For many years, the Tylers were one of Pine Valley's most wealthy and prominent families. Dr. Charles Tyler was the patriarch of the clan. The kindly Chief of Staff at Pine Valley Hospital, Charles suffered an exhausting marriage to irrepressible busybody Phoebe English, herself an offspring of one of Pine Valley's founding families. Phoebe and Charles raised two children of their own—Lincoln, a prestigious lawyer, and Anne, who was killed by a car bomb meant for her political-candidate husband, Paul Martin. When Charles Tyler's son, Charles, Jr. (from his first marriage) and his wife were killed in a plane crash, the Tylers also took grandson Chuck Tyler into their sprawling home in one of Pine Valley's most affluent sections. Through the years, many more memorable characters populated the Tyler mansion: among them Phoebe's naughty niece, Brooke English, Phoebe's second husband con artist Langley Wallingford, and his illegitimate daughter, sweet Hillary Wilson.

Socialite Phoebe English Tyler Wallingford (left) considered herself the toast of the town. A member of Pine Valley's elite Daughters of Fine Lineage, Phoebe traced her roots back to the Mayflower. Phoebe savors wealth, stature—and an occasional bit of the bubbly!

Dr. Charles Tyler proudly acknowledged the accomplishments of his son Lincoln (right), who established a successful law firm in Pine Valley back in the early 1970s.

Lincoln Tyler's first wife Amy was *All My Children*'s first heroine. A liberal activist in the anti-war movement, Amy often angered her conservative mother-in-law, Phoebe.

Daughter Ann Tyler Martin shared few happy times with her husband, dancing teacher Nick Davis. Their marriage crumbled when Nick, wrongly believing he was sterile and could never give Ann a child, asked her for a divorce.

Phoebe fought a losing battle to keep grandson Chuck away from former teenage hooker Donna Beck. Against Phoebe's wishes, they married.

Phoebe worried incessantly about her daughter, Ann. In this 1973 photo, she anxiously listens in on a telephone conversation between Ann and her then-husband, Paul Martin.

The Families

After his ill-fated first marriage to Donna, Chuck Tyler tried to rewrite the book of love by marrying troubled young Carrie Sanders (right), a young woman who had grown up in an abusive home. Her marriage to Chuck, though short-lived, provided Carrie with the only family stability she had ever known.

After living away from Pine Valley for several months, Lincoln Tyler returned to town and fell in love with Kitty Shea Davis (right). Despite Phoebe's disapproval of the poor but charming Kitty, Lincoln married her and they lived happily until Kitty's untimely death in the summer of 1977

Phoebe always looked out for the best interests of her trusted chauffeur and confidante Benny Sago. Street-wise Benny loved and married hooker-with-a-heart-of-gold Estelle Tuggle (below).

Brooke English finally tamed her wild ways when she settled down (for a time) with solid Tom Cudahy (below). Together they had a daughter, Laura. Though their marriage ended, they remain close friends.

After her divorce from Charles, Phoebe fell victim to petty thief turned big-time con artist, Langley Wallingford. In hot pursuit of Phoebe's fortune, the roving-eyed swindler married the wealthy dowager and moved right into her mansion.

Langley sweet-talks Phoebe

December 1979

Langley
You're living in the wrong age, my sweet. In another time when beauty was more appreciated, your face alone would have inspired painters and poets, not just a humble scholar like myself.

Phoebe:
Oh, Langley!

In the late 1970s, Charles Tyler found himself in the middle of a messy triangle when he fell deeply in love with his trusted friend and longtime secretary Mona Kane. Phoebe, who by now had become an overbearing alcoholic, fought unsuccessfully to hang on to Charles.

Phoebe's sassy goddaughter, Cecily Davidson, shook up the staid Wallingfords when she moved into the manor.

Phoebe adored her brother, Ed English, but she was wary of his wife, Peg. And rightly so! It came as quite a shock to the clan when Peg was revealed to be the notorious "Cobra," head of an international drug cartel.

In 1984, the Wallingfords hosted Langley's teenage daughter Hillary Wilson as a house guest.

Brooke was never happier than when she posed for this photo with her infant daughter Laura in 1985. Sadly, Laura was killed in a drunk driving accident several years later.

Though she truly loved Tad Martin, Hillary married Bob Georgia (above) because she wrongly believed he was fatally ill with leukemia. Shortly before the wedding, Bob went into remission but neglected to tell Hillary, who went through with the marriage.

The Kane Family

When it comes to her family, Erica Kane is a lioness. The incomparable Ms. Kane will go the extra mile to protect, defend and support the members of her close-knit den. When her brother Mark became addicted to drugs, Erica stood right by his side on the grueling road to recovery. And when she suspected that her long-lost father, Eric Kane, was alive, she stopped at nothing to find "daddy" and bring him back to Pine Valley.

Erica proved how strong her family ties were when her daughter Bianca fell ill with Reye's Syndrome. During those trying hours, she quickly and totally put her little girl's welfare above her own. But when a family member crosses Erica, watch out! Bad-seed daughter Kendall Hart found that out when she plotted to steal Erica's husband, Dimitri.

And no one could really appreciate how Erica grew to become the woman she is without meeting her saintly and long-suffering mother, Mona. She singlehandedly raised Erica while doling out a bottomless supply of motherly love. With a hell-raising daughter like Erica, that was hard work.

Erica's long-lost relatives seem to come out of the woodwork. In January 1977, the first kin to pop into town was Erica's half-brother, Mark Dalton (below, center), a promising young composer. Neither Erica nor Mark knew they were related, so they dated for a spell. But their budding romance came to a screeching halt when Mona informed a stunned Erica that she and Mark were siblings.

In one of the few times in her life she's ever been outwitted, Erica was bamboozled when her mousy, long-lost sister, Silver Kane (above), showed up at her door and quickly insinuated herself into Erica's life. Silver turned out to be an impostor named Connie Wilkes.

Erica was scandalized when Mona announced her intention to marry her boss, the newly divorced Dr. Charles Tyler (right), Phoebe Tyler's ex-hubby. Erica scandalized? Now that's a switch!

Mona Kane was an inspiration to her daughter (above). She was everything Erica didn't want to be—sweet and dull.

ALL MY CHILDREN

Erica found love with businessman Travis Montgomery, and together they had a daughter, Bianca (above). They later divorced, but when Bianca fell ill with Reye's Syndrome, Erica remarried Travis to give her daughter a stable family life. It was one of the few unselfish things Erica has ever done. The second marriage didn't last either, however, for Erica was in love with Travis's brother Jackson, and they were having an affair.

As Bianca grew up, Erica demonstrated that she can actually care about someone other than herself (above). In fact, she has often turned into a lioness over her child's well-being.

Since childhood, the driving force in Erica's life was the relationship with her father, movie director Eric Kane, who abandoned her as a young girl. In 1989, she confronted her demons when she found her daddy working as a circus clown named Barney (above).

In a rare family portrait taken in 1993 (right), Erica is joined by the women in her family: from left, her saucy daughter Kendall, her late mother Mona and her pride and joy, Bianca.

The Families

The Cortlandt Family

Palmer Cortlandt rules his family and his enviable financial empire with an iron hand. Born Pete Cooney in Pigeon Hollow, West Virginia, Palmer is a self-made man who rose from his humble beginnings to amass great wealth—only to lose his fortune time and time again. Palmer's stately home, Cortlandt Manor, has been the site of family feuds, memorable marriages—and a murder or two! Children, nieces, nephews, wives and other relatives may come and go, but one thing never changes at Cortlandt Manor—Palmer. He's as caustic and cantankerous as ever. But somewhere beneath that crusty exterior beats a heart of gold.

Palmer dominated his diabetic daughter Nina (below), keeping the teenager sheltered from the world, especially young men—until an attack of appendicitis put her in the hospital, where she met and fell in love with Dr. Cliff Warner. Of course Palmer objected.

Daisy Murdoch was Palmer's first wife and perhaps his greatest love. When she had an affair early in their marriage, Palmer banished Daisy, telling their daughter Nina that her mother was dead. But upon her return, the passion between "P.C." and "D.C." burned hotter than ever!

No man could ever be good enough for Palmer's daughter. From the leather chair in his library, he hatched scheme after scheme to keep Cliff and Nina apart.

Assuming the identity of Monique Jonvil, Daisy returned to Pine Valley and quickly developed an unbreakable bond with her unsuspecting daughter, Nina.

Cliff escorted Nina to her nineteenth birthday bash. The event was one of the grandest affairs ever held in the Cortlandt Manor ballroom.

In 1982, Nina and Cliff celebrate Nina's adoption of their son, Bobby.

Palmer's maid and two-time mother-in-law Myra Murdoch discovered love in her golden years with the Cortlandt family chauffeur, Jasper Sloan. They married in 1984.

Ross Chandler turned out to be Palmer's long-lost son, from his long-ago liaison with Adam Chandler's sister, Lottie. Adam raised Ross to despise his life-long enemy Palmer (below).

In 1983, Palmer and Donna pose with son Palmer John (above). Sadly, the infant (actually Chuck Tyler's natural son) died in a fire at the Chateau restaurant.

In 1985, gold-digger Cynthia Preston wormed her way into Palmer's life and soon became the third woman to become Mrs. Palmer Cortlandt (above).

Palmer adopted Cynthia Preston's son, Andrew (below), and groomed him to be his successor at the helm of the Cortlandt empire. However, the young man's bright future was dimmed when he was sent to jail for his role in the death of Alex Hunter.

One of Pine Valley's most beloved couples was gloriously reunited in dramatic fashion when Dr. Cliff Warner raced alongside a moving train and proclaimed his love to Nina.

Natalie Hunter nursed Palmer back to health after a near-fatal gunshot wound. While living at Cortlandt Manor, she engaged in a steamy affair with Ross Chandler, and when it ended, she married Palmer on the rebound in 1987.

Here's a proud Palmer in 1989, surrounded by his newly united family—niece Dixie, nephew Will and niece Lanie (below). Palmer welcomed his three relatives from West Virginia into his home, and, as he always does, began to meddle in their personal lives.

In the fall of 1989, the Cortlandt clan gathered in the garden to wish a happy fourth marriage and a fond farewell to Cliff, Nina and Bobby.

They say opposites attract! Petulant Palmer and eccentric Opal (above) proved the point when they fell in love in 1990. Palmer's ex-wife Daisy played matchmaker for the unlikely couple.

Just as he'd done five years before, Palmer escorted niece Dixie down the aisle when she married Tad Martin again in May 1994 (left).

The Families

The Chandler Family

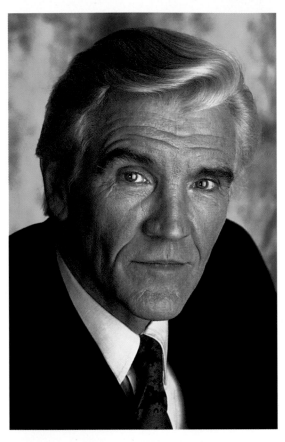

Adam Chandler is outrageous. Adam Chandler is flamboyant. Adam Chandler always does the unexpected. When this silver-haired sultan arrived on the scene in 1984, few knew the tremendous impact he would have on the people of Pine Valley. The brooding, self-absorbed Chandler blew into town and immediately set out to rule the roost by ruthlessly manipulating everyone who came into contact with him. It's his way or no way!

The greedy Mr. Chandler thinks nothing of using others as pawns in his pursuit of power. Power and money are the instruments he uses to control the people in his life, and he cares little about the emotional torture he inflicts upon his victims. But Chandler does have some redeeming qualities. Adam's a family man who dearly loves twin brother, Stuart, his daughters, Skye and Hayley, his son, Adam, Jr., and his nephew, Ross. And he's been known to pour on the charm to win the hearts of a bevy of beautiful brides like Erica, Brooke, Natalie and Gloria. He adores his family, he worships women, but more than anything else—Adam loves Adam!

Adam Chandler loved Erica Kane (below), but what he loved even more was making Erica miserable. And nothing could make Erica unhappier than being married to Adam.

Adam raised Ross Chandler, his late sister Lottie's illegitimate son by Palmer Cortlandt—a fact that Adam went to great lengths to keep secret from his nephew.

Stuart Chandler is as kind as Adam is heartless.

Ross Chandler enjoyed fleeting happiness with wife Ellen and their adopted daughter, Julie (below). The happy family atmosphere fell apart when Julie stumbled upon her father raping Natalie Hunter.

Adam abandoned his daughter Skye at age five and didn't see her until she returned to Pine Valley seeking daddy's love. They reconciled, and proud papa Adam congratulated Skye on her marriage to Tom Cudahy. Moments later, Adam stunned the guests at Skye and Tom's wedding reception when he announced his engagement to Tom's ex-wife, Brooke English. Now that's keeping it all in the family!

Adam's illegitimate daughter Hayley was a ghoulish sight when she first turned up with that silky mane of dyed-black hair. Tough-as-nails Hayley had a chip on her shoulder the size of Plymouth Rock—though you'd never know it from this sweet smile.

Happiness finally came to Stuart Chandler in 1987 when, while teaching art courses, he met delicate Cindy Parker (left), whose son Scott was his student. Despite the actions of some ignorant people, including Stuart's niece Skye, who tried to drive Cindy out of Pine Valley because she had contacted HIV from her drug-addicted husband, Fred, they shared a tender courtship. They got married, and when Cindy died of AIDS, Stuart adopted Scott.

Adam always gets what he wants, and in 1990 he wanted to get his greedy hands on Natalie Hunter's money. Using every trick in the book to woo Nat away from her true love, Trevor Dillon, Adam took Natalie to the Justice of the Peace for a quickie wedding before she could change her mind. Trevor arrived moments too late to stop the nuptials.

Alcoholic Arlene Dillon Vaughan rediscovered her long-lost love, Adam (above), when he was in the midst of an ugly divorce from Natalie, her brother Trevor's fiancé. Adam pretended to fall in love with Arlene and plotted to set Trevor up on a phony drug charge. When Arlene backed out of the scheme, Adam fiercely told her he had no use for a lush like her!

Adam would do practically anything to pry his son Junior (left) away from the child's mother, Dixie. When they divorced, Junior became the focus of a bitter custody battle.

Sultry and sexy Gloria Marsh captivated both Stuart and Adam. For the first time since Cindy's death, Stuart Chandler fell in love. Stuart saw a kernel of goodness in the troubled young nurse, and they were engaged. At the same time, Gloria developed a tempestuous relationship with Adam. "I wouldn't date you if you were the last man on earth!" uttered Gloria to Adam (left). But she did! And Gloria eventually gave in to Adam's pursuit and married him!

The Families

The Marick Family

With the early Nineties came a new core family to *All My Children*, the Maricks, who lived at Wildwind, a secluded mansion on the outskirts of Pine Valley. The first Marick we met was Dimitri, a dark, mysterious and dashing prince who rescued Natalie Hunter heroically from the bottom of a well and nursed her back to health in the safe confines of his stately manor.

In time, more and more of Dimitri's secretive past unfolded as we met Edmund Grey, who led a successful crusade to prove that he, like Dimitri, was a rightful son of the late millionaire Hugo Marick. We were spooked by Dimitri's mysterious maid (and mother-in-law) Helga. We were shocked by the unexpected return of his comatose wife, Angelique. And we were taken by surprise by the revelation that Dimitri had a son, Anton Lang, whom he'd never known about. We journeyed to the Marick family's ancestral home in Budapest and followed Dimitri through a whirlwind courtship with Erica Kane that began with a sizzling affair and nearly ended with a horrifying knife wound to the chest. The Maricks have been rocked by brotherly battles and scandalous affairs, stabbings and sacrifices.

Dimitri rescued Natalie Hunter from a well, where she'd been imprisoned by her crazed sister, Janet. Struck by Natalie's uncanny resemblance to his comatose wife, Dimitri brought her back to recuperate at the Wildwind Mansion where they encountered Natalie's former fiancé, Trevor Dillon (below).

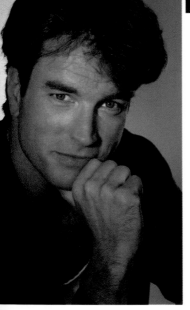

Journalist Edmund Grey discovered he was Dimitri Marick's half-brother.

A hush fell over Dimitri and Natalie's engagement party when, at the stroke of midnight, Helga wheeled in Angelique—her daughter and Dimitri's wife—who had recently awakened from a fifteen-year coma.

Edmund and Dimitri's late father, Hugo Marick, appeared as his domineering self in 1992 flashbacks.

Dimitri's mother-in-law, Helga, held a deep dark secret—she was the only person who knew the truth that Edmund Grey was Hugo Marick's illegitimate son—and Dimitri's half-brother. And to keep the secret safe, Helga burned Hugo's will.

The Families

Erica Kane proved her sure and steady hand when she sexily shaved off husband Dimitri's beard.

Journalist Edmund Grey came to Pine Valley in search of a story, and along the way, found the love of his life—or at least one of the loves of his life—Brooke English. Edmund begged Brooke to marry him, but her answer was a resounding, "No!"

The news that Anton Lang was his long-lost son came as quite a shock to Mr. Marick. He didn't even remember sleeping with the boy's mother, Corvina. Why? It seems Corvina seduced and got pregnant by a drunken Dimitri, who recalled none of their carnal encounter.

On the rebound from Brooke, Edmund married Maria Santos (above), a breathtakingly beautiful surgeon who had recently relocated to Pine Valley from her native Texas. Maria loved Edmund dearly; but she held on to her lingering doubts that Edmund still carried a torch for Brooke.

In 1992, bad blood often boiled over between brothers Edmund Grey and Dimitri Marick (left). These lifelong enemies finally reconciled in Budapest when Dimitri discovered that Edmund was truly his half brother and the rightful heir to the Marick estate.

The Families

Chapter 3

THE LOVERS

ove has always been an essential element in the lives of *All My Children*. It motivates the action in almost every story. Regardless of the pain and heartache that follow, Pine Valley-ites relentlessly pursue love. For the past 25 years, *All My Children* has courageously presented love stories in every form imagineable, representing every age and ethnic group. It takes chances with controversial couplings that in the end prove successful.

Always a popular theme, young love thrives in Pine Valley. *All My Children* has produced its share of star-crossed lovers: Greg and Jenny, Angie and Jesse and Nina and Cliff are just a few. Beginning with Tara and Phil, the show has handled its young couples responsibly and truthfully while they deal with issues from peer pressure to unplanned pregnancy to marriage and divorce. They have felt the joy and pain of first love and learned to love again.

We have also seen the wisdom of love the second time around. Ruth and Joe, both previously married, found long lasting happiness that has survived the traumas of parenthood and aging with grace. We've witnessed the melting of hearts with Phoebe and Langley, Palmer and Opal as they discover love is still alive in the autumn years. May/December romance has been played out with Mark Dalton and Ellen Shepard, Charlie Brent and Erica Kane.

Love rarely conquers all in Pine Valley. While there have been moments when the course of true love has run smooth, it doesn't always last. The demise of love sometimes comes with the entrance of a third party, generating stories of love triangles fraught with jealousy, obsession and hate. As in real life, love is complicated in the town of Pine Valley.

When two people finally do get together on *All My Children*, it is with pomp, circumstance and something unexpected, for a Pine Valley wedding is an event. Of the many, Cliff and Nina's fairy-tale celebration may be the most memorable. Nina's father Palmer suspended his interference in their lives for one blessed day when love reigned supreme.

After years of being subject to the overprotective Palmer, Nina Cortlandt met and fell in love with Dr. Cliff Warner. Palmer's machinations kept them apart, but eventually they cleared the way to be together. One and all gathered to toast Cliff and Nina's happy future after their lavish wedding on the grounds of Cortlandt Manor.

Falling in love is wonderful. The experience can be even more sweet when you're young and in love. Over the past 25 years, audiences have watched *All My Children*'s youthful couples discover that incredible feeling all for themselves. Holding hands, gazing into each other's eyes as they recite the poetic words of Browning or Wordsworth, these innocent youngsters seem blissfully unaware of life's pressures as they fall hopelessly, impetuously in love. Along the way, they capture our hearts, too. The more labyrinthine their struggle for happiness, the harder we pull for these kids to get together. More often than not, love does not conquer all in Pine Valley. The electric spark of youthful adoration fades and these young lovers move on to other romantic conquests, leaving us with little else but everlasting memories of love in bloom.

Frail teenager Nina Cortlandt fell instantly in love with handsome Dr. Cliff Warner (left) while she was his patient. Suffering from appendicitis, Nina was rushed to Pine Valley Hospital where the attending physician, young Dr. Warner, soothed her worries. Nina's obsessive father, Palmer Cortlandt, tried every trick in the book to break up the lovers, though they eventually cleared the way to marry. And marry. And marry. And marry! After four tries, Nina and Cliff are happy forever!

Tara Martin and Phillip Brent (above) were *All My Children*'s original teenage sweethearts. They fell in love and were planning to marry until Phillip found out the awful truth that his "Aunt Amy," not Ruth Brent, was actually his mother. This shocking revelation drove Phillip to suffer a breakdown, and he rejected a heartbroken Tara. It took years before they were able to work out their many problems and find happiness with each other.

While Devon Shepherd was in love with Dan Kennicott, she entered into a relationship with Wally McFadden (above) by whom she became pregnant. Though they were never truly in love, these innocent kids decided to marry for the sake of their baby. Their devotion was sorely tested by Devon's affairs and alcoholism, which eventually caused the union to crumble.

Jesse and Angie's first kiss

June 1982

Angie:
I liked you so much when I first met you.

Jesse:
But I treated you so bad.

Angie:
I was being a snob. Trying to impress you with what a smart student I was.

Jesse:
You can't help it if you're born smart.

Angie:
I never had a best friend like you have with Jenny. Jenny is a very special friend to me, too, but I think of you differently.

Jesse:
I guess I feel kind of different about you, too.

Angie:
Oh, Jessie. Do you?

They kiss

Jesse:
I guess I got me somebody?

Angie:
I guess I do too!

The heartbreaking romantic saga of streetwise Jesse Hubbard and beautiful, brainy Angie Hubbard proved to be one of the most popular in *All My Children*'s first quarter-century on the air. In the beginning, their devotion was tested sorely and often by Angie's stuffy father Les Baxter, who was determined to keep his darling daughter away from "that delinquent." Eventually, they overcame life's obstacles, and, with their son Frankie, Jesse and Angie found happiness—though it all ended much too soon when Jesse, a police officer, was killed in the line of duty.

The Lovers

Love finally did conquer all in the case of star-crossed lovers David Rampal and Melanie Cortlandt (right). Their plans for a rosy future were halted in the fall of 1989 when David fell into a deep depression over the death of his mother, Marissa. When David refused to allow Lanie to help him deal with his demons, they broke up, but they eventually found their way back to each other. Though they moved away from Pine Valley, all reports indicate that David and Melanie are as much in love as ever.

Here's an offbeat love story: Flighty and rich teenager Cecily Davidson informed tough-guy Nico Kelly that if he married her, she would come into her trust fund and they'd both be rich. Of course, they wouldn't have to consummate the marriage, just live together! Sexual tension filled the air as Nico and Cecily carried on their marriage of convenience, slowly but surely, however, they did what neither wanted—they fell in love!

Beautiful, young, innocent Julie Chandler believed she loved decent Charlie Brent with all her heart. Everyone thought these cute kids would be together forever, but the relationship came to an end when Julie found herself overwhelmingly attracted to devil-may-care rogue Nico Kelly.

The tumultuous courtship of Brian Bodine and Hayley Vaughan (left) began at Pine Valley High School where, for a school project, they became "parents" to a sack-of-flour "baby" they named "Spike." Though they cared deeply for each other, a flurry of insurmountable problems—especially Hayley's alcoholism and Brian's relationships with An-Li and Dixie—drove this attractive couple apart for good.

Anton Lang and Kendall Hart (below) are an unlikely couple. They are not, and will never be, sweet and starry-eyed kids experiencing the first blush of love. He was a highly volatile young medical student, and she was an angry young woman determined to get revenge on her long-lost mother, Erica Kane. Both in search of love, they arrived in Pine Valley in 1993 as strangers in a strange town. When they met, sparks flew immediately, though they seldom seem to enjoy each other's company—except beneath the sheets.

Cupid fired his mighty arrow straight at love-struck teenagers Greg and Jenny. Lasting love is never easy to find, but it's even more difficult for two sweet and innocent kids from opposite sides of the track. Blue-blooded Greg was born into one of Pine Valley's founding families, while Jenny Gardner was the daughter of the incorrigible Ray Gardner and his tacky wife, Opal. Viewers pulled for these tortured teens to get together, but family, friends, jealous lovers and their own misguided pride worked to keep them apart for years.

Just when it seemed that Jenny and Greg had secured their happy future, tragedy struck. Jenny's former fiancé Tony Barclay discovered that Jenny, Greg and Tad planned an afternoon of jet-skiing at a nearby lake. Insanely jealous, Tony plotted to kill Greg by rigging his jet ski to explode. His plans backfired when Jenny and Greg switched skis and she became the unwitting victim. Their time together was short, but Greg and Jenny's pure devotion to each other will linger in viewers' hearts forever.

Love bloomed in the spring of 1982 for Greg Nelson and Jenny Gardner (left).

Greg defied his mother's wishes and took Jenny, not Liza, to the Pine Valley High School prom (right). While Liza stewed and plotted her next scheme to drive them apart, Greg and Jenny danced the night away.

At the Glamorama, beautician Opal Gardner gladly applies the finishing touches to her daughter's flawless face before a date with her "rich" boyfriend, Greg.

Greg's snooty mother Enid Nelson tried to impress upon her son the importance of marrying the "proper" young lady (right). To Enid's tastes, Jenny didn't fit the bill and she tried to push Greg into the arms of longtime family friend Liza Colby.

Jenny's Final Words
May 1984

Jenny: Don't cry. It's all right, Greg. You make me so happy.

Greg: I love you.

Jenny: Promise me...your dreams... don't give up your dreams.

Greg: Our dreams. Our dreams!

Jenny: Not anymore. I want you to hold on to them. You go on dreaming. You go on with your life.

Greg: You aren't going to die, Jenny. You aren't going to die...

Jenny: Say it. Promise.

Greg: I promise. But you're not going to die, honey.

In 1983, Greg suffered a fall that left him paralyzed from the legs down. Not wanting to be a burden to the girl he loved, Greg drove Jenny away. As the president of the previous graduating class, Greg attended Jenny's high school graduation, and awkwardly posed with his estranged girlfriend.

JENNY CLOSES HER EYES AND THE HEART MONITOR STOPS BEEPING.

At Pine Valley Hospital, a disbelieving Greg clutches Jenny's hand as her life slips away.

Greg's rejection eventually drove Jenny to agree to a hasty wedding with her fellow model, Tony Barclay (above). This elaborate wedding was "arranged" by Olga Svenson, Jenny and Tony's modeling agent, and would have taken place if Greg hadn't, in dramatic fashion, burst into the ceremony and convinced Jenny to come back to him.

Greg, Jenny and their best pal, Jesse Hubbard, made a fabulous threesome in 1982. The following year, Jesse met Angie, and the threesome became a foursome.

Liza Colby was all too eager to get her claws into Greg. And Liza was so fiercely jealous of Jenny Gardner that she "fixed" the Miss Junior Pine Valley contest so that she, and certainly not Jenny, would win.

Greg and Jenny finally married, but their happiness didn't last long. In an insane act of vengeance, Jenny's jilted fiancé, Tony Barclay, rigged Greg's jet ski to explode. In a tragic twist of fate, Jenny and Greg switched jet skis. Jenny's craft exploded, and she was critically injured (left).

The Lovers

Brooke English never let Adam get away with anything. In love and war, Brooke proved that the best defense is a good offense.

Gloria Marsh fell in love with Stuart Chandler because he was the first man to see the good in her. When she was with Stuart's brother Adam, Gloria felt something else—passion! So Gloria jilted Stuart and married Adam. Their stormy marriage, fraught with love, war and infidelity, continued up until the day that Gloria and Adam were to renew their vows. Instead of pledging her love to Adam, Gloria humiliated her husband in front of their friends and family and stormed out on her deceitful husband.

It took a shipwreck for sophisticated Natalie Hunter and gruff cop Trevor Dillon to admit their love for each other.

Here's a recipe for romance: take one red-blooded male and one fiery female, mix them together in a zesty storyline, then sit back and watch them sizzle! Stormy, volatile love affairs are the stuff that soaps are made of, and *All My Children* has had no shortage of tempestuous relationships. There's no sure-fire way of telling what makes a couple click, but more often than not it has something to do with the heat they generate together.

Take the impassioned pairing of Brooke English and Adam Chandler. For years, Brooke was involved with soft-spoken "nice guy" Tom Cudahy. As they grew apart, Brooke became a savvy career woman with a taste for strong, powerful men. Millionaire Adam Chandler fit the bill perfectly! Adam and Brooke were a couple for the 1990s. Both had plenty of drive, ambition and sexual energy. And they fought like crazy! When Adam hired Brooke to run *Tempo* magazine, he never expected his new editor to be so tough and independent. When Adam stole a story off Brooke's desk and published it without her consent, she furiously quit on the spot. He had found his match! On the day his daughter Skye married Tom, Brooke's ex, Adam surprised Brooke with a proposal of marriage. Even more surprising, she accepted! For a while, Brooke brought out Adam's good side, but before long, they were back to their old ways—fighting and loving, loving and fighting. Their combustible relationship couldn't last. But for the short time Brooke and Adam were together, they were hot, hot, hot!

When smart and sophisticated Natalie Hunter met brawny policeman Trevor Dillon, she despised him at first. But that didn't stop him from pursuing his golden-haired "doll." He did everything in his power to win her over, and his insufferable pursuit drove Nat nuts! Still, it appeared to her close friend Donna Tyler that Natalie was actually eating up all of Trevor's attention. To get away from him, Natalie took a boat trip, not knowing that Trevor was captaining the craft. When a storm blew in, Natalie and Trevor found themselves shipwrecked on a tropical island. Alone together, it was inevitable that they would put down their swords and take a romantic roll in the sand.

In love and war, *All My Children*'s couples have endured turbulent times. Here's a look at some of the more hot-blooded pairings.

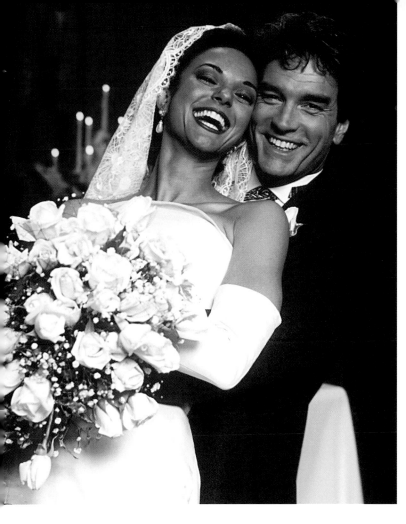

Charlie Brent knows how to woo a woman. The handsome private eye pulled out all the stops in his pursuit of Hayley Vaughan (above). Moonlit strolls along the beach and candlelit suppers were just part of Charlie's romantic offensive. To top off his amorous quest, Charlie pulled a kitten out of his kit bag and brought a smile to Hayley's face. How could a girl say no?

Edmund + Maria = passion! Even after they married, the writer and the doctor continued to steam up our TV screens with their lusty interludes (above).

Ellen Shepherd was years older than Mark Dalton (below), so their May/December romance caught friends and family by surprise. Their passion was furious, their love strong, but Mark's immaturity (and an affair with teenager Pamela Kingsley) led to the end of their first marriage. Years later, Mark and Ellen found their way back to each other, and to this day, they are together.

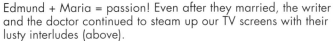

Behind his wife Phoebe's back, Langley Wallingford enjoyed a rollicking affair with the family maid, Opal Gardner (above). Their wacky romance stopped cold when Opal demanded that Langley divorce Phoebe and marry her. When Langley refused to give up his meal ticket, Opal blackmailed her lover.

The Lovers

Caught in the middle of a three-way romance, Erica came up with an outrageous strategy to deal with the two brothers who loved her—she would date them on alternate nights!

There are often many romantic entanglements along the road to happiness. Pine Valley's most memorable love stories have been especially complicated when they involved two men and a lady. Or two ladies and a man. Yes, some of *All My Children*'s most scintillating romances involve three participants in stories fraught with jealousy and passion.

Consider the tangled threesome of Travis, Erica and Jackson. She was his brother's wife, so Jack maintained a "hands-off" policy with Erica Kane. But Jack's attraction for Erica grew, especially after they survived a plane crash together, taking shelter in a deserted cabin in the desert and sharing a sleeping bag for warmth. This incident ruffled Travis' feathers, provoking a bitter rivalry between the two brothers that didn't end when Travis divorced Erica. Tickled by Jack's interest, Erica was ready to respond. Following him to a Paris hotel, she donned a blonde wig, grabbed a feather duster and transformed herself into Jack's very own French maid, "Corinne." Jack, who had been a confirmed bachelor, proposed to her. And just when she accepted, Travis decided he wanted Erica back! And he had a strong supporter in their daughter, Bianca. But Erica desperately wanted Jackson, and whatever Erica wants, she usually gets. But Bianca wanted Erica to get back with her daddy, and more importantly, Bianca really, really, really didn't want Erica to marry Uncle Jack.

Then Erica came up with a preposterous plan—she would date Travis and Jackson on alternate nights! Finally Erica was forced to make a choice when Bianca nearly died of Reye's Syndrome. She acceded to her daughter's wishes and remarried Travis. That's when this triangle became a quadrangle! After Travis cheated on Erica with his ex-wife Barbara, Erica cheated on him with Jack. Soon both her marriage and her affair ended in court. Losing Bianca to Travis in a bitter custody battle, Erica blamed Jack for not lying for her on the witness stand. She simply couldn't love him after that! Or could she? Four years later, Jack found himself back in bed with Erica, and this time, he was the (married) man in the middle. Another triangle? Indeed. So goes the geometry of Pine Valley.

In the mid-1980s, French-Canadian hunk Jeremy Hunter see-sawed between two bitter rivals, Erica and Natalie. For a while, Natalie had the upper hand when she got Jeremy drunk, then convinced him that he had made her pregnant. Jeremy returned to Erica, only to eventually marry Natalie.

Famed womanizer Tad Martin faced a dilemma when he fell in love with Hillary Wilson, only to ruin everything by impregnating Dottie Thornton. Hillary stood on the sidelines and urged Tad to do the right thing by marrying Dottie. When Dottie lost the baby, their loveless marriage went down the drain, and Tad reunited with Hillary.

In 1992, Livia Frye found herself torn between two lovers. The men—Lucas Barnes (father of Livia's teenage son Terrence) and handsome Tom Cudahy—both loved her, but Livia could choose but one. What to do? Sorry, Lucas, Livia chose Tom.

Erica and Brooke fight over Jackson

Erica: How in the world could Jack be taken in by the likes of you? You've always been such a loser!

Brooke: You'd better be very careful.

Erica: Oh, really. Careful of who? What— a common slut?

BROOKE SLAPS ERICA

Attracting a man is easy for Erica. Winning his affection? A piece of cake. But dealing with her longtime rival, Brooke English, now that's work. In 1991, Jack was the man who provoked a battle between the warring women.

The Lovers

Natalie never got over her undeniable feelings for Jeremy. Even during her short-lived 1988 marriage to millionaire Palmer Cortlandt, Natalie still pined away for Jeremy, whom she had loved since they were both teenagers in their native Canada.

In 1978, Donna Tyler (standing) saw an unmarried Tara Brent as a real threat to her marriage to Dr. Chuck Tyler—despite Chuck's protestations and reassurances that he was a one-man woman. In late summer, Donna's fears were realized when Chuck and Tara gave in to their long-suppressed passion and made love in the Tyler cabin at Willow Lake.

Adam Chandler desperately wanted a male heir, and when his infertile wife Brooke couldn't provide him with a child, Adam lured the hopelessly lovesick Dixie Cooney (left) into a night of passion in the Chandler Mansion boathouse. The scheme worked, temporarily, when Dixie became pregnant and gave birth to Adam, Jr. Adam gained a son, but the scheming Chandler eventually lost the love of both women.

Natalie Hunter was once again at the center of a combative triangle in 1990 (above). She had strong feelings for Trevor Dillon, but they were always too busy fighting to admit their mutual attraction. At one point, Trevor (at right) accused his rival, Adam Chandler, of pursuing Natalie for her money. And Trevor was right, which only angered Natalie more. To spite him, Natalie capped her dalliance with Adam by eloping with him!

Two handsome men, one confused lady. In 1993, Brooke was in the center of her own love triangle (right). On one side was Tad Martin, the father of her son Jamie, who wanted Brooke to marry him. On the other side was Edmund Grey, the former lover she had never really gotten over. In May, a wistful Edmund was left out in the cold when Brooke accepted Tad's proposal and became his wife.

𝔈𝔵𝔱𝔯𝔞𝔳𝔞𝔤𝔞𝔫𝔱 and spectacular or sweet and simple—*All My Children*'s glorious weddings are among the most unforgettable in soap opera history. Viewers followed the fairytale courtships of their favorite couples in eager anticipation of the day when they would finally become man and wife. Unforeseen obstacles often prevented the lovers from taking that walk down the aisle, but, in nearly every case, the cherished moment finally arrived without incident. Here they are—the lavish ceremonies, the breathtaking gowns and the most beautiful vows. Relive the magic of *All My Children*'s greatest weddings all over again!

Joe and Ruth (1972)
Widower Dr. Joe Martin worked side-by-side with married nurse Ruth Brent at Pine Valley Hospital. After Ruth's husband Ted Brent was killed in a car accident, doctor and nurse fell in love and got married in a simple ceremony at the Martin home (left).

Phillip and Tara (1976)
After his presumed death in Vietnam, her marriage to Chuck, his marriage to Erica and their own illegitimate child, Pine Valley's first young lovers, Phil Brent and Tara Martin, finally cleared the way to make their turbulent relationship legal (below).

Chuck and Donna (1977)
Wealthy Dr. Chuck Tyler defied his snobby grandmother, Phoebe, and married former teenage prostitute Donna Beck. Sadly, the marriage ended in divorce.

Jeff and Mary (1973)
After his rocky first marriage to Erica Kane, Dr. Jeff Martin found happiness with sweet nurse Mary Kennicott.

Tom and Erica (1978)

On September 6, 1978, Erica Kane married former football hero Tom Cudahy (above) on the rebound from her failed affair with Nick Davis. Tom and Erica's union suffered irreparable damage when he wanted a baby, but she wanted a career.

Ellen and Mark (1989)

The story of an older woman accepting the love of a younger man culminated in the marriage of Ellen Shepherd and Mark Dalton (above). They divorced soon after but rekindled their romance and remarried in 1989.

Chuck and Donna 2 (1990)

After years apart, Chuck and Donna proved that a strong love can still burn bright when they remarried, with Donna's daughter Emily Ann and Dr. Joe Martin in attendance (left).

The Lovers

Phoebe and Langley (1980)
Con artist Langley Wallingford romanced lonely divorcee Phoebe Tyler (above) for her money, <u>then</u> fell in love with her! Phoebe's son, Linc, and Langley's sworn enemy, Myrtle, were on to Langley's scheme, but he persuaded them all that he could make his new bride happy.

Cliff and Nina (1981)
Dr. Cliff Warner and Nina Cortlandt married in a beautiful ceremony on the grounds of Cortlandt Manor. Bride and groom were overjoyed, though Cliff worried all through the ceremony about the baby nurse Sybil Thorne told him she was carrying.

Frank and Nancy (1980)
An anguished Dr. Frank Grant came close to leaving Pine Valley when his ex-wife Nancy accepted Dr. Russ Anderson's proposal of marriage. As their wedding drew near, Nancy realized she still loved her ex-husband Frank, and they remarried in a Thanksgiving wedding (above).

Cliff and Nina 3 (1988)

Cliff and Nina married four times over a ten-year period! Here, in wedding number three, they pledge their love to each other in a chic ceremony at New York's Tavern on the Green (above).

Erica and Travis (1990)

Though she loved Jackson Montgomery, Erica Kane remarried her ex-husband Travis Montgomery because that's what their daughter, Bianca, wanted her to do. On May 21, 1990, Erica sacrificed her own feelings and tied the knot with her daughter's father (above).

Greg and Jenny (1984)

Jenny Gardner, a girl from the wrong side of the tracks, and Greg Nelson, the prodigal son of one of Pine Valley's snootiest families, overcame insurmountable odds to became man and wife (left).

The Lovers

Stuart and Cindy (1989)
It's only fitting that two of Pine Valley's most adored citizens, Stuart Chandler and Cindy Parker (left), would become man and wife. A few short months later, Cindy died of AIDS, but these two special people shared enough love to last through eternity.

Dixie and Adam (1989)
Everyone warned Dixie Cooney to stay away from Adam Chandler (above). They said he wanted her only because Brooke English couldn't conceive the child he so desperately wanted. Dixie got pregnant—and then got betrayed!

Palmer and Opal (1990)
It was months in the making, but Opal Purdy finally persuaded Palmer Cortlandt that they shared a special, offbeat kind of love. Will, Tad and Dixie stood by as the bride and groom spoke their solemn vows (left).

Trevor and Natalie (1992)
The first time Trevor Dillon married Natalie Hunter, he was really marrying Janet Green, who threw Natalie down a well and transformed herself into the spitting image of her sister. Here, Trevor married his favorite blond—this time for real!

Dimitri and Erica (1993)
In a ceremony fit for royalty, Erica Kane and Dimitri Marick held their flowery spring wedding at Wildwind, the groom's gothic estate.

The Lovers

Adam and Gloria (1993)
Adam Chandler surprised his bride-to-be Gloria Marsh by flying the wedding guests out to sea to join the couple in a fabulous wedding aboard a luxury yacht (above).

Tom and Livia (1992)
Pine Valley turned out in style for the elegant wedding of Tom Cudahy and Livia Frye. The stylish reception featured a touching duet between Livia and special wedding guest Peabo Bryson.

Edmund and Maria (1994)
A horse-drawn carriage brought Edmund Grey and Dr. Maria Santos to their wedding in style on March 11, 1994.

Tad and Dixie (1994)

Is marriage better the second time around? Tad and Dixie endured hardship, trauma and years of separation before, at long last, tying the knot again on May 16, 1994.

Tom and Barbara (1989)

Though he wasn't the father of her unborn child, gallant Tom Cudahy agreed to marry Barbara Montgomery (below). But Barbara went into labor during the ceremony and they finally married at the hospital—while Barbara was giving birth!

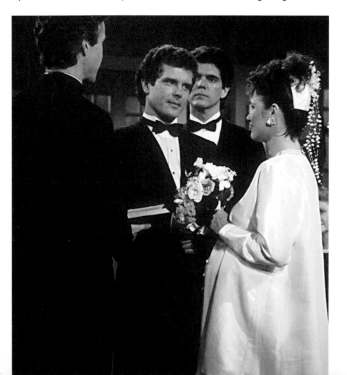

Charles and Mona (1980)

After divorcing his busybody wife Phoebe, Dr. Charles Tyler found everlasting love with his secretary, Mona Kane.

The Lovers

Cliff and Nina's Glorious Wedding Day

The bridal party arrives at the ceremony via a horse-drawn carriage.

The lovely bride prepares to walk down the aisle.

Of all the soap-opera weddings, Cliff and Nina's storybook spectacular may have been the most lavish. It was certainly one of the most memorable. Viewers followed every romantic twist and turn in this classic tale of a patient who fell instantly in love with her charming prince of a doctor.

Dr. Cliff Warner and Nina Cortlandt were destined to be together from the moment they met. But Nina's overbearing, overprotective father, Palmer Cortlandt, did everything in his power to keep them apart. In scheme after scheme, Palmer succeeded in separating the sweethearts. First he hired a private investigator to unearth a secret in Cliff's past that would discredit the good doctor in Nina's eyes. Unable to find a scandal in Dr. Warner's unsullied background, Palmer manufactured one of his own. Mr. Cortlandt paid Cliff's former girlfriend Janice Rollins $10,000 to claim that Cliff fathered her illegitimate son then abandoned her to move to Pine Valley. Nina was devastated and broke up with Cliff, but ultimately she found her way back to the man she loved. Palmer then reached a new low in treachery by allowing Nina to believe that she was going blind, then persuaded her to break up with Cliff so that she would never be a burden to him. When that plan misfired, Palmer came to see that neither his money nor his power could match the love that Cliff felt for Nina. Granting a temporary truce in his vendetta, Palmer allowed the lovebirds to proceed with an elegant wedding on the grounds of his sprawling estate. And what a wedding it was!

"This is the happiest day of my life," exclaims Nina to her bridal party. (From Left: Peggy Warner, Daisy Cortlandt, Nina, Brooke English)

"I am Mrs. Clifford Warner, and that has such a beautiful sound to it," says Nina to her new husband Cliff as they celebrate their union with a bit of the bubbly.

One and all gather to toast Cliff and Nina's happy future.

179

The Lovers

Chapter 4

VILLAINS, ROGUES & VIXENS

Pine Valley might be a kinder, more peaceful place to live without a villain or two stirring things up. Or a rogue complicating the lives of a few women in town—or a vixen some men. But it certainly wouldn't be as interesting. *All My Children* has developed some of the most malevolent, despicable characters in daytime, lacking standards, conscience and restraint and shamelessly conniving without a thought for the innocent parties involved. Some, like Billy Clyde Tuggle, come to town to plant seeds of destruction and are quickly gone—only to reappear when the dust settles. Others have chosen to stay permanently, constantly wreaking havoc upon the fair citizens of Pine Valley. Adam Chandler is one such schemer, and his wealth and power make him a formidable opponent. His constant acts of betrayal and twisted perception of love bring endless pain and heartache.

Though age has softened him, Tad Martin will forever be known as one of Pine Valley's most prolific cads. He spent years scheming and manipulating women of all ages, blinding them with his charm. Audiences have been shocked, entertained and enthralled by this many-faceted character.

Of all the bad and beautiful ladies of Pine Valley, the most outrageous and unforgettable is Erica Kane. One of daytime's most enduring characters, she has charmed and plotted her way into the lives of almost every man in Pine Valley. She has met her match on more than one occasion—but not for long. These willing adversaries usually realize the fight is fixed and bow out before they get in any deeper. Audiences have applauded her gumption and admonished her gall. Erica Kane is the very embodiment of vixen and is a most integral force on *All My Children*.

Adam Chandler tore apart the lives of two women he supposedly loved: his wife, Brooke English, a strong woman unafraid to challenge the ruthless tycoon but also unable to have children, and innocent Dixie Cooney, the lovesick young woman who could give Adam his male heir. He left Brooke and got what he wanted from Dixie, who he then tried to have committed to mental hospital.

What would Pine Valley be without a dirty villain or two stirring things up? Much too pleasant a place to live! These rotten scoundrels pop into town, wreak havoc on the fair citizens, but then, thankfully, they're sent to the slammer, carted off to the funny farm or ceremoniously bumped off. But some of these bad guys and gals have a nasty habit of turning up weeks, months or even years later to undertake another round of vicious vendettas.

Billy Clyde Tuggle
No daytime bad boy was more contemptible than Billy Clyde Tuggle (left). Once a pimp for his wife Estelle, sleaze-ball Billy tried to bury her alive when she fell in love with Benny Sago. Like a bad penny, Billy turned up again in 1990 to make Donna Tyler's life a living hell.

Kent Bogard
Corrupt cosmetics baron Kent Bogard (above) didn't realize how good he had it while dating his client, Erica Kane. If only he hadn't entered into a sneaky affair with the notorious Connie Wilkes, Kent might be alive today. Because when Erica found out, she shot him. Accidentally, of course. But the results were the same—Kent was stone-cold dead.

Zach Grayson
Gigolo. Pimp. Extortionist. Murderer. Zach Grayson (left) had a rap sheet as long as his arm. The law never caught up with Zach, but on April 12th, 1985, his evil deeds did! Daisy Cortlandt was found standing over Zach's dead body holding a bloody knife. But Daisy didn't kill him—Marian Colby did! Grayson had been blackmailing Marian, and when she fell behind in her payments, she stabbed him to death. In self-defense, of course.

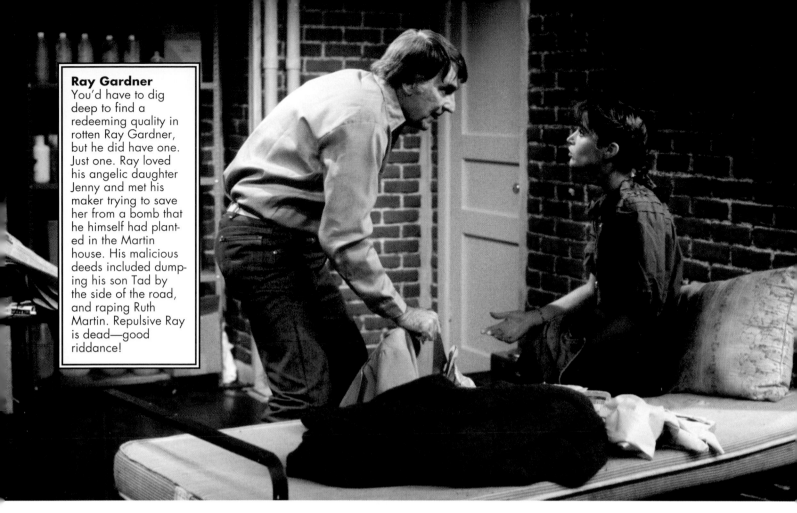

Ray Gardner
You'd have to dig deep to find a redeeming quality in rotten Ray Gardner, but he did have one. Just one. Ray loved his angelic daughter Jenny and met his maker trying to save her from a bomb that he himself had planted in the Martin house. His malicious deeds included dumping his son Tad by the side of the road, and raping Ruth Martin. Repulsive Ray is dead—good riddance!

Carter Jones
Carter was a deeply disturbed master of mind games who came to town to terrorize and emotionally intimidate his ex-wife, attorney Galen Henderson. Later, Carter turned his mad intentions to the blind Natalie Dillon and *Loving*'s Dinah Lee Mayberry before landing where he remains to this day—in jail!

Lars Bogard
Cosmetics magnate, bon vivant, millionaire, Nazi. Yes, Nazi. Lars's secret past was discovered by Erica Kane and Palmer Cortlandt who journeyed to South America and watched the sinister war criminal fall to his death off the back of a boat. Bogard's body was supposedly minced into a million pieces by the boat's propeller, but did we ever see his corpse? Afraid not.

Will Cortlandt

Nearly everyone in town had reason to despise wicked Will Cortlandt, the ruthless fellow who raped Gloria Marsh and turned Hayley Vaughan into a drunk before luring her into a loveless marriage. A crowbar to the head, administered by Janet Green, brought Will's reign of terror to an abrupt end.

Sean Cudahy

Slimy Sean Cudahy was a ladies' man who enjoyed romantic conquests, good times and money—especially other people's money! In 1981, Sean was sent to jail for the murder of Sybil Thorne, and upon his release, he returned to his wicked ways. In 1990, Sean broke the heart of young Cecily Davidson by sleeping with her mother.

Langley Wallingford

Phoebe thought she was marrying a noble Professor, but little did she know that her husband-to-be, Langley Wallingford, was really oily con artist Lenny Wlasuk, who once snatched Myrtle Fargate's purse at a carnival. Lenny set out to fleece Phoebe out of her family fortune, but along the way, something strange happened—he fell in love with his prey!

Wade Matthews

As the song says, he was "just a gigolo." When Phoebe's marriage to Langley hit the skids, the wealthy dowager fell for the boyish charms of Wade Matthews (above), a crafty con artist. Smooth as silk, Wade had a mission: Marry the old broad, rob her blind, then hop the next flight to Rio. And he nearly succeeded—until Phoebe's ex, Langley, saved the day by stopping Wade at the airport and forcing him to confess at gunpoint.

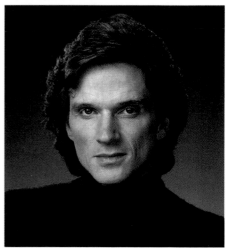

Creed Kelly

There's more than meets the eye to handsome Creed Kelly (above), the public relations executive who befriended runaway Julie Chandler in 1987. Creed, hell-bent on getting revenge on his former lover Elizabeth Carlisle, attempted to seduce, ravage and ultimately kill her daughter, Julie. The madman escaped punishment by parachuting from a plane, and to this day, he is still at large.

Tony Barclay

Handsome and kind, model Tony Barclay made a major about-face when his beloved bride-to-be, Jenny Gardner, jilted him at the altar and ran off with her first love, Greg Nelson. Slipping into psychosis, Tony plotted to kill Greg, but his murder plot backfired and Jenny became his unwitting victim.

Villains, Rogues & Vixens

Eddie Dorrance

Eddie was the kind of guy who gives show biz a bad name. As the ruthless manager of singer Kelly Cole, Eddie pushed his client to exhaustion, then doled out amphetamines to keep her at the top of her game. At the same time, this wheeler-dealer consorted with the likes of conman Langley Wallingford before finally being murdered in cold blood by the hostess of the Chateau, Claudette Montgomery.

Ted Orsini

Twisted Ted Orsini lured his look-a-like, Tad, to Canada for what Tad thought was a hunting trip. Little did Tad know that *he* was the prey and the woman they both loved—Dixie—was the prize.

Craig Lawson

Crafty Craig Lawson came to town to console Tad Martin's "widow," Dixie. Claiming that he and the "late" Tad Martin had been buddies, Craig quickly became Dixie's hero, her closest confidante and eventually her husband. Dixie was as shocked as anyone else when her new husband turned out to be a two-bit con artist.

Richard Fields

Fields was a popular Hollywood matinee idol with a dangerous depravity—he liked young girls. Years ago, Fields raped a teenage Erica Kane, who blocked out her memories of the gruesome encounter after giving birth to a daughter, Kendall.

Dr. Damon Lazarre

Dr. Lazarre, the guru-like leader of a religious cult, came to Pine Valley in the summer of 1987. Among Dr. Lazarre's more wicked deeds was brainwashing the real Silver Kane into shooting her sister Erica. He toppled off a bridge, but like so many villains, Damon's body was never recovered.

Stan Ulatowski

While in jail for covering up the killing of Silver Kane, Palmer Cortlandt met safe-cracker Stan Ulatowski. When both men were released, Palmer hired his former cell-mate to work at Cortlandt Manor. Within months, "Mr. U" fell in love with Opal Purdy and tried to eliminate his competition, Palmer, by poisoning his old pal.

Les Baxter
How could sweet Angie Baxter have had such a deceptive daddy? Les Baxter (above) ruled his family with an iron hand and later was revealed to be a black-market-baby ringleader named Mr. Big. Baxter's reign of terror came to a bitter end when, in a fight to the death with his son-in-law Jesse Hubbard, he fell down a flight of stairs and died.

Janet Green
She's back! With a new face but the same bizarre attitudes, Janet "From-Another-Planet" Green (above) reappeared in Pine Valley in 1994. Wacky Janet achieved soap infamy by throwing her sister Natalie down a well and taking her place in Trevor Dillon's bed. And who will ever forget when she killed Will Cortlandt with a crowbar? After serving a prison sentence, Janet picked up where she left off by worming her way back into Trevor's life and disposing of his dog, the lovable Harold, by drugging the pooch and shipping him off to California in a moving van.

Connie Wilkes
Connie nearly pulled off the ultimate con when she moved in on Erica Kane by masquerading as Silver Kane, her mousy sister. Connie insidiously attempted to drive Erica crazy and even had the gall to seduce Erica's boyfriend, Kent Bogard.

Peg English
Poor Brooke English! She grew up believing that Peg English (above) was her loving, albeit stuffy, mother, only to learn that Mom led a secret life as "Cobra"—the leader of an international drug cartel. And Brooke received a double whammy when she discovered that Peg was not her mother after all, but a woman who deeply resented raising her husband's illegitimate daughter.

Helga Voynitzeva
Dimitri Marick's mother-in-law, Helga Voynitzeva, did a number of nasty deeds before she tripped and fell to her death in Budapest. Perhaps Helga's most despicable act was luring Erica Kane into a crypt and locking her inside—alongside the rotting corpse of the late Hugo Marick.

Villains, Rogues & Vixens

There are two words guaranteed to make any Pine Valley mother shudder—Tad Martin! Though in recent years he has matured into a responsible young man, Tad will forever have a tough time living down his undisputed reputation as Pine Valley's most lovable lady-killer. You see, Tad Martin was born to manipulate. Cast off by his low-life parents, Ray and Opal Gardner, Tad Gardner was adopted by the warm and supportive Martins. But in his deep subconscious, he always questioned his worthiness. As a rebellious teen, Tad habitually took shortcuts and used people to his own advantage. As a young adult, he demonstrated a distinct lack of moral fortitude by deflowering every pretty girl who crossed his path.

As played by two-time Emmy winner Michael E. Knight, Tad remains one of daytime's most complex yet comedic characters. Say what you will about this romantic rogue, but when Tad Martin believes in something, he will stop at nothing to achieve his goal. The same kooky guy who thinks nothing of donning a chicken suit to propose to his lady love won't think twice about bravely risking his life to keep her safe from harm. There's only one Tad—he's smooth, he's funny, and we can't help but love him.

Tad dated Dottie Thornton (below) for only one reason: money. Dottie's mother, Edna Thornton, paid Tad big bucks to date her daughter to boost the overweight teenager's confidence. Soon, Tad was compelled to marry Dottie for yet another reason—she was pregnant with his child—which she lost in a miscarriage.

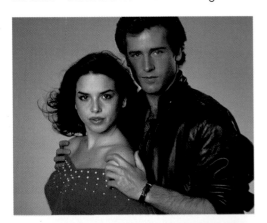

"What light through yonder window breaks?" In 1984, Tad spoke those classic words to Hillary Wilson (left) when they played star-crossed lovers Romeo and Juliet in a Pine Valley High School production of Shakespeare's time-honored play.

Tad proved his mettle when he carried on a secret affair with middle-aged Marian Colby while at the same time romancing her teenage daughter, Liza (below).

Tad and Hillary (left) strike an optimistic pose on their February 1985 wedding day at the Wallingford Mansion. The couple had planned to marry in a grand church wedding, but Tad, locked in a bank vault by robbers, failed to show for the ceremony. Their happiness—and their marriage—ended when Tad soon returned to his womanizing ways.

190

Tad grew close to Dixie Cooney Chandler (above) when he heroically rescued her from the clutches of her first husband, Adam Chandler, who tried to have Dixie committed to an asylum. They married for the first time in December 1989.

Suffering from amnesia, Tad hitchhiked out to California's Napa Valley (left), where he met up with Nola Orsini, the owner of one of the country's finest vineyards. A stunned Nola believed that Tad was really Ted, her son who was kidnapped as a child. Though Tad wasn't really Nola's son, they developed a close bond that continued until her death in 1993.

When Tad offered Jane Cox a job in May 1994, he had no idea that his new employee was actually Janet Green (above), the very same woman (with a new face) who killed Dixie's brother, Will Cortlandt.

Devoted fans of Tad and Dixie were less than thrilled when Tad wedded the mother of his son, Brooke English, on May 28, 1993 (above). Their marriage was short-lived.

Seriously injured in a tornado, Tad had a fantastic out-of-body experience in which he encountered his late sister Jenny, the dearly departed Nola Orsini, and his *not*-so-dearly-departed father, Ray Gardner, who appeared as the chauffeur from hell.

The Rogues

Vixens

They're bad and they're beautiful. They're the women who know what they want—and they'll do whatever it takes to get it. On *All My Children*, many a luscious lady has used her wiles to captivate a Pine Valley man. Check out this all-star cast.

Brooke English

Way back in 1976, wealthy young Brooke English (left) used her sex appeal to spin the heads of two eligible boys—virginal student Dan Kennicott and sensual grease monkey Benny Sago. Spoiled and hungry for fun, Brooke pitted the two boys against each other and enjoyed the best of both worlds.

Liza Colby

Liza had a naughty habit of toying with the affections of already-attached men. The guy she wanted most of all was Greg Nelson, but he only had eyes for Jenny Gardner. Greg refused to fall for Liza, but his college roommate, the nerdy Alfred Vanderpoole, developed a huge crush on the blond vixen (below).

Claudette Montgomery
Claudette (above) saw an opportunity to marry a rich widower when she chased after Lincoln Tyler. Even before his wife Kitty's corpse was cold, Claudette was all over the lonely Linc, who was not immune to her charms. In a wily attempt to snare him, she offered to totally redecorate his apartment—and, of course, she had very special plans for his bedroom.

Cecily Davidson
Cecily (left) used sex as a weapon to keep Charlie Brent and Julie Chandler apart. Though Cecily wasn't sleeping with Charlie, she bragged to everyone that she was, and the lying Jezebel made sure that the news of Charlie's fictitious affair reached Julie, who was devastated by her boyfriend's "infidelity."

The Rogues

Ceara Connor

Ceara (above) loved men, and she loved money. And there was nothing she wanted more than a man with money. She found just the guy in Jeremy Hunter's rich young son David, though he had no desire to tie the knot. What's a girl to do? To make David jealous, Ceara dated every eligible gent in town. Eventually she did get married—not to David, but to his *father*, Jeremy!

Barbara Montgomery

Barbara, Travis's ex-wife, had a mind for business and a body for sin. And she used both to considerable advantage to upset Erica Kane by luring Travis into intimate dinners that were "strictly business." But try convincing Erica!

Taylor Roxbury Cannon

Taylor would do anything to attract a man—even change careers. The object of her affections—Derek Frye—was a cop, so that's what Taylor decided to become. Though she denied it, Taylor's interest in police work was really an interest in Derek. But Derek was more interested in fellow officer Mimi Reed!

Julia Santos

Ever since Julia Santos's first appearance (wearing nothing but a skimpy towel), she has tried to catch the eye of every man in town. Too bad for Julia that most of them were already in love with other women.

Sybil Thorne
A nurse by day and a temptress by night, Sybil Thorne tried for months to lure Dr. Cliff Warner into her bed, and finally succeeded when, in a weak moment, he gave in to temptation. Unfortunately for Cliff, Sybil became pregnant from this one-night stand.

Skye Chandler
When it came to bewitching handsome guys, here's one vixen who knew that the sky's the limit! Skye Chandler (above) used her steamy sexuality to hunt down and capture handfuls of guys. Among her quarry were Mitch Beck, Tom Cudahy, Travis Montgomery and Jeremy Hunter, all of whom in time became wise to Skye's wicked ways.

Natalie Marlowe
Natalie may have been married to the wealthy Alex Hunter, but she lusted for his son, Jeremy—even when she was carrying Alex's baby. With almost as many husbands to her credit as Erica Kane, Natalie finally tamed her restless soul by marrying Trevor Dillon, who was everything she ever wanted in a man.

Kendall Hart
Kendall (left) lusted after Dimitri Marick, but her desires were one-sided because Dimitri was married—to Kendall's mother, Erica. Did this stop this Lolita from pursuing her prey? No way. Through a sizzling series of lies and schemes, Kendall sabotaged Erica and Dimitri's marriage.

The Rogues

She's the sexy seductress you love to hate. For 25 years she has gone through men and marriages in a never-ending search for love. She's the scheming Erica Kane, played to perfection by the one-and-only Susan Lucci.

From vixenish teen to vampy young woman to vulnerable lover to vital mother, Erica is daytime television's most original character. But for all her ego and self-confidence, she's really as insecure as the rest of us. Erica is afraid she might be unlovable. It's a fear she's had since the day her father, movie director Eric Kane, walked out on the family when she was just a little girl. That's what drives her to do the things she does on such a grand scale. Larger than life, Erica is out there every day fighting, plotting and grabbing for love and romance, fame and fortune. You never know what Erica's going to do next! But whatever it is, you can bet there's a man involved. Erica needs a man in her life. She's just built that way: passionate, tempestuous. And the way she drives men wild, they want to either kiss her or kill her. But when life kicks her—which it does with alarming regularity—she kicks back! That's why they love her—and so do we.

In the course of Erica's journey, she's found herself in some predicaments that most women would run from. Like falling for Nick Davis (above). Nick was more than just a father figure—he was her mother's best friend!

What went wrong with Erica's first marriage, to Dr. Jeff Martin? Among other things, Erica quickly became bored with being a doctor's wife, preferring the allure of her glamorous modeling career. The marriage suffered another major blow when she chose to have daytime television's first legal abortion.

In February 1988, Erica had an incredible dream in which she encountered nearly all the men in her past. From left, Nick Davis, Phil Brent, Jeremy Hunter, Brandon Kingsley, Adam Chandler, Tom Cudahy and the woman of the hour, Erica!

In 1973, Erica made the tragic mistake of getting intimately involved with Jason Maxwell, the powerful head of her New York modeling agency. Married at the time to hard-working Dr. Jeff Martin, she began an affair with Jason—but he soon turned up stone-cold dead.

Erica on Erica

"I'll warn you, I've got claws!"

"The real me is sweet and innocent and vulnerable."

"I present an alluring, gorgeous love goddess image to my public."

"I'm Erica Kane. I'm an American Beauty."

"I am Erica Kane. Men flock to me like moths to a flame!"

"I'm not out to win any popularity contests."

"I won't let anyone destroy me!"

199

When Erica decided to become an actress, she wanted an Oscar. But she wound up with an *Adam* (right). Chandler, that is. Here was a man every bit as clever and cunning as she was, lying and scheming to get what he wanted—and what he wanted was Erica. In 1984, he got her!

The year was 1978, and after two marriages, one abortion, one miscarriage, one nervous breakdown and an affair or two, Erica fell for the innocent smile and athletic physique of former star football quarterback Tom Cudahy.

Still married to Tom Cudahy in 1981, Erica began an affair with Brandon Kingsley, the head of Sensuelle Cosmetics. Brandon neglected to tell Erica one pertinent little piece of news: that he was a married man!

Erica on Men:

"I really hope I can find a man who shares my values, my hopes. A man who will give me the baby I so desperately want."

"I used every feminine wile to get you to want me, Jack. And you know what? It worked."

"He is just a man, and I am Erica Kane. Need I say more?"

"You are the meanest man I have ever slept with."

"I know when a man loves me."

"Brandon turns me on like no man ever has!"

"I don't have to bait a trap to get a man."

"The day I need a married man to dangle romance in my face, then drop it all to go rushing back to his wife, is the day I need to be committed!"

At the height of her modeling fame, Erica's career fell apart when she was charged with the murder of her fiancé, Kent Bogard. Kent died when Erica confronted him at gun-point over his affair with the incorrigible Connie Wilkes. In the ensuing struggle, the gun went off, killing Kent. Erica was eventually cleared of all charges.

Erica's greatest love of all may have been world-traveling writer Mike Roy, who never tried to change her flighty and egocentric ways. Though he never allowed her to get away with any bull, Mike loved Erica just the way she was. With Mike, Erica found out she was capable of love, but sadly, their time together was short because Mike was killed.

Erica's priceless putdowns:

"In her own peculiar way, Brooke is a rather good-looking girl."

"I will thank you to mind your business, Barbara."

"Brooke, you're nothing but a husband-stealing little tramp!"

"You sneaky little brat, Brooke."

"Silver, you'll rue the day you crossed Erica Kane!"

"Kent Bogard, I wouldn't go out with you if you were the last man on earth!"

"Unlike you, Brooke, I have a man who adores me."

"You have messed with me for the last time, Brooke. This is war!"

"Natalie, you are a slut!"

Erica has a nasty habit of falling for the wrong man. Some had wives, others had problems. Jeremy Hunter had taken a holy vow of celibacy, but she promptly made him break it.

Erica and Jackson Montgomery make quite a pair! Their on-again, off-again romance is volatile and never boring.

Married man Dimitri Marick pursued Erica, and although she cared for him deeply, she refused to become a mistress again.

The men may come and go, but Erica's female rivals seem to stick around forever. No one has feasted on more of Erica's leftovers than Brooke English, and to this day, Brooke remains a thorn in her side.

Chapter 5

BEHIND THE SCENES

Since *All My Children* premiered on January 5, 1970, more than 6,450 episodes have been produced. Every day, five days a week, without reruns or seasonal hiatus, the hard-working group of contract actors, day players, directors, technicians, hair and makeup artists, costume and set designers, stagehands and production staff work round-the-clock to bring Pine Valley to life.

The faces we know best are those of the actors who portray our favorite characters on *All My Children*. We know all about their lives in Pine Valley, but what we aren't privy to are their real lives. Each of them has an endless supply of stories of their time in Pine Valley—and outside of it. Their auditions; the first day on the set; relationships with fellow cast members and crew; behind the scenes action—from practical jokes to filming love scenes; and some of their real life moments through the years, all provide a wealth of rarely recounted tales. Their memories are presented here in all their humor and tenderness.

Through the years, *All My Children* has welcomed stars from every part of the public arena—from Olympic athletes to Wall Street wonders, film stars to political dignitaries. Many who appear as guests are long-time fans of the show. Some of the world-famous names who have paid visits to Pine Valley are Oprah Winfrey, Donald Trump, Carol Burnett, Boomer Esiason and Elizabeth Taylor.

All My Children has inspired fierce loyalty among its legions of viewers. Through the years, we've come to regard the residents of Pine Valley as members of our own families, so clearly do they represent them. With every episode, we are drawn into the intimate workings of their make-believe lives. Thousands of *All My Children* viewers have had the rare opportunity to meet their favorite actors in person. For the people on the street, these star encounters are truly thrilling. Read on to find out some of the questions they ask—and the answers they receive.

James Kiberd (Trevor) looks to the heavens for inspiration as he prepares to tape a scene.

A Day in the Life of All My Children

The genius behind *All My Children*, Agnes Nixon.

Each day, five days a week, a new one-hour episode of *All My Children* is rehearsed and taped inside ABC's cavernous "TV 23," a block-long facility housing the cast and crew that make up the fictional town of Pine Valley. Over 250 hours of original programming are produced each year, and there are no reruns or lengthy hiatus for the hard-working group of actors, technicians, artists and writers who assemble each weekday to bring *All My Children* to life.

It takes hundreds of people to make the show happen. In addition to the 35 to 40 contract actors with ongoing histories and interwoven plots, there are about 50 "day players" (actors with minor roles), over 50 crew members (technicians, hair stylists, makeup artists, wardrobe and set designers), 35 members of the production staff and nearly 75 stagehands and electricians.

Putting together a one-hour soap is a 24-hour operation. In a normal day, an episode begins shooting in the late afternoon and concludes in early evening. But taping has been known to continue into the wee hours when special scenes, such as fires, storms or parties, require careful set-up. The instant a show "wraps," a team of stagehands converges upon the studio floor to dismantle the sets, move them out and erect the next day's sets. *All My Children* begins anew!

Makeup artist Norman Bryn applies the finishing touches to Dondre Whitfield (Terrence).

James Mitchell (Palmer) relaxes between scenes in his second-floor dressing room, which is adorned with a wall-sized poster of Palmer in action with his former wife, Daisy.

Here's what happens at *All My Children* during a 24-hour period:

3:00 a.m. The lighting director and stagehands arrive to hang and focus lights for the day's episode.

7:00 a.m. The director (one of three who alternate in the position) arrives to inspect the sets.

7:30 a.m. Actors arrive and begin their first, or "dry," rehearsal in a bare second-floor rehearsal hall.

8:00 a.m. Wardrobe staff arrives and begins distributing costumes to actors in their dressing rooms. Truck drivers begin picking up props at theatrical prop houses for the following day's episode. Editors begin the process of assembling the scenes from the previous day's show.

8:00 a.m. to 7:00 p.m. The previous day's sets are moved from the studio to a warehouse. In late afternoon, sets for the next day's show are trucked to a studio loading dock.

8:30 a.m. Engineers arrive to set up and adjust the cameras.

9:00 a.m. Makeup and hair stylists arrive and begin to beautify the cast. Stagehands, who have been on the job for hours, go to lunch.

10:00 a.m. Production assistant makes any necessary changes in that day's script and places preliminary production instructions into the next day's script.

10:00 a.m. to 12:00 p.m. Action shifts to the third-floor studio for camera blocking. Actors go through their lines during this first rehearsal on the set for the benefit of the director and camera operators.

Wardrobe assistant Mark Klein delivers freshly pressed costumes to the cast.

Emmy-winning costume designers Carol Luiken and Charles Clute design (and shop for) the outfits worn by the cast.

Director Conal O'Brien directs the studio traffic in one of Pine Valley's frequent courtroom scenes (below).

Makeup artist Jennifer Aspinall double-checks a Polaroid photo to insure that the jagged scar she's applying to Sydney Penny's face (Julia) looks exactly the same as it did the day before.

11:30 a.m. Director's technical meeting takes place for the next day's show.

12:00 p.m. Actors break for lunch. Sound effects are set up. Makeup, hair and wardrobe are completed.

1:15 p.m. Dress rehearsal takes place. The entire show is performed in full makeup and costume.

3:00 p.m. Before taping the show, the director gives his final performance "notes" to the actors. Engineers double-check and adjust the videotape recording machines.

4:00 to 7:30 p.m. Lights, camera, action! *All My Children* is taped. Wardrobe personnel pick out costumes for the next day's episode.

7:30 p.m. to 1:00 a.m. Stagehands dismantle sets and move them out of the studio, readying the stage for the next day's sets.

1:00 a.m. to 3:00 a.m. Cleaning staff arrives to restore the studio to its original luster.

James Kiberd (Trevor) and his assistant, Penny Templeton, sit down to a hot lunch in his dressing room.

The prop department mixed over a ton of oatmeal (flavored with cinnamon) to simulate quicksand for this dramatic scene in which John Callahan (Edmund) rescued Julia Barr (Brooke) from the murky mess (below).

Susan Lucci (Erica) and Walt Willey (Jackson) in action.

David Canary (Adam) and Teresa Blake (Gloria) team up in private to rehearse their scenes.

Behind the Scenes

Deep in thought, Susan Lucci (Erica) receives a last-minute touch-up before taping her scene.

Shooting a scene with twins Stuart and Adam Chandler requires a stand-in—and some technical wizardry. Here, Richard Green stands in for Stuart while cameras tape David Canary as Adam (below). Moments later, Canary will change into his Stuart costume and the scene will be re-shot from another angle.

During an idle moment, actress Jill Larson (Opal) reads her fan mail.

Director Chris Goutman turns chaos into order during the taping of Tad and Dixie's 1994 wedding (above).

Just as they've been doing for the past 25 years, original cast members Ray MacDonnell (Joe) and Mary Fickett (Ruth) get together to practice their dialogue (above).

Kelly Ripa (Hayley) finds a cozy dressing room perch to relax and study her lines.

From her office one-half block away from the studio, head writer Megan McTavish dreams up future twists and turns of the storyline.

Each week, casting director Judy Blye Wilson receives thousands of resumes and photographs from aspiring actors hoping to land a role on the soap.

Executive Producer Felicia Minei Behr oversees every facet of the production process, which includes welcoming guest star Kaye Ballard to Pine Valley.

One of three cameras records this scene featuring actors Richard Shoberg (Tom) and Walt Willey (Jackson) (left).

Walt Willey (Jackson) reclines in comfort as he reads over his daily script.

213

Off-Camera Moments

The cameras may stop rolling, but the fun never stops. When the day is done, the cast of *All My Children* ventures out of Pine Valley and into the real world. Here are some memorable snapshots of off-camera moments through the years.

Is that Myra Sloan directing traffic? Yes. On days off from the studio, actress Elizabeth Lawrence (left) volunteered her time as a member of the New York City Auxiliary Police Department (1983).

Richard Shoberg (Tom) enjoyed a soothing dip in the pool during a break in taping sequences on the Caribbean island of St. Croix (1978) (below).

Gillian Spencer (Daisy) and James Mitchell (Palmer) traveled to New York City's Bide-A-Wee Animal Shelter to adopt two cuddly kittens. In the story, Palmer gave Tweedle-dee and Tweedle-dum to Daisy to replace her dearly departed cat, Bonkers (1985) (below).

It was a banner day on New York's Columbus Avenue when actors Darnell Williams (Jesse), Kim Delaney (Jenny), Marcy Walker (Liza) and James Mitchell unfurled a computer-printed banner sent in by a zealous fan who proclaimed, "SAVE JESSE, RETURN JENNY, NAIL LIZA, ABORT PALMER" (1982).

The *All My Children* softball squad posed for this team picture before heading for a game in New York's Central Park (1990).

Behind the Scenes

Taylor Miller (Nina) and Peter Bergman (Cliff) (above) hammed it up on the streets of New York while taping an ABC promo for the new fall season (1981).

Mark LaMura (Mark) and Kathleen Noone (Ellen) cuddled atop the *All My Children* float in a Knoxville parade (1981) (left).

Popular Tasia Valenza (Dottie), Michael E. Knight (Tad), Ruth Warrick (Phoebe), James Mitchell (Palmer) and Julia Barr (Brooke) met the press (below) when ABC introduced the *All My Children* game (1985).

Jean LeClerc played Jeremy during the week, but on weekends the handsome French-Canadian played gentleman farmer on his farm outside Montreal (1988) (below).

Candice Earley (Donna) led a group of soap opera singers (above) in a fund-raising extravaganza benefitting flood victims in Johnstown, Pennsylvania (1977).

New York Mets superstars Daryl Strawberry and Keith Hernandez welcomed soap superstar Susan Lucci to baseball's Shea Stadium (1989).

Behind the Scenes

Family Feud host Richard Dawson offered roses (and of course, a kiss) to the team of Julia Barr (Brooke), Dorothy Lyman (Opal), Debbi Morgan (Angie), Marcy Walker (Liza) and Ruth Warrick (Phoebe) (1983).

The late makeup artist Sylvia Lawrence, Agnes Nixon, Mary Fickett (Ruth), Ray MacDonnell (Joe), Susan Lucci (Erica) and Ruth Warrick (Phoebe) all participated in the cake cutting as *All My Children* celebrated the taping of its 5000th show (1989).

On location in Maine, James Kiberd (Trevor) shields fair Kate Collins's porcelain skin from the hot summer sun (1990).

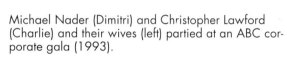

Michael Nader (Dimitri) and Christopher Lawford (Charlie) and their wives (left) partied at an ABC corporate gala (1993).

Shari Headley (Mimi) watches in amusement as Kelly Ripa (Hayley) shows her the latest dance craze (below) at an ABC holiday party (1993).

Backstage Memories

As All My Children *celebrates its 25th anniversary, past and present cast members reflect on their Pine Valley years.*

Candice Earley (Donna Beck Tyler): I remember when Verla Grubbs, played by the one and only Carol Burnett, asked my character to sing a little song for her at the Chateau. I looked out into the audience and stared straight into a pair of the most  gorgeous violet eyes. They belonged to Elizabeth Taylor, who had popped into Pine Valley to say hello to Carol and stayed for my song. That was a glorious night for Donna and a dream come true for me!

Richard Van Vleet (Dr. Chuck Tyler): Chuck should never have lasted as long as he did, because he was supposed to die 20 years ago! Before I was even cast in the role, the writers had made up their minds to kill the character off! Evidently, they liked me enough to rewrite the story and I actually got to do the death scene, but fortunately for me, we played it as a fantasy.

Ellen Wheeler (Cindy Chandler): I'll never forget the day that we taped the scenes in which a fire destroyed the Hubbard house, because that day was so long! To insure our safety, the technicians spent hours setting up the scene, while we actors patiently waited and waited. Finally, I went out and bought a book of crossword puzzles—really easy crossword puzzles. Anything to pass the time as I waited to face my towering inferno.

Larkin Malloy (Travis Montgomery): I loved Travis's elegant executive office at Montgomery Enterprises. In fact, I felt so comfortable on the set that I went out and ordered the same furniture for my apartment. Travis didn't always have the best business sense, but the guy had good taste.

Michael Brainard (Joey Martin): The actors on *All My Children* get most of the credit, but the guys behind the camera were just as responsible for making us look so good. So every once in a while, I tried to sneak in a little tribute to them on the air. Like the time I mentioned Joey's friends Hank and Joe—who just happened to be our cameramen. They loved it!

Robin Christopher (Skye Chandler): I will never forget the day that Skye married the man of her dreams, Tom Cudahy. I experienced many of the same emotions that a real bride feels on her wedding day, like real tears. From the  moment I walked onto the set, I couldn't stop crying.

Michael E. Knight (Tad Martin): Way back in the beginning, Tad was just too cool when it came to pick-up lines. Get this—one time I swaggered up to that gorgeous blonde ice princess, Liza Colby, and said, "I really dig you, baby. I'm not feeding you a line, I'm giving it to you straight." Well, let me tell ya, folks, there was no way that I could say a line like that with a straight face. So I threw in a couple of wisecracks and—I've been doing it ever since.

Michael Brainard (Joey Martin): I drove my producers crazy when, right in the middle of our taping day, I came down with a case of everyone's least favorite childhood disease—chicken pox! Of course, my castmates avoided me like the plague until the writers wrote me out of the show and sent me home to recover. But I was itching to get back!

 **Julia Barr** (Brooke English): I still get choked up when I think of the time that our writers had me choke on a piece of food so that Tom Cudahy could demonstrate the brand-new Heimlich Maneuver. I know we were performing a valuable public service, but I was terrified! I've had a terrible fear of choking ever since!

Maurice Benard (Nico Kelly): One of my favorite times was the three weeks Nico spent on the critical list at Pine Valley Hospital. For an actor used to learning 30 pages of dialogue a day, the critical list is the place to be. You just show up at the studio and go straight to bed. I just popped on my headphones and grooved on tunes all day. Not bad!

Dondre T. Whitfield (Terrence Frye): Everybody here at the studio has a specific job to do. Like the paint guy. He's this dude who sits in a little room surrounded by hundreds of cans of paint. Like a fireman, he waits and waits—until the moment our director sees some dirt or a smudge on one of the walls of the set. The director yells, "Get the paint guy," who springs into action, racing to the set with a brush and just the right color to restore Pine Valley to all its chromatic glory.

Debbi Morgan (Dr. Angie Hubbard): Once, I gave a real scare to the director because just as the show was about to be taped, I was nowhere to be found. As precious minutes passed, he put out a frantic SOS. The cast and crew searched everywhere and finally found me—fast asleep on the floor of my dressing room. I was on the set in a flash, with a trail of clothing following me!

Susan Lucci (Erica Kane): I owe so much to our ingenious creator, Agnes Nixon! Agnes introduced humor and tongue-in-cheek wit to daytime TV, and I've been the lucky recipient of much of that wonderful comic writing.

James Mitchell (Palmer Cortlandt.): It's never easy memorizing 30 pages of dialogue. So I'll let you in on a little secret. Every once in a while, I scribble a key word somewhere on the set, like on the back of the antique Chinese plates that sit on Palmer's mantlepiece. If you ever catch me pondering those plates, you'll know why!

Winsor Harmon (Del Henry Hunkle): When I think of *All My Children*, I think of Susan Lucci. So as you might imagine, it was scary meeting her in person because I think she's the best actress on the soaps. It's amazing to watch Susan become Erica every day at the studio. We'll be talking in the makeup room and she's just so sweet and sincere, then she goes before the cameras and suddenly she's that scheming Erica! Let me tell you, it's an amazing transformation!

Cady McClain (Dixie Martin): I may have been the only actor over the age of sixteen who didn't have a driver's license. And that became a problem when the *All My Children* script required me to drive a car! At 7:15 the next morning, I was at the DMV taking a test for my learner's permit. Then I enrolled in a driving school and hit the streets with my instructor. The irony of the whole thing is that I only had to drive 50 yards in the scene before a stunt driver took my place!

Kelly Ripa (Hayley Vaughan): During my first three months on *All My Children*, I wore a long black wig that made me look like Morticia from *The Addams Family*! On my first day on the show, the hairdresser asked, "Do you want to do the wig now?" To which I replied, "Wig? What wig? Nobody told me about a wig!" Oh, I just knew that my parents were going to take one look at my frightening hairdo and say, "What has New York done to our little girl?"

Ruth Warrick (Phoebe Tyler Wallingford): Phoebe's a grande dame, but our real grande dame is the woman who weaves our magical stories—the incredible Ms. Agnes Nixon. The name Pine Valley is actually derived from  the place Agnes calls home, the Delaware Valley. The name of the house she lived in many years ago was called Pine Cottage. Put the two names together, and you get Pine Valley!

Larkin Malloy (Travis Montgomery): I'm a pretty good driver, but Travis was supposed to be a champion. So to get ready for the big racing scene, I went to Formula One Racing School. Getting in that car and hitting the track at 150 miles an hour was one of the most exciting things I've ever done.

Matt Servitto (Trask Bodine): Unlike those rich Cortlandts and wealthy Wallingfords, my character didn't have the money to dress for success! So when our costume department went shopping for my wardrobe, they didn't go to Saks or Bloomies. No, my torn shirts and ripped jeans come from some of New York's seediest T-shirt and biker shops. And an old, weathered Army jacket I wore came from my own private collection!

Matt Servitto (Trask Bodine): My character had one of the quirkiest names on daytime TV! I mean, have you ever met anyone named Trask? Or Bodine? Well, our head-writers did! Actually, one of the writers chose the name Trask because he had a boyhood friend named John Trask, and another writer picked Bodine because she thought it sounded "macho and cool." All I know is that people chuckled when they heard the name! But they didn't forget it!

James Kiberd (Trevor Dillon): Trevor was only supposed to last a mere twelve days. So what did I have to lose? Without telling anybody, I slicked back my hair, grew several days of stubble, and played the role looking...well, slimy! It must have worked! Because instead of giving me a reprimand, the producer gave me a pat on the back...and a contract offer that I couldn't refuse!

Larkin Malloy (Travis Montgomery): When Travis was kidnapped, I was supposed to look beaten and disheveled. So my producer asked me not to shave for two painfully long weeks! You can bet that I felt just as uncomfortable as I looked because New York was in the midst of a heat wave and my itching and sprouting whiskers drove me crazy.

Sydney Penny (Julia Santos): You may have noticed that my character wears clothes that are designed to attract the attention of the opposite sex. I don't actually choose Julia's wardrobe—that's the job of our costume designer, Carol Luiken. Carol dresses our cast from head to toe, down to the last detail. And details are important to her. In fact, one of Carol's pet peeves is flat pocketbooks. She can't stand to see characters carrying pocketbooks that are obviously empty! So whenever Carol sees one of us carrying a bag that looks like a pancake, she races onto the set and stuffs it with tissue paper. Well, she must be doing something right, judging from the three Emmys on her desk!

Cady McClain (Dixie Martin): Soap-opera pregnancy is great! The fun part for me was wearing a big, fluffy pillow under my clothes for twelve hours a day. The only problem I had was hunger—I guess I thought I was really eating for two!

Michael E. Knight (Tad Martin): For years, David Canary and I shared a dressing room, which we both thought was hilarious because our characters hated each other. But fortunately, David and I got along, which is a good thing—because I had to stare at his mug for twelve hours a day!

Shari Headley (Mimi Reed): As Mimi, I was bitter enemies with Taylor Roxbury Cannon. Funny thing is, in real life, I am best buds with Ingrid Rogers, who plays the role. Most of the time we were able to separate our real lives from our soap lives, but trying to balance this love/hate relationship wasn't always easy. One time, I was smiling at Ingrid during a scene when suddenly I thought to myself, Wait a minute, I can't do that! I'm supposed to hate her!

Tommy Michaels (Timmy Hunter): My dressing room is one of the most popular places for the *All My Children* cast to hang out. Not because of me, but because of my Nintendo! When I brought it to the studio, I never realized that all my castmates would be stopping  by to play video games. Don't get me wrong, I love the company. But I'm still in school, so when I'm not studying my lines, I'm doing my homework!

James Mitchell (Palmer Cortlandt): My favorite scene was the one where, during a Christmas Eve snowstorm, Palmer Cortlandt was forced to deliver his own son! I have to admit—I couldn't sleep a wink on the night before we taped that scene. I know it seems silly, but the miracle of birth is very exciting—even when it's all just make-believe!

James Kiberd (Trevor Dillon): I live about half my life in my dressing room here at the *All My Children* studio. That's why I've equipped the place with all the comforts of home—a refrigerator, microwave, blender, steamer and a toaster. (I love to eat—can you tell?) Every day, my assistant and I do a formal lunch with table linens and a full set of china. Nice, eh? Hey, maybe I oughta start taking reservations!

John Callahan (Edmund Grey): I presented quite a challenge to our costume designer, Charlie Clute, when my character, Edmund, posed as a sleazy gigolo. You see, Charlie usually shops for wardrobe in places like Saks Fifth Avenue. But where do you shop for a sleazy guy who wears leather and gold chains? Charlie found just the place in a bizarre little shop in Greenwich Village where they stocked the perfect outfits for my character—along with a selection of sex toys and edible undergarments!

John Callahan (Edmund Grey): My name was nearly mud the time I took a plunge into quicksand! Fortunately, I didn't have to wallow in real mud during the long hours of rehearsal and taping that scene. To simulate quicksand, our prop department mixed up 1500 pounds of oatmeal, cinnamon and cocoa puffs in a pool—and I just jumped in! After playing scene after scene in the sticky mixture, I stepped outside for a breath of fresh air, only to get nibbled on by every dog in New York!

Michael E. Knight (Tad Martin): Tad was originally brought to *All My Children* as a villain, which meant that, before long, he was bound to die a horrible death. So to survive, I took the advice of my castmate Dorothy Lyman, who told me that if I wanted to say something funny, I should just say it. The writers must have liked what they saw because before long, Tad became a scoundrel—with a sense of humor.

Felicity LaFortune (Laurel Banning Montgomery): I won't forget the time I had to carry a corpse around Pine Valley. The prop department wanted to make our corpse-carrying look as realistic as possible, so they went out and rented a dummy from a company that makes them for automobile crash tests! So if you ever need a fake corpse of your own, just check the yellow pages for Dummies on Demand!

James Kiberd (Trevor Dillon): I've had my share of good times here on *All My Children*. But let me tell ya, it was no fun doing the shows surrounding the death of Trevor's wife, Natalie. They were tough scenes to do—especially the one where I had to break the news to our son, Timmy, that his mom wasn't going to make it. That stuff was so emotionally intense that we didn't rehearse it. There was no way we could practice such powerful stuff—we just

had to go out there and do it! From what they tell me, there wasn't a dry eye in the studio that day.

Jill Larson (Opal Cortlandt): Wasn't it W.C. Fields who once counseled actors never to work with dogs or children? His point was that they steal the scene from you! Frankly W.C., I've had no problems with the kid who plays my son. Maybe that's because I hardly ever see him! His birth was accomplished with a teddy bear, and he's never there during rehearsals because we practice our lines with a plastic doll. Just before taping, they thrust a real, live child in my arms and shout, "ACTION!" So I really have to be on my toes.

Jill Larson (Opal Cortlandt): You gotta love soap opera food, because it's not always what it appears to be. For instance, you know those elegant party scenes where everyone's dining on caviar and champagne? Instead of fish eggs, we're actually chowing down on a mixture of blackberry jam and currants, topped off with bottles of bubbly ginger ale. Yumm!

Elizabeth Lawrence (Myra Sloan): I spent years lurking about the Cortlandt estate in my long black gown, always up to my gray bun in gothic intrigue. Finally, the writers decided that my character needed a spiffy new wardrobe and a shorter hairdo. Well, I wore the

new clothes, but I steadfastly refused to let them cut my hair—so I wore a wig.

Shari Headley (Mimi Reed): You know what really blew me away? Meeting Adam Chandler in the flesh! I'm a big *All My Children* fan, so I was a little nervous to do a scene with Adam because I expected the actor to be a tyrant like his character! But let me tell you, David Canary is a real cool guy. He's not at all like that ruthless Adam.

Eileen Herlie (Myrtle Fargate): I've become the resident protector of all the children on *All My Children*! At one time or another, they all move into my boarding house. One of our prop men calls me the "Mother Teresa of Pine Valley!" I was especially fond of Francesca James, the Emmy-award winning actress who played both Kitty and Kelly. Nowadays, she works behind the scenes as the Producer of *General Hospital*!

Kiss and Tell

Are those intimate love scenes as hot as they look?
Here are the sexy secrets from the stars themselves.

Peter Bergman (Dr. Cliff Warner): Nina and Cliff's first kiss was memorable for both of us. We both dreaded it, but when the moment finally came it was beautiful. Our lips met in a soft, tender kiss. It was perfect. Until our lips parted and there was a tiny bridge of saliva stringing between us. We remained in character until I delivered my line, and the bridge started bouncing! That broke everyone up!

Cady McClain (Dixie Martin): When you're doing a scene with Michael Knight, you never know what to expect. Like the time I was supposed to act embarrassed when Opal caught us kissing. On the first take, the director didn't think I seemed embarrassed enough, so Michael told him, "Don't worry, I'll take care of it." So during take two, Michael reached behind me and unhooked my bra! I was beet red—but hey, the scene worked!

Paige Turco (Lanie Cortlandt): My audition called for me to kiss Trent Bushey, the handsome actor who played David Rampal, whom I'd never met. I was so nervous! My mouth was so dry that when our lips finally met, they stuck together!

Kate Collins (Natalie Dillon): My *All My Children* love scenes were always an adventure. Like the time Jean LeClerc (Jeremy) and I were in bed kissing, and just when we were getting to the sweet part, the headboard fell off the back of the bed—and we went with it. Head first! The director screamed "CUT!" and stopped the tape, but no one could stop our hysterical laughing!

Liz Vassey (Emily Ann Sago): Back when I auditioned, I was lucky to share a smooch with Nico, played by Maurice Benard. My friends back home in Tampa, Florida, were so jealous! And they should have been, because it was hot! Unfortunately for me, not only did Nico and I never kiss on the show, we never even had a meaningful conversation!

Lindsay Price (An-Li): When I began playing An-Li, I was only fifteen and Matt Borlenghi, who played my leading man, Brian, was 24. So when it came time to do our first love scene, I was petrified. And most of all, I worried what my mom would say. I nervously handed her the love-scene script and announced, "Read this and please don't get mad." I expected her to say, "I'm calling the producers!" but luckily, Mom understood that I was just doing my job!

Robin Christopher (Skye Chandler): On my second day on *All My Children*, I was asked to do a steamy love scene, and just the idea of it frightened me. You see, I'm a nice old-fashioned girl, so I was really shocked when the director asked me to make out ferociously with Brian Fitzpatrick, who played Mitch Beck, in front of 40 leering stagehands. I was mortified—but I did it—for all of America to see.

Cady McClain (Dixie Martin): I sometimes got the giggles when I had to cuddle and kiss Matt Borlenghi, who played Brian. To be honest, the love scenes were a little uncomfortable to do, because off camera, Matt and I were good friends. So just before our love scenes, we'd shake hands, pat each other on the back, then go for it! I always told his girlfriend not to watch the show because I didn't want her to hate me!

Misadventures on the Set

You never know what's going to happen in the course of taping five one-hour episodes of All My Children *every week. The show you see at home may look smooth as silk, but that's because the flubbed lines, the backstage gaffes and the hilarious goofs are cut out before* All My Children *ever reaches the air. Here, the stars relive their most memorable bloopers.*

Ray MacDonnell (Dr. Joe Martin): As an actor trying to sound like a doctor, I spend lots of time practicing the names of all those medical tongue-twisters. Like Nina's "debilitating diabetic retinopathy" and Erica's "tenacious case of toxemia." The toughest was the time I had to explain that Phillip's illness was caused by "fumes from a faulty flue in the furnace." It took me six tries to get that one right!

Susan Lucci (Erica Kane): One of the most harrowing adventures that ever happened to me was the time Michael Nader and I were supposed to tape a scene in which Erica and Dimitri take a leisurely, romantic boat tour along the Danube. Little did we know that our speedboat driver was practicing for Hungary's version of the Indianapolis 500! As soon as we stepped into the boat, our speedy guide hit the throttle and took off! That first take was not the one that aired, because we both looked frightened to death!

Kelly Ripa (Hayley Vaughan): During a scene I accidentally caught my finger in the door in Myrtle's kitchen. It began to swell up immediately, but I still attempted to say my next line which was supposed to be a perky "Good Morning!" But it came out more like a painful cry, along with a flood of tears. I tried to hold them back—but it hurt!

Susan Lucci (Erica Kane): I still remember the time that Erica risked life and limb to rescue Jeremy Hunter from prison in a daring helicopter escape. A stunt woman was supposed to fill in for me, but standing there on the prison roof, with the wind whipping and the snow falling, I guess I got a little carried away! So I tried to climb the ladder that dangled from the chopper! In an instant, our horrified director threw himself at my feet to hold me down before I really got carried away.

Eva LaRue (Dr. Maria Santos): I'm a top-notch neurologist on *All My Children*. But as an actress, all of that medical jargon gives me a headache! You see, my brain just doesn't want to remember the lingo, like Natalie's hematoma of the I-don't-know-what, and my favorite disease—Ted Orsini's rare case of "Tripomitosis"—which means sleeping sickness. Try pronouncing that one! Why couldn't I just say "sleeping sickness?" So the next time you hear me stumbling over someone's dreaded disease, please remember—I'm not a doctor, I just play one on TV!

Trent Bushey (David Rampal): I had the honor of taping the last scene—a bed scene!—in *All My Children*'s old studio before it was torn down. And strangely, I almost had nothing to wear! You see, my wardrobe had accidentally been packed up and shipped to the new studio—so we rummaged through the garbage and found an old pair of dirty sweat pants. Despite the smell, I put 'em on and did the scene—because as they say, the show must go on!

Jean LeClerc (Jeremy Hunter): We shot an elaborate fox hunt on Long Island. It was supposed to be spring, but let me tell you, the day we shot the scene, it felt more like the dead of winter. We were freezing. My teeth chattered so, I was amazed I could speak my lines. Susan Lucci and I shivered in our heavy winter coats and dreaded the moment we'd be needed on camera without them. But we survived!

Robin Christopher (Skye Chandler): Skye spent a lot of time in comas, beginning with a car accident that put her in a coma for a week, and then a near-fatal fire that left my character comatose for three months. I got so tired of lying there that I once dozed off in the middle of a scene. When one of my fellow actors began delivering his lines, I woke up with such a start that I nearly jumped out of the bed!

Shari Headley (Mimi Reed): I was trying my best to act like a genuine police officer when I interrogated Tad Martin, played by Michael Knight. He looked at me and asked, "Hey what gives you the right to question me?" At which point I whipped out my badge and flashed it in his face—but it was upside down. Without missing a beat, Michael nonchalantly turned the badge around and said, "OK, Officer Reed." It was very funny. So funny, in fact, that they left it in the show!

Richard Van Vleet (Dr. Chuck Tyler): All of our fights were choreographed with split-second timing, but on one occasion things almost went awry! In a fight with Billy Clyde Tuggle, he was supposed to flip me over and try to smash a shovel on my head! But he accidentally knocked the wind out of me, and when I looked up,  the shovel was coming right at my face! Fortunately, I swerved out of the way just in time!

Kelly Ripa (Hayley Vaughan): The most fun I've ever had was when Dom DeLuise made a guest appearance as a traffic cop in a scene with me. Actually, the scene was very hard for me because Hayley was supposed to be frantic, but Dom was just too hilarious! He was ad-libbing like crazy, and every time I felt a giggle coming on, I'd turn away from the camera and put my hand over my mouth! I was supposed to be hysterical, but I was hysterically laughing!

Kelly Ripa (Hayley Vaughan): I love to eat, so our writers are always creating scenes where I inhale everything in sight! Like the time I was busy eating so much delicious popcorn that I forgot to say my next line! Our director, who's in the control booth, came over the P.A. and announced, "Kelly, could you help us out here and say your line?" I was left with food—and my foot—in my mouth!

Kate Collins (Natalie Hunter): My romantic roll in the sand with Trevor Dillon was right out of *From Here to Eternity*. Ha! The scene was actually more reminiscent of *Arachnophobia*! But instead of hairy spiders, our tormentors were mosquitoes. Millions of them! If you opened your mouth, you inhaled mosquitoes! We sprayed on so much bug repellent that by the time it came to tape our big beach-front love scene, we couldn't breathe from the fumes.

Ruth Warrick (Phoebe Tyler Wallingford): I remember my first day on the *All My Children* set. The wardrobe mistress was fixing a broken zipper on my slacks when I was called to the set. Well, when you hear your name, you go. And I went. And so, there was the very proper Phoebe—in rehearsal for the first time—caught with her pants down!

Jill Larson (Opal Cortlandt): Opal likes to eat the strangest things—like peanut butter-and-bologna sandwiches! One day, the prop guys actually made me a real one and I didn't find out about it until I took the first bite—on tape. Yeccchhh! Opal may love the combination of peanut butter and bologna, but I found it to be a horrifying experience.

Richard Van Vleet: (Dr. Chuck Tyler): I loved going to Switzerland! But we should have left our snow-suits back in Pine Valley—because, at the time, Europe was having a heat wave! But with the help of some plastic icicles and a batch of man-made snow, we made Switzerland look like a winter wonderland. No one ever knew the difference.

Jean LeClerc (Jeremy Hunter): Jeremy and Natalie's wedding was a glorious affair, but I remember that neither one of us got to taste the cake! Kate Collins and I were whisked away from the set to take pictures, and when we got back, our wedding cake was history. And I was hungry, too!

Julia Barr (Brooke English): I still remember the time that Brooke went for a romantic skinny dip with her boyfriend, Dan Kennicott, in Aunt Phoebe's pool. That sizzling scene may have looked provocative on the air, but it was freezing in the water. After four hours in an unheated pool, we ended up saying lines like, "Isn't this w-w-wonderful?"

Eddie Earl Hatch (John Remington): I faced some emotion-packed scenes during my year on *All My Children*. Like the time I told Angie the sorrowful tale of my sister's death. I was supposed to cry real tears, but all that pent-up emotion came running out my nose. I didn't have a tissue so I did the only thing I could think of—I grabbed my tie and used it to wipe my runny nose. Yeah, I know it sounds awful, but on the soaps, the show must go on.

Shari Headley (Mimi Reed): Mimi was supposed to be a pilot, and the truth is, I hate flying! And the plane I was supposed to be flying wasn't even real—just a set that was constructed here at the *All My Children* studios. Still, I was absolutely nauseated during the scene. So, I made sure I knew all my lines so we got it in one shot. I don't think my stomach could have handled another take!

Kate Collins (Natalie Hunter): Viewers saw my character kill Silver Kane in self defense, but what you didn't see was the trouble we had getting Silver to die! No matter how many times I pulled the trigger on that prop gun, it just wouldn't fire. It took ten tries before Silver went out with a bang!

Nancy Addison (Marissa Rampal): I lived out my fantasies playing a secret agent. We even stole a page from a James Bond novel when I was supposed to swallow a deadly cyanide capsule. The scene worked like a charm except for one thing—I couldn't swallow the pill. I played the entire scene with the poison pill—which was just sugar—tucked under my tongue.

Taylor Miller (Nina Cortlandt): The kind of storybook romance that Nina had with Cliff wasn't as easy as it looked. In one fantasy scene, Peter Bergman led me out of the fog to a bed covered with beautiful satin sheets. But when he put me down on the bed, I slid off it and landed on my you-know-what!

Richard Van Vleet: (Dr. Chuck Tyler): Even after 20 years, fans never seem to forget the time I rescued Donna from her rotten pimp Tyrone, who was played by a terrific actor named Roscoe Orman. The funny thing is, at the same time he was also playing Gordon, the nicest guy on *Sesame Street*! But soon, young children who watched both shows began to confuse the two characters. They thought Gordon was Tyrone! So Roscoe made a tough decision, and for the kids, he left *All My Children*.

Behind the Scenes

The Joke's On You!

*Who are the all-time practical jokers
in the* All My Children *cast?
Which stars are the class clowns?
Here, the stars relive their favorite pranks.*

Lonnie Quinn (Will Cortlandt): Michael Knight pulled a practical joke on me when I was taking a long, hot shower—which was a little too long for Michael's liking, because when I reached for my towel, it was gone. So was my  robe. I had to sneak back to my dressing room wearing only a smile. I never did get him back for that one!

Cady McClain (Dixie Martin): When they met, Tad and Dixie really had a case of puppy love. So once Michael Knight played a joke on me by coming onto the set dressed up like a toy poodle on a leash, complete with a cute little ribbon in his hair. He's one sick puppy—but he always makes me laugh!

Mark LaMura (Mark Dalton): Once, in rehearsal, I donned a long, flowing, platinum wig and the "cutest" little dress and pranced my way through Foxy's Bar. Hey, I must have looked pretty good because for months, the director jokingly asked when that "blond bombshell" was coming back.

Kathleen Noone (Ellen Dalton): Mark LaMura, who played my husband Mark, could never remember the line, "I love you." So one time, just to get through the scene, I wrote "I love you" on my eyelids, and when the moment came, I closed my eyes  to give him his line. It didn't work because we both started laughing.

What's it like to be a bonafide soap star?
All My Children's actors have real lives, too—and real families!
Are the people of Pine Valley stars at home? Here's what
they have to day about their real-life dramas.

Alan Dysert (Sean Cudahy): When my son Cody was three, he loved to watch *All My Children* with me—especially when Adam, Dixie and Palmer were on the screen. But every time I came on, he demanded that I turn on *Sesame Street*. And every time I kissed one of my leading ladies, he'd hit me!

Tommy Michaels (Timothy Hunter): My friends think that it's awesome that I'm a TV star. They say, "Wow, you must make a lot of money," and I tell them the truth—I do, but I'm saving it all for college.

Susan Pratt (Barbara Montgomery): When she was five, my daughter Sophia loved to help me practice my lines—but only if she could play Erica, her favorite character. If I was on the show, she got bored and asked me, "Mommy, is *One Life To Live* on soon? I want to see Tina! She's exciting."

John Wesley Shipp (Carter Jones): I've played all sorts of wonderfully different characters over the years, but the slimy, sleazy, psychotic roles like Carter seem to be my good-luck charm. In fact, they've won me two Daytime Emmy awards for my roles on *As The World Turns* and *Santa Barbara*. My grandmother told me, "John, you got two Emmys for playing bad guys! I don't know what that says about you, but be sure to say you didn't get it from your grandmother!"

James Patrick Stuart (Will Cortlandt): Will lived in a mansion, but when I first started working on *All My Children*, I lived on a couch! You see, I was cast on a Friday in L.A. and reported to work in New York on Monday. Who had time to find an apartment? So, for a while, I camped out with a friend of a friend of a friend. And I told everyone I lived on a park bench.

Kelly Ripa (Hayley Vaughan): Pine Valley is not all that different from the town I grew up in in New Jersey. My father jokes that there are more people living in my apartment building in New York than in our entire hometown. It was big news when I got the part on *All My Children*, everyone was shouting, "Did You hear about Kelly?" No one needed to ask "Kelly who?" because there was only one Kelly in town—me!

Richard Shoberg (Tom Cudahy): I guess I'm a lot like the nice guy I play. Back in 1978, Tom was a bachelor and so was I. Since then, we've married and raised two children. But the similarities end right there. You see, I'm still happily married to my one and only wife, Varaporn, while Tom has walked down the aisle five times! Some quick math tells me that's almost one wife every three years! I'd say that's just a little above the national average!

Kelly Ripa (Hayley Vaughan): Well, my character was once into shoplifting, but it's not something I do. But try telling that to the security guard at one of New York's finest stores. The guy recognized me from the soap and proceeded to follow me wherever I went! I tried to explain that I'm not really a kleptomaniac, but all he said was, "Sure, toots!"

Kathleen Noone (Ellen Dalton): One of my concerns in real life was and is the energy problem. I took it right to Pine Valley and talked our executive producer into letting Ellen and Mark purchase daytime's first—and only—solar home. I'm proud that Ellen was such a positive role model over the years.

How did your favorite All My Children
actors get their start on the show?
Here's the inside information.

Susan Lucci (Erica Kane): My first day as Erica was nerve-wracking. As a first-time soap opera actress, I was on probation for my first five shows. I never knew if they liked me or didn't like me. But I suppose, after 5185 shows, they must think I'm doing something right.

Rosa Nevin (Cecily Davidson Kelly): I was living in Los Angeles when I got the role of Cecily, and I thought, Great, ABC is just a few blocks away. Wrong! Little did I know that *All My Children*'s studios were 3000 miles away—in New York! So on two days notice, I pulled up stakes and moved cross country!

Rudolf Martin (Anton Lang): Just moments before taping my first scene with Susan Lucci, I introduced myself by saying, "Hello, my name is Rudolf, and I play Anton." In the scene Erica was supposed to say to her husband, "I just met Anton, and he's very nice." Instead Susan mixed up my real name with my character name and said, "I just met Rudolf, and he's very nice." Of course, the director yelled, "Cut!" Frankly, I was flattered, because Susan rarely forgets her lines.

Genie Francis (Ceara Connor): I'll never forget my first meeting with *All My Children*'s creator, Agnes Nixon. Ever since I was a teenager, I'd played nice girls, but over lunch, she told me all about a new character she'd created just for me. She was so excited to tell me about Ceara—whom she conceived as an opportunist driven to make it big. Because Agnes was so enthusiastic, so was I. I couldn't wait to sink my teeth into such a meaty role.

Eva LaRue (Maria Santos): I owe a bit of thanks to the *All My Children* writers for creating such an intriguing role and asking me to play it—without an audition. You see, they already knew my work because I'd recently screen-tested for two other parts—Kendall and Laurel—but both roles went to other actresses. Finally, the producers called me about Maria and basically said, "Here's the role—do you want it?" My answer, of course, was a resounding yes.

Tonya Pinkins (Livia Frye): If the fates had been different, I might have become the first Angie Hubbard on *All My Children*. You see, back in 1981, I was up for the part of Angie, but Debbi Morgan accepted the role at the last minute. I was heartbroken because I've been a huge fan of the show since I was eight years old. I know everything there is to know about Pine Valley—I even remember every one of Tom Cudahy's ex-wives!

William Christian (Derek Frye): I originally came on the show as a "day player"—that's someone playing a very small role for a day or two. But the writers liked my scenes so much that I got a wife, a family and a 1991 Emmy nomination!

Taylor Miller (Nina Cortlandt): I'd never heard of *All My Children* when I came to New York to audition, so I wasn't very nervous. But I had no idea how many actresses wanted this plum part. One month later, just as I was about to go home to Texas, I heard that I'd won the role. The rest is history!

James Kiberd (Trevor Dillon): As a very scared young actor, l played a character named David Duncan on *All My Children* for one day. I was terrified! I had these two long scenes with Nina Cortlandt, and I was so bad, I went out of the studio in tears, swearing I'd never act again! It just "shows to go ya," anyone can overcome their fears!

Eileen Herlie (Myrtle Fargate): I have had a remarkable run here, considering that I was scheduled only for a short stay in Pine Valley. You see, I'd never done television before *All My Children*. I thought, Soap opera? Oh no, it's not my cup of tea!  Well, I quickly discovered that I like the brew and the crew—and I've been happily here ever since.

 **James Patrick Stuart** (Will Cortlandt): I was really intimidated on my first day in Pine Valley. That is, until Michael Knight (who plays Tad) offered to take me to breakfast, and Susan Lucci knocked on my door and said, "Hi, I'm Susan. If you need anything, I'm just down the hall!" They really made me feel welcome.

Kate Collins (Natalie Hunter): Just before I got the part of Natalie, I was a struggling actress auditioning like crazy and working as a freelance secretary to make ends meet. Believe me, I watched every penny! But as soon as *All My Children* called, I decided to splurge a little. I took my first paycheck, ran right to Bloomingdales' men's department and treated myself to a cashmere sweater!

Jean LeClerc (Jeremy Hunter): I'll let you in on a little secret. When I arrived in New York to audition and was told I would be screen-testing with Susan Lucci, I had no idea who she was. Growing up in Canada, I had never heard of the formidable Erica, and I was most surprised to meet this very tiny person who created such a stir.

 **Walt Willey** (Jackson Montgomery): My first professional acting job was playing a customer at Foxy's Bar. I was one of those happy folks you always see in the background. You could hardly call it acting. I felt more like a breathing prop! But as a struggling actor just getting started in the business, working on *All My Children* was a dream come true.

Dondre Whitfield (Terrence Frye): When I came to *All My Children*, my castmates teased me because I didn't have anything in my dressing room. It was empty. I kept it that way because I felt that if I got too comfortable, I wouldn't work as hard.

Over the years, *All My Children* has been a who's who of who's hot as stars from the silver screen and the political world, as well as Wall Street whizzes and Olympic athletes—many of them die-hard fans of the show—have all made guest appearances.

Actress Maureen O'Sullivan, who played Jane in the Tarzan movies, appeared as Mrs. Whelan, the landlady who harbored Erica while she was on the run after Kent Bogard's death.

Movie legend Elizabeth Taylor surprised her dear friend Carol Burnett by strolling onto the *All My Children* set during dress rehearsal—wearing Carol's charwoman costume! Elizabeth stayed to do a quick cameo at the Chateau with Verla and Myrtle.

Donna Hanover Guiliani, the wife of New York City Mayor Rudolph Guiliani, guested as a local TV reporter in a scene with Erica Kane. The role was an easy one for the Big Apple's First Lady, who has been a local TV news anchor for more than twenty years.

Swimming champion Summer Sanders, winner of four medals in the 1992 Summer Olympics, showed up at Pine Valley Hospital to visit the children in the pediatric ward. On hand to greet her were Stuart Chandler and nurse Gloria Marsh.

Actor/comedian Jerry Stiller appeared as a slick-talking theatrical agent in scenes with Hayley Vaughan. Stiller's real-life wife, Anne Meara, appears in the semi-regular role of Wildwind maid Peggy Moody.

The Fans

PAUL ANKA

"I watch the show when I can, and of course my family watches it, too. So when *All My Children* called and asked me to do a part, I was delighted to say yes, because I knew I'd get the chance to meet Susan Lucci. I'm a big fan of hers."

It wasn't "puppy love" when Charlie Brent took Erica Kane out for a night on the town and encountered talented singer/songwriter Paul Anka at Nexus.

DONALD TRUMP

"Candidly, this is what I remember about my appearance on *All My Children*. My driver pulled up at ABC, I dashed out of the car, and before I knew what happened, I was in the studio standing in front of a camera and reading a line off a cue card. I shook hands with a few people, ran out the door, jumped back in my car, and I was gone. You have to remember, I'm a busy guy!"

How's this for a dynamic duo? Erica Kane and millionaire Donald Trump! The real estate mogul popped into New York's Nexus to say hi to Charlie Brent and, of course, his old chum, Erica.

Erica created a local scandal when she trashed her mother—and the rest of Pine Valley—during an interview with talk show host Dick Cavett.

Erica nearly caught a pass from football quarterback Boomer Esiason during his 1988 post-Super Bowl appearance in Pine Valley.

Glamorous supermodel Cheryl Tiegs was among the celebrities who attended the star-studded opening of Erica's disco.

At a benefit engagement at the Chateau, Erica introduced pop star Stevie Wonder, who encouraged Pine Valley-ites to be sure they "Don't Drive Drunk."

In January 1982, Broadway's legendary Gwen Verdon portrayed Brandon Kingsley's uptight sister, Judith. Among her acquaintances were Palmer Cortlandt and Dr. Chuck Tyler.

Dashingly handsome race car driver Danny Sullivan gave Erica Kane driving tips during his May 1987 cameo appearance at the Montgomery Cup Ball.

When music professor Mark Dalton turned his attentions to song writing, he called upon his friends Melba Moore and Lesley Gore to perform one of his tunes.

Erica Kane welcomed talk-show hosts Regis Philbin, Kathie Lee Gifford and former Miss America Carolyn Sapp to a Pine Valley society bash.

The Fans

Whenever she's in need of financial advice, Erica consults with her savvy friends, Capital Cities/ABC CEO Tom Murphy and one of America's wealthiest gentlemen, Omaha investor Warren Buffett.

DOM DELUISE

"When they asked me if I'd like to do the show, I said, 'Oh, yeah, great! I'm going to enjoy being on because a lot of my friends are big fans, and they can watch me.' In my scene, there was a guy with a donkey, so I kept saying, 'Get your ass off my street!' There was a real donkey there, so I could get away with that line! I had fun, and I was really surprised by how many people saw it. Not just my friends, but people stopping me on the street, cab drivers yelling to me. It was amazing!"

Livia Frye's old friend Peabo Bryson joined the bride in a duet during the reception following her wedding to Tom Cudahy.

Larger-than-life funny man Dom DeLuise portrayed a wacky traffic cop during Hayley Vaughan's Caribbean kidnapping in 1991.

In 1984, Adam Chandler wooed and wowed Erica Kane by introducing her to New York City Mayor Ed Koch.

Singer Jimmy Buffett stopped into Foxy's Bar in Center City to sample the margaritas and chat with Benny Sago.

JIMMY BUFFETT

"On the morning of my cameo, I got to spend the day in Pine Valley behind the scenes and even sat on Nina's bed. It was a blast. Then I had to go to work. My big scene came in Foxy's, which was the kind of place I felt comfortable in. Good type casting, too. I played a bar fly glued to a pin ball machine and had a brief conversation with Benny about his gambling as he went looking for Estelle. My only regret was not meeting Billy Clyde, who still is one of the most memorable characters I have ever seen. It was too short a stay, and I was much too quickly back out on Columbus Avenue into what passes for the real world."

In 1981, Erica Kane was practically floating on air when five beefy football players from the New Orleans Saints hoisted her aloft while shooting a cosmetics commercial inside the Superdome.

Long before she became a national celebrity, Baltimore newscaster Oprah Winfrey popped up in a quick cameo when she introduced herself to Pine Valley's Pamela Kingsley. Blink and you missed her!

PATRICK WAYNE
"Working on *All My Children* proved to be a very enlightening experience. Never having worked in daytime prior to this stint, I never really appreciated the work involved in putting a show on each day. For starters, you do a new play every day. And when you start rehearsal in the morning, the final product may be substantially different from the script you were given to learn the night before. My hat goes off to these performers and the life they bring to these shows on such short notice. They're worthy of my highest esteem."

In 1990, Erica went on a cruise, and in typical fashion, she flirted with Captain Nil Lindstrom, played by guest star Patrick Wayne. Soon after setting sail, the Captain proposed to a flabbergasted Miss Kane! She graciously declined.

Gossip maven Virginia Graham was a frequent guest, playing a nosy, busybody talk show host—herself!

1989's Mrs. Homemaker USA pageant was emceed by the king of beauty contests himself, Bert Parks. Bert posed with contest winner Cecily Kelly and warbled those memorable words, "There she is, Mrs. Homemaker USA."

VIRGINIA GRAHAM

"Working on *All My Children* was hysterical fun! One of my funniest scenes was the day Erica was about to marry Adam. I was the gossip columnist and they wouldn't let me into the wedding, so I beat up Adam's henchman and broke in shouting, 'What's going on here?' People wrote from all over the country that it was the funniest show they'd ever seen."

On Broadway and the silver screen, he showed us "how to succeed in business without really trying." On *All My Children*, gambling was Robert Morse's business when he portrayed Benny's bookie, Harry.

Fans

Without question, Carol Burnett is *All My Children*'s number-one fan. The comedienne rarely, if ever, misses an episode of the show, and if she has to miss it, she'll do whatever she can to catch up. In 1986, she joined the cast for two weeks as Verla Grubbs, the long-lost daughter of Langley Wallingford.

CAROL BURNETT

"One summer, my girls, my husband Joe Hamilton and I went to Europe. We were in London, Paris, Rome, and all the way through the trip, my PR guy Rick Ingersoll, who knew how much I would miss *All My Children*, sent me a telegram every week about what was going on in Pine Valley. It would read something like 'Erica is doing blah-blah-blah. Palmer Cortlandt has done this to Nina, etc.' Well, finally we're at Lake Como and very early one morning, there's a knock at our door. The hotel manager is standing there white as a ghost with this telegram in his hand. He says, 'We have some very bad news. Erica has been kidnapped by Adam. Someone else is in a coma from an auto accident. And another person is in jail and looking for a lawyer.' I practically fell down, I was laughing so hard."

Fan-tastic Tales

Thousands of All My Children *viewers have had the once-in-a-lifetime opportunity to meet their favorite stars in the flesh. How do the actors feel about greeting their adoring public? Check out these fan-tastic encounters.*

Ingrid Rogers (Taylor Roxbury Cannon): I must be doing a good job of playing a bad girl because a woman once came up to me on the subway and said, "You're such a horrible child on the show!" I took that as a real compliment!

James Patrick Stuart (Will Cortlandt): I went out for a night on the town with a couple of buddies, and we ended up at a strip club. I said, "I can't go in there. I might get recognized!" Well, they convinced me to go in, and, of course, the lady right on stage looked down at me and said with a bump, "Aren't you on *All My Children*?" I wanted to crawl under the table!

James Kiberd (Trevor Dillon): I haven't met too many people who are as wild and crazy as Trevor— that is, until I went to my first pro football game. There were 74,108 screaming fans there, and talk about excited! I mean, the whole crowd was shouting, "Trevor!" I took one look around and couldn't help but yell, "Yeah! Party!"

Debbi Morgan (Dr. Angie Hubbard): In an airport waiting area, I was hiding out behind a hat and a pair of sunglasses when I noticed a woman who was dressed just like me and was acting just like me. We peeked at each other once—then again. Finally, she came over, whipped off her sunglasses and said, "Hi, I'm Whitney Houston, and I know exactly what you're doing—because I'm doing the same thing!"

Michael E. Knight (Tad Martin): When I first joined the show, fans were always confusing me with Michael Knight, the character David Hasselhoff played on *Knightrider*. You know, the guy with the talking car. I got a bunch of letters from kids asking me for a picture of that damn car. So I sent them one of me standing in front of a beat-up Volkswagen. It didn't talk, but it got great mileage!

Gillian Spencer (Daisy Cortlandt): *All My Children* fans have never forgotten Daisy's precious cat, Bonkers. Or should I say, our producer's cat, because the kitty in question was actually the pride and joy of our executive producer at the time, Jackie Babbin. Years after Bonkers had gone to cat heaven, people are still asking about him. And wouldn't you know it, that cat got more fan mail than I did!

Jean LeClerc (Jeremy Hunter): I once sold myself at auction to two wonderful women from Chicago who bought me for $6,000 apiece! The Cystic Fibrosis Foundation gladly took their money, and they took a first-class trip to New York for a lavish lunch with me. Imagine—$6,000! I never realized I was such an expensive date!

James Patrick Stuart (Will Cortlandt): Because of *All My Children*, I was invited to a party at the White House in 1991. I was a nervous wreck. Though I must admit, I acted pretty cool when I met President and Mrs. Bush. But when I bumped into Supreme Court Justice Sandra Day O'Connor at the buffet, I said something idiotic like, "Uh, you look familiar. Are you a friend of my mom's?"

James Mitchell (Palmer Cortlandt): In real life, I'm recognized all the time by police officers, cabbies and athletes. Though my favorite was the man who came up to me on the street and said, "I can't believe it. You're Palmer Quartermaine from *One Life To Live!*" I just smiled because, well, he was close enough.

 **Lauren Holly** (Julie Chandler): On the show, Julie had lots of run-ins with Cecily, played by Rosa Nevin. Off-camera we were the best of buddies, but try telling that to the little old woman who followed the two of us through Macy's. Everywhere we went, she was right on our tail. Finally, she got me all alone and whispered, "What are you doing with that awful Cecily? Don't you know she's trying to steal your boyfriend?" I just thanked her for the tip, and she happily went on her way.

Mark LaMura (Mark Dalton): When the storyline called for Mark to become addicted to drugs, I set out to make my portrayal as realistic as possible. To prepare for the role, I spent several weeks undercover observing the scene in New York's seediest areas. I did my best not to get noticed, but one night, a cop pulled me aside and asked, "Hey, ain't you on *All My Kids*? We watch you every day at the station house." What a way to blow your cover!

Candice Earley (Donna Beck Tyler): Playing a teenage prostitute had its embarrassing moments. One night, I was innocently walking home from the studio when a cop stopped and arrested me—he swore I was a want-  ed prostitute. Believe me, it took a lot of convincing to prove to him that I wasn't a hooker—I just played one on TV!

James Kiberd (Trevor Dillon): When Trevor was a cop, it came in handy for me. Like the time a real policeman pulled me over for speeding. I was prepared to have the book thrown at me, but instead, the cop took one look at me and said, "Are you in a rush, Officer Dillon?" And he let me off with just a warning!

Matt Borlenghi (Brian Bodine): For the entire time I was on the show, I could never get used to the fans treating me like I was somebody special. It just blew me away—especially when they asked for my autograph. One girl told me that she was just a typ- ist and I told her, "Yeah, but I'm sure you're a better typist than I'll ever be. So why don't we trade signatures?" I've been doing it ever since, and you oughta see my autograph collection.

 **Dondre T. Whitfield** (Terrence Fry): I was shocked to be invited to appear on a TV talk show dealing with people who have secret crushes. I told them I didn't have a secret crush on anyone, but they explained that someone had a crush on me! My secret admirer turned out to be a nice girl named Tisha who knew everything I had ever done in my career, which was kind of freaky. Later, I met her mom, and we all went out to dinner and had a great time.

 **Susan Lucci** (Erica Kane): When we took the show on the road to the beautiful city of Budapest, I never expected to be recognized because the Hungarians have never seen *All My Children*—or so I thought. I was barely off the plane when a woman came rushing up to me asking, "Is it you—Susan Lucci?" It seems that one of her favorite things to do when she's in the States is to watch me on *All My Children*. So after a big hug, my new Hungarian friend shuffled me through the airport so her friends could meet a "famous American television actress!"

Alan Dysert (Sean Cudahy): The first time I left the show in 1981, I moved to Nashville to start my own music publishing company. But I could never escape Sean! You see, every time I walked into a record executive's office for a  "high-powered" meeting, the secretary would practically attack me. I think every secretary in Nashville is an *All My Children* fanatic.

 **Sarah Michelle Gellar** (Kendall Hart): On a plane, a flight attendant came running up to me said, "Oh my god! I love you. You're the best thing on the show!" And as I was signing an autograph for her, she told me how sorry she was that my show had been canceled. Canceled? "Yeah, *Life Goes On*. It's such a good show." I probably should have signed Kellie

Martin's name because that's who she thought I was—one of the stars of *Life Goes On*. I was so embarrassed, but as they say—life goes on!

Ray MacDonnell (Dr. Joe Martin): I was riding the crosstown bus, and a woman with a hacking cough sidled up to me and asked me for medical advice. She knew I was an actor, but insisted that after all these years of playing a doctor, I must know a remedy for her ailment. Well, I leave medical care to the experts—though I actually felt a twinge of guilt that I wasn't able to help her.

Jill Larson (Opal Cortlandt): In recent years, Opal has mellowed, but she'll always be a bit tasteless because the viewers won't have it any other way. In fact, there's an organized club of *All My Children* fans dedicated to that very cause. Anytime our costume designer tries to dress me in something sophisticated, they write in urging that we KEEP OPAL TACKY!

Dondre T. Whitfield (Terrence Frye): If you ever see me driving on the highway, just keep on going. The other night, I'm driving along and this car comes right over to my side at about 65 miles an hour and one of the females in the car says, "Aren't you Terrence? Oh, my God!" And her car was swerving all over the road. I quickly said, "See ya!" and pulled out of there quick! Man, it's dangerous being a "celebrity!"

James Kiberd (Trevor Dillon): At the University of Nebraska, I walked by a group of students who were watching *All My Children* in the student union. So I decided to have a little fun. I pulled up a chair and waited for them to notice me. I waited…and waited, but their eyes were glued to the tube—not to me! I grunted and coughed until someone finally looked over—and shrieked "Trevor!" Boy, was that fun!

Paige Turco: My character, Lanie, was a talented pianist—which was a bit difficult for me because I'd never played piano in my life. But I was convinced I could fake it. Just play some music, and *don't show my hands!* But I learned a quick lesson that you can't fool the audience. I received a letter from an eagle-eyed fan who noticed that I was looking at the wrong keys.

Alan Dysert (Sean Cudahy): I used to get great fan letters, especially when Sean was really bad. One lovely mom from Cleveland wrote me to say that if I ever came near her daughter, she'd "tan my hide!" I'm not sure what that means, but I've steered clear of the entire state of Ohio ever since.

Ray MacDonnell (Dr. Joe Martin): Joe's been dispensing advice for 25 years, so sometimes fans will write me with advice. Like the fan who told me to check into Dr. Chuck Tyler's medical records because in one short summer, Chuck went from folding towels as a hospital orderly to performing brain surgery as a full-fledged doctor. Well, they say anything can happen in Pine Valley—and it usually does!

The Fans

Chapter 6

AMC TRIVIA

There's so much to know about the making of *All My Children* and all that's happened on the show since its premiere 25 years ago: How and why it was created by the legendary Agnes Nixon, bits about the characters and the actors who portray them, facts about the fictional town of Pine Valley, the real stories behind the legends and myths, and plot points from long-ago. With the trivia list that follows, you can learn all you wanted to know about *All My Children*. Or take the quiz and test your knowledge of the show!

A testament to the consistently high caliber performances of its actors and the quality plots and dialogue of its talented writers, is the fact that *All My Children* has received more than 35 Emmy awards as well as hundreds of nominations—including fourteen for Susan Lucci (Erica Kane) and seven for James Mitchell (Palmer Cortlandt)—during its first quarter century on the air. With his four awards, David Canary (Adam and Stuart Chandler) has won more Emmys than any other actor. A complete listing of *All My Children*'s Emmy honors follows, along with some of the winners' touching and gracious acceptance speeches.

If it's not on the page, it's not on the stage. Credit for *All My Children*'s riveting stories and richly drawn characters must go to the talented staff of writers, led by Agnes Nixon (front row, second from left.) In 1988, the entire team posed together after winning the Emmy for Outstanding Writing.

All My Children premiered on ABC on January 5, 1970.

Agnes Nixon created the storyline bible for *All My Children* several years before its sister show *One Life To Live,* but that show premiered two years before *All My Children.* After the successful premiere of *One Life,* she submitted the concept of *AMC* to ABC.

The four original cast members who remain today are Mary Fickett (Ruth Martin), Ray MacDonnell (Dr. Joe Martin), Ruth Warrick (Phoebe Tyler Wallingford), and Susan Lucci (Erica Kane).

A total of 15–20 million television viewers watch *All My Children* every weekday.

Casting Director Judy Blye Wilson sifts through 5,000 photos and resumes per month from ambitious actors.

It costs nearly $30,000 to shoot one episode of *AMC.* This figure represents the use of the soap's New York City studio and the salaries of all the backstage technical personnel. Actors, writers and producers' salaries are extra.

Susan Lucci wears a size-4 dress.

The makeup department of *AMC* uses an average of a quart of foundation each month.

Most babies and toddlers on *AMC* are played by twins.

The *AMC* studio has 34 dressing rooms, including two large ones for extras.

At 6'3", Walt Willey (Jackson Montgomery) is the tallest actor on the show.

On January 5, 1995, *AMC* taped its 6450th episode.

Originally a half-hour show, *AMC* went to the current hour length in April 1977.

Before joining *AMC,* Dondre Whitfield (Terrence Frye) was known to prime-time audiences for his role as Robert on *The Cosby Show.*

Susan Lucci is half-Italian and half-Swedish.

Ruth Warrick (Phoebe) made her film debut in *Citizen Kane* with Orson Welles (1940) and went on to appear in 29 more movies until 1952.

The character Ceara Connor, formerly played by Genie Francis, was named after Agnes Nixon's oldest granddaughter Ceara, who is in her early twenties. Ceara is a old Irish name meaning "woman with a spear."

Constructing a new set costs anywhere from $5,000–60,000.

One of the oldest props on the show is a framed photo of Kay Campbell, who played Kate Martin until her death in 1985.

One of the most expensive props ever used by *AMC* was a Lear jet on which Erica Kane and Jackson Montgomery once flew—and crashed. To show the "wreckage," a real plane was purchased by the show and banged up.

When *AMC* moved from one studio to another, Adam Chandler's massive desk broke and had to be reconstructed from its shattered pieces.

The food consumed by the characters on the show is real. Every dish is ordered in triplicate, in case retakes are required.

35 stunt people were used in the elaborately staged tornado that struck Pine Valley in the summer of 1994, with ten video cameras recording the action.

Until 1994, the oldest set still in use was the Martin living room, which remained virtually unchanged until its destruction in the tornado.

Every *AMC* script is divided into six acts and a prologue.

Richard Shoberg (Tom Cudahy) is a talented singer/guitarist and has written a number of songs.

The exterior of Pine Valley University is really New Jersey's Princeton University.

The exterior of Cortlandt Manor is a real mansion called Waveny in New Canaan, Connecticut.

James Kiberd (Trevor Dillon) is married in real life to Susan Keith, who plays Shana Vochek on *Loving,* where they met when he was playing Mike Donovan on that show.

There is an average two- or three-week lag between the taping of an episode and the date it's aired on TV.

Among the film credits for Cady McClain (Dixie Martin) are the role of Peter O'Toole's daughter Tess in *My Favorite Year.*

Timothy Busfield, who played Elliot Weston on *thirtysomething,* was once an extra on *AMC.*

Ed O'Neill of *Married with Children* once played a private eye hired by Palmer Cortlandt.

Felicity LaFortune (Laurel Montgomery) began her career as an opera singer. Vocal cord problems cut short her budding musical career.

Tonya Pinkins (Livia Frye) won a Tony Award for her starring role in the Broadway musical, *Jelly's Last Jam.*

Walt Willey (Jackson Montgomery) is a stand-up comic who has headlined in hundreds of comedy clubs across America.

The typical *AMC* script is 80 pages long.

Mary Fickett (Ruth Martin) was the hostess of a network morning show called *Calendar* in the early 1960s.

A popular brand of frozen fish sticks are used in place of chicken fingers at the Chicken Shack.

It takes about 450 lights each day to tape one episode of *AMC.*

There are an average of 45 different music cues used in each show.

Jill Larson (Opal Cortlandt) played Ursula Blackwell, *One Life To Live's* mad bomber, in the late Eighties.

When the outside of the Pine Valley Inn is shown, you're actually seeing the exterior of the Governor's mansion in Trenton, New Jersey.

David Canary (Adam/Stuart Chandler) played Candy in the popular Sixties western series, *Bonanza.*

When a cast member leaves *AMC,* his or her photo isn't removed from the show's opening until the official end of the actor's contract cycle.

According to a *USA Today* survey, *AMC* is the TV program most often taped on VCRs in the United States.

Over 250 people work on the show.

The real name of the character Langley Wallingford (Louis Edmonds) is Lenny Wlasuk. In real life, Wlasuk is the last name of a woman that used to live next door to Agnes Nixon in Syracuse, New York.

All regular cast members are dressed head to toe by *AMC's* costume department, but extras wear their own clothing.

AMC is shown not only in England, but in France, Israel and Italy, where it's dubbed into the native languages.

Robin Mattson (Janet) is a gourmet cook. In 1993, she completed the Gastronomic Directives Course at the Los Angeles International Culinary Institute.

James Kiberd (Trevor Dillon) was honored with the prestigious Danny Kaye Award at the National Convention of the U.S. Committee for UNICEF, for his *Knots for Tots* program. Fans send ties for Trevor to wear on the show, which are then personally autographed by James and sold. All proceeds go to UNICEF.

The six men who married Erica are Jeff Martin, Phil Brent, Tom Cudahy, Adam Chandler, Travis Montgomery and Dimitri Marick.

It takes an average of fifteen minutes for each performer to be made up for the camera.

Dr. Clader, the doctor who delivers all of Pine Valley's babies, is the actual name of Agnes Nixon's personal obstetrician.

In Italy, *AMC* is called *La Valle dei Pini.*

Pies and cakes on the Valley Inn dessert cart are fabulous fakes purchased from a distributor in California. Real desserts wouldn't hold up under the hot studio lights.

In 1994, Kelly Ripa (Hayley Vaughan) became co-host of *Music Scoop,* a syndicated music video series.

One of the costume department's most radical alterations was the wedding dress for Opal Cortlandt (Jill Larson), which was cut down from a larger size, and excess beads were taken off the front to make it look simpler.

Eileen Herlie (Myrtle Fargate) is a distinguished Shakespearean actress. She played the role of Gertrude in Shakespeare's *Hamlet* twice: opposite Sir Laurence Olivier in the movie version (1948) and with Richard Burton in the 1964 Broadway production.

Due to union regulations, when a door is needed for a new set, it can't be bought in a store, but must be constructed by the show. Each door can cost anywhere from $2,500–3,000.

All the show's props are stored in a cavernous warehouse where everything from Laura Cudahy's cemetery headstone to copies of Erica's autobiography, *Raising Kane,* are found.

James Mitchell (Palmer Cortlandt) danced in the famous dream sequence of the classic movie musical *Oklahoma!*

There are seven commercial breaks during an hour-long episode of *AMC.*

AMC constructs at least 1,000 new sets every year, most of them temporary.

In 1991, Ruth Warrick (Phoebe) received her certification as a licensed metaphysical teacher from Unity School of Practical Christianity in Lees Summit, Missouri.

For its socially relevant storylines, *AMC* has received awards from the Juvenile Diabetes Association, The Wilmer Eye Clinic, The Reye's Syndrome Foundation and the Alliance for Gay Artists in the Entertainment Industry.

AMC receives approximately 3,000 letters a month, 2,000 of them for the actors.

Top mail-getters among actors varies according to what's happening on the show, but Susan Lucci (Erica) and James Kiberd (Trevor) consistently receive boxloads of fan mail.

Erica Kane once claimed to have attended the famous 1969 Woodstock rock concert.

The most famous *AMC* myth: that Bobby, Joe Martin's teenage son, went upstairs to wax his skis in 1970 and was never heard from or seen again. In truth, he went away to camp.

The *AMC* costume department buys five dozen new pairs of stockings a week.

Though she has put her stamp on the role, Julia Barr didn't create the character Brooke English. It was originated by Elissa Leeds, who later played Frisco's manager, Steffi Brands, on *General Hospital.* At that time, Julia was starring on *Ryan's Hope* as mob princess Reenie Szabo.

AMC's Executive Producer Felicia Minei Behr met her husband Bob 25 years ago when she was associate producer and he was a cameraman on the show.

Winsor Harmon (Del Henry) was born in Crowley, Louisiana, at the exact moment that President John F. Kennedy was assassinated.

Christopher Lawford (Charlie Brent) is the son of the late Peter Lawford and Patricia Kennedy Lawford.

In high school, Winsor Harmon watched *AMC* every day. During the summers, he'd tape the show, then get together with friends to see what schemes Erica, Palmer and Adam were up to.

Julia Barr (Brooke English) once played Erica Kane. When David Canary tested for the role of Adam, Susan Lucci wasn't available, so Julia stepped in and played Erica in an audition scene with Adam.

The costume department doesn't make the actors' clothing. They buy all the outfits from department stores and boutiques.

Grant Aleksander (Alec McIntyre) and his actress wife Sherry Ramsey are active members of People for the Ethical Treatment of Animals (PETA) and the nurturing owners of many cats and dogs.

Ingrid Rogers (Taylor Cannon Barnes) appeared in the feature film *Carlito's Way* opposite Al Pacino, Sean Penn and Penelope Ann Miller.

Mrs. Valentine (Alyce Webb), Phoebe Wallingford's seldom seen housekeeper, was named after the housekeeper of a friend of Agnes Nixon.

Two *AMC* associate directors, Shirley Simmons and Barbara Martin Simmons, are sisters-in law.

Tad and Dixie's favorite song is "You are My Sunshine." He once gave his beloved wife a music box that played the tune.

Agnes Nixon derived the name Pine Valley from her family's own home on the Main Line in Philadelphia. "The name of our house is Pine Cottage," says Agnes. "There are pines everywhere on the land, and we live in the Penn Valley. So I put them together."

At fourteen, Sydney Penny (Julia Santos) appeared in the miniseries *The Thorn Birds* as young Meggie.

Erica and Travis's first wedding ceremony was unofficial. While hiding from the evil Dr. Damon Lazarre, they married themselves in a secret cellar vault (1987).

Richard Shoberg (Tom Cudahy) played football at Michigan's Albion College, but after getting battered and beaten for a year, he decided acting was a much safer game.

Julia Roberts once auditioned for a role on *AMC.* She didn't get it.

Shannon Doherty *(Beverly Hills, 90210)* screen-tested but failed in her bid to win a role on *AMC.*

Erica Kane has the largest wardrobe of any character on *AMC.*

Ray MacDonnell has been a leading soap star for over 35 years. Before joining the original cast of *All My Children,* he was a fixture on *Edge Of Night* for eight years as family man Phil Capice.

Dr. Maria Santos was originally scheduled for a story with Trevor Dillon. Only after the writers witnessed the tremendous on-screen chemistry between actress Eva LaRue (Maria) and John Callahan (Edmund Grey) were storyline plans altered to create a love story for the duo.

The costume department stocks 125 wedding bands.

The rock band Urge Overkill are big fans of the show. In 1994, they recorded a hit song named after their favorite character: "Erica Kane, Erica Kane."

Pine Valley, which is on Pennsylvania's Main Line, is across the river from *One Life To Live*'s Llanview, which is located near the Chestnut Hill area outside of Philadelphia.

Every *AMC* script is available on microfilm at the Annenberg School of Communications library at the University of Pennsylvania in Philadelphia.

Sarah Michelle Gellar (Kendall Hart) was a competitive ice skater for three years, placing third in a New York State regional competition.

Eva LaRue (Dr. Maria Santos) co-hosted *The New Candid Camera* with Dom DeLuise.

During taping, a painter sits just offstage at all times to touch up smudges or scuff marks on the sets.

According to a national survey, *AMC* is the favorite soap of the players in the National Football League (NFL).

The All My Children Quiz

1. The bullet that killed Jesse Hubbard was meant for someone else. Who was the intended victim?
2. What is Palmer Cortlandt's real name?
3. Who was the real mother of Cliff's son, Bobby?
4. Who is Jamal's natural father?
5. Where did Adam and Dixie enjoy their first night of illicit passion?
6. Angie and Jesse Hubbard were once part owners of what Pine Valley establishment?
7. Who turned out to be Bonnie McFadden's secret friend, Willie?
8. Who suffered a severe facial laceration during Pine Valley's devastating tornado of '94?
9. How did Mimi Reed determine that Danielle wasn't Lucas's daughter but Derek's?
10. When Erica stabbed Dimitri, whom did she really think she was attacking?
11. Who was Benny Sago's first wife?
12. What was the name of Kate Martin's late husband?
13. What was the name of Erica's autobiography?
14. Where did Maria and Del first meet?
15. What was the name of Daisy's cat?
16. What phony first name did Erica use when she applied for a job as a Sea City waitress?
17. To what foreign land did a grief-stricken Erica retreat after Mike Roy's tragic death?
18. Where did Travis Montgomery move when he left Pine Valley?
19. What is the name of Timmy Dillon's dog?
20. What animal bit Erica when she was stranded in the wild after a plane crash?
21. Who had fun playing a sexy French maid named Corinne?
22. Who was the bartender at Foxy's?
23. What does Opal call her special chicken recipe?
24. What is Hayley's nickname for her Uncle Trevor?
25. By what nickname does Trevor call Hayley?
26. What is Tad and Dixie's favorite fast food?
27. What was Tad wearing the first time he proposed to Dixie?
28. What is Tad and Dixie's favorite sunny song?
29. Whose murder did Tad witness when he was a boy?
30. What magical Disney song played in the background the first time Charlie and Hayley made love?
31. Who collapsed at Natalie and Jeremy's 1988 wedding?

32. What is the name of the magazine on which both Brooke and Erica have served as editor?
33. Palmer is Ross Chandler's father. Who was Ross's mother?
34. Why was Janet Green's face covered with bandages for several weeks?
35. What was the name of Tom Cudahy's sports bar?
36. What sneaky trick did Adam pull on Erica when they were getting divorced?
37. Which four characters have been in Pine Valley since the day *All My Children* began?
38. Palmer and Adam grew up in what West Virginia town?
39. What is the name of Dixie and Del's father?
40. What near-tragedy happened to Brooke while investigating the site of the proposed Willow Lake Retirement Community?
41. Who fathered Dixie's son?
42. Which popular character had a twin sister named Karen Parker?
43. What was Laurel Banning Montgomery's real name?
44. When they first fell in love, why didn't Jeremy and Erica make love for months?
45. Which football quarterback once asked Erica for a date?
46. Who founded the Glamorama beauty salon?
47. Why did Verla Grubbs (Carol Burnett) come to Pine Valley?
48. What shocking discovery did Edmund and Maria make on their honeymoon in Budapest?
49. What did Eric Kane do for a living?
50. What is name of Pine Valley's daily newspaper?
51. When Erica found her long-lost father, what was he doing for a living?
52. Why was Kendall Hart sent to jail?
53. What medical need caused Del Henry to seek the help of his sister, Dixie?
54. Myra Sloan was more than Palmer's housekeeper. What was their relationship?
55. In what sleazy bar did Palmer work while suffering from amnesia?
56. What was found at the bottom of Palmer Cortlandt's pond?
57. Who romanced Erica while she was a Sea City waitress?

58. Why did Nico and Cecily leave Pine Valley?

59. Where did Edmund Grey locate his old friend, Peggy Moody?

60. Who runs The Boutique?

61. Where did Myrtle and Langley meet?

62. What was the name of Phoebe's newspaper advice column?

63. What is the name of Phoebe's seldom-seen society friend?

64. Who kidnapped Erica in Budapest?

65. Who schemed successfully to replace Erica Kane as CEO of Enchantment Cosmetics?

66. Who defended Erica Kane when she was charged with attempting to murder Dimitri?

67. What Napa Valley winery does Tad operate?

68. How did Tad lose his memory?

69. What was Mimi Reed's high-flying hobby?

70. At first, why didn't Dimitri believe that he was Anton's father?

71. Where did Janet Green keep her sister Natalie prisoner?

72. What kind of dogs does Palmer keep on the grounds of his estate?

73. Who shocked Pine Valley when she married Will Cortlandt?

74. Who married Tom Cudahy while she was in labor?

75. Who disguised himself as a hospital orderly and befriended an unsuspecting Natalie?

76. What was Mona Kane's first clue that Kendall Hart was Erica's daughter?

77. Which character had daytime television's first legal abortion?

78. For what medical reason did Travis and Barbara Montgomery conceive a second child?

79. Who left Tad a fortune and a winery in her will?

80. Why did Palmer deliver Opal's baby?

81. In his will, what piece of real estate did Hugo Marick leave his son Edmund?

82. Why did Laurel Banning spend so much time at the Smith Barry Institute?

83. What are the first names of Phoebe's two children?

84. Which notorious villain posed as John Henry, the owner of the Cyclops nightclub?

85. Who paid Tad to date Dottie Thornton?

86. How many men has Dixie Cooney married?

87. How many men has Phoebe Tyler married?

88. Who won the title, Man of Enchantment?

89. Ruth Martin once enjoyed a sizzling affair with a doctor. What was his name?

90. Why didn't Opal attend the funeral of her beloved daughter, Jenny?

91. When Natalie married Trevor, who was her maid of honor?

92. Attorney Paul Martin once traveled to *One Life To Live*'s Llanview to defend someone against murder charges. Who was Paul's client?

93. During his childhood, Charlie Brent was known by a different first name. What was it?

94. "Tad" is a nickname. What is Tad's first name?

95. Why did Erica and Travis seem so surprised moments after the birth of their daughter, Bianca?

96. Though she loved Tad, why did Hillary agree to marry Bob Georgia?

97. Who are Adam's two daughters?

98. Why did Nick Davis propose to Erica?

99. Can you name all five of Tom Cudahy's wives?

100. Who rejected Sean Cudahy at the altar?

1. John Remington (a.k.a. Remy)
2. Pete Cooney
3. Sybil Thorne
4. Alec McIntyre
5. In the Chandler boathouse
6. The Steampit disco
7. Stuart Chandler
8. Julia Santos
9. DNA testing
10. Richard Fields
11. Estelle La Tour
12. Henry
13. *Raising Kane*
14. In college
15. Bonkers
16. Sally
17. Tibet
18. Seattle, Washington
19. Harold
20. A snake
21. Erica
22. Hughie
23. Purdified Chicken
24. Porkchop
25. Tinkerbell
26. Chicken fingers
27. A bright yellow chicken costume
28. "You Are My Sunshine"
29. Mary Kennicott
30. "A Whole New World"
31. Natalie's ex-husband Palmer Cortlandt
32. *Tempo*
33. Adam Chandler's sister, Lottie
34. Janet had plastic surgery to give herself a new face.
35. The Goalpost
36. He sent his twin brother Stuart to the Caribbean to sign the divorce papers.
37. Erica, Phoebe, Ruth and Joe
38. Pigeon Hollow
39. Seabon Hunkle
40. She fell into quicksand.

41. Adam Chandler
42. Cindy Chandler
43. Carla Benton
44. Jeremy had taken a holy vow of celibacy.
45. Boomer Esiason
46. Opal Gardner
47. She was searching for her long-lost father, revealed to be Langley Wallingford.
48. They learned that Anton is Dimitri's son.
49. He was a movie director.
50. The Bulletin
51. He was Barney, a circus clown.
52. Kendall committed perjury during Erica's attempted murder trial.
53. He needed a kidney transplant.
54. Myra was Palmer's mother-in-law.
55. Foxy's
56. Silver Kane's body
57. Dave Gillis (a.k.a. Steven Andrews)
58. They went on a world tour when Cecily won the Miss Homemaker contest.
59. In a nursing home
60. Myrtle Fargate
61. At a carnival, where they both worked
62. Dear Aggy
63. Juanita Ramsey
64. Edmund Grey
65. Alec McIntyre
66. Livia Frye and Trevor Dillon
67. Orsini Vineyards
68. He fell off a bridge after a fight with Billy Clyde.
69. Piloting planes
70. He didn't remember sleeping with Anton's mother, Corvina. She seduced him while he was drunk.
71. In the bottom of a well
72. Dobermans
73. Hayley Vaughan

74. Barbara Montgomery
75. Carter Jones
76. Mona noticed that Kendall had a birthmark exactly like the one on the baby Erica gave up for adoption.
77. Erica Kane
78. Travis and Barbara conceived a child as a bone marrow donor for their daughter Molly.
79. Nola Orsini
80. A snowstorm prevented them from going to the hospital.
81. The Wildwind Mansion
82. Her autistic daughter, Lily, was being treated there.
83. Lincoln and Anne
84. Billy Clyde Tuggle
85. Dottie's mother, Edna
86. Four —Adam, Tad, Craig, Brian
87. Three—Charles Tyler, Langley Wallingford, Wade Matthews
88. Charlie Brent
89. Dr. David Thornton
90. She was somewhere in the Australian outback and couldn't be located.
91. Natalie's best friend, Donna Beck Tyler
92. Victoria Lord Buchanan
93. Philip
94. Thaddeus
95. They were expecting a boy!
96. Because she believed Bob was dying of a fatal blood disease and wanted to make his last days happy ones.
97. Skye and Hayley
98. Nick proposed to a deathly ill Erica to give her reason to live. He later reneged.
99. Erica, Brooke, Skye, Barbara, Livia
100. Cecily Davidson

All My Children's *Emmy Awards*

A Complete Listing
1973–1994

𝕿𝖍𝖗𝖔𝖚𝖌𝖍 𝟏𝟗𝟗𝟒, *All My Children* has been honored with over 35 of the prestigious golden statuettes and hundreds of nominations, including fourteen for Susan Lucci (Erica Kane) and seven for James Mitchell (Palmer Cortlandt). With his four awards, David Canary has won more Emmys than any other actor. So here's to the winners!

Award Year: 1972–1973
Outstanding Achievement By Individuals In Daytime Drama
Winner: Mary Fickett

In 1973, *All My Children*'s Mary Fickett became the first daytime soap actor to receive an Emmy for her role as Ruth Martin. Ms. Fickett's award, given for Outstanding Achievement by Individuals in a Daytime Drama Series, was presented during the primetime ceremony held in Los Angeles. Strangely, Ms. Fickett was the only actor up for the award. Four directors and two set designers were her competition.

Award Year: 1979–1980
Outstanding Performance By An Actress In A Supporting Role
Winner: Francesca James as Kelly Cole

Award Year: 1979–1980
Outstanding Performance By An Actor In A Supporting Role
Winner: Warren Burton as Eddie Dorrance

Award Year: 1979–1980
Outstanding Achievement In Technical Excellence

Winners: Joseph Solomito, Howard Zweig: *Technical Directors;* Lawrence Hammond, Robert Ambrico, Dianne Cates–Cantrell, Christopher N. Mauro, Larry Strack, Vincent Senatore: *Electronic Cameras;* Albin S. Lemanski: *Audio Engineer;* Len Walas: *Video Engineer;* Diana Wenman, Jean Dadario: *Associate Directors;* Roger Haenelt, John L. Grella: *Videotape Editors;* Irving Robbin, Jim Reichert: *Music Composers;* Teri Smith: *Music Director*

Award Year: 1979–1980
Outstanding Achievement In Design Excellence
Winners: William Mickley: *Scenic Designer;* William Itkin, Donna Larson, Mel Handelsman: *Lighting Directors;* Carol Luiken: *Costume Designer;* Sylvia Lawrence: *Makeup Designer;* Michael Huddle: *Hair Designer;* Hy Bley: *Graphic Designer*

Award Year: 1980–1981
National Academy Of Television Arts And Sciences Trustees Award
Individual: Agnes Nixon

At the Eighth Annual Daytime Emmy Awards in 1981, *All My Children*'s creator, Agnes Nixon, was given the prestigious National Academy of Television Arts and Sciences Trustees Award. In presenting the award, Barbara Walters noted that Ms. Nixon was both the first writer and the first woman to be so honored by the Academy.

Award Year: 1980–1981
Outstanding Achievement In Technical Excellence
Winners: Joseph Solomito and Howard Zweig: *Technical Directors;* Lawrence Hammond, Dianne Cates–Cantrell, Robert Ambrico, Christopher Mauro, Larry Strack, Salvatore Augugliaro, Vincent Senatore,

Thomas Mcgrath: *Electronic Cameras;* Len Walas: *Senior Video Engineer;* Albin S. Lemanski, Peter Bohm, Charles Elsen: *Senior Audio Engineers;* Barbara Wood: *Sound Effects Engineer;* Diana Wenman, Jean Dadarlo: *Associate Directors;* Roger Haenelt: *Videotape Editor*

Award Year: 1980–1981
Outstanding Individual Achievement In Any Area Of Creative Technical Crafts
Winners: Tobert Hoffman: *Technical Director, Remote;* Anthony Gambino, Lawrence Hammond: *Electronic Cameras*

Award Year: 1981–1982
Outstanding Actress In A Supporting Role
Winner: Dorothy Lyman as Opal Gardner

In the spring of 1982, Supporting Actress winner Dorothy Lyman received the first of two consecutive Emmys for her portrayal of wacky Opal Gardner. The following year, Dorothy became the first *All My Children* actress to receive the Outstanding Actress Award.

Award Year: 1981–1982
Outstanding Achievement In Technical Excellence
Winners: Joseph Solomito, Howard Zweig: *Technical Directors;* Diana Wenman, Jean Dadarlo, Barbara Martin Simmons: *Associate Directors;* Lawrence Hammond, Robert Ambrico, Larry Strack, Vincent Senatore, Jay Kenn, Trevor Thompson: *Electronic Cameras;* Len Walas: *Senior Video Engineer;* Al Lemanski, Charles Elsen: *Audio Engineers;* Roger Haenelt: *Videotape Editor;* Barbara Wood: *Sound Effects Engineer*

Award Year: 1982–1983
Outstanding Achievement In Design Excellence
Winners: William Mickley: *Scenic Designer;* William Itkin, Donna Larson, Donald Gavitt, Robert Griffin: *Lighting Directors;* Carol Luiken: *Costume Designer;* Sylvia Lawrence: *Makeup;* Scott Hersh: *Makeup Designers;* Richard Greene: *Hair;* Robert Chiu: *Hair Designers;* Teri Smith: *Music Director;* Sid Ramin: *Music Composer*

Award Year: 1982–1983
Outstanding Achievement In Technical Excellence
Winners: Howard Zweig, Henry Enrico Ferro: *Technical Directors;* Diana Wenman, Jean Dadario: *Associate Directors;* Lawrence Hammond, Robert

Ambrico, Trevor Thompson, Vincent Senatore, Robert Ballairs, Thomas French, Richard Westlein: *Electronic Cameras;* Len Walas: *Senior Video Engineer;* Fran Gertler, Kathryn Tucker–Bachelder: *Audio Engineers;* Roger Haenelt: *Videotape Editor;* Barbara Wood: *Sound Effects Engineer*

Award Year: 1982–1983
Outstanding Actor In A Supporting Role
Winner: Darnell Williams as Jesse Hubbard

Award Year: 1982–1983
Outstanding Actress In A Daytime Drama
Winner: Dorothy Lyman as Opal Gardner

Award Year: 1983–1984
Special Classification Of Outstanding Individual Achievement
Winners: Paul Colton, Jack Hughes: *Audio Mixers*

Award Year: 1983–1984
Outstanding Individual Achievement In Any Area Of Creative Technical Crafts
Winner: Everett Melosh: *Lighting Director*

Award Year: 1983–84
Outstanding Achievement In Any Area Of Creative Technical Crafts
Winner: Dick Roes: *Audio*

Award Year: 1984–85
Outstanding Lead Actor In A Drama Series
Winner: Darnell Williams as Jesse Hubbard

Awarded his second Emmy in 1985, as Outstanding Lead Actor, an emotional Darnell Williams (Jesse Hubbard) seemed completely stunned as he thanked everyone who "helped me get a bookend." He concluded, "It's hard to thank everybody and think at this moment. I'm shaking, my shoes are wet, I'm gone! Thank God, thank everybody, thank you!" Two years earlier, Darnell won as Outstanding Supporting Actor.

Award Year: 1984–1985
Outstanding Drama Series Writing Team
Winners: Agnes Nixon, Clarice Blackburn, Lorraine Broderick, Carlina Della Pietra, Susan Kirshenbaum, Victor Miller, Elizabeth Page, Elizabeth Wallace, Wisner Washam, Mary K. Wells, Art Wallace, Jack Wood: *Writers*

Award Year: 1985–1986
Outstanding Lead Actor In A Drama Series

Winner: David Canary as Adam and Stuart Chandler

Award Year: 1985–86
Outstanding Younger Leading Man In A Drama Series
Winner: Michael E. Knight as Tad Martin

In 1986, Michael E. Knight (Tad Martin) posed backstage with fellow winner David Canary (Adam Chandler) after nervously accepting his first Emmy as Outstanding Younger Leading Man. The following year, Michael won again and offered this heartfelt thanks: "Since Tad Martin slithered out of town in December, I've had a lot of time to think about what the experience of working at *All My Children* meant for four years, and the only word I can come up with is wonderful. At the risk of sounding like a broken record, I would like to thank everybody at 101 W. 67th Street, upstairs and down, you're all fantastic. I miss you very much, and I love you all."

Award Year: 1986–1987
Outstanding Supporting Actress In A Drama Series
Winner: Kathleen Noone as Ellen Chandler

Award Year: 1986–1987
Outstanding Younger Leading Man In A Drama Series
Winner: Michael E. Knight as Tad Martin

Award Year: 1987–1988
Outstanding Lead Actor In A Drama Series
Winner: David Canary as Adam and Stuart Chandler

David Canary has won an unprecedented four Emmy Awards as Outstanding Lead Actor. Not expecting to win in 1988, he confessed to the audience that he hadn't prepared a speech. Still, he spoke eloquently as he related a unforgettable dream he'd had: "I did have an actor's nightmare the other night. I found myself in the wings of a theater, preparing to go on for my final recital, my final test, at a conservatory of music. I had one little piece of sheet music, it was a pop song. I couldn't find the sheet music, I couldn't remember the name of the song, and I was in my underwear. I woke up wondering why I had this nightmare of unpreparedness, and now I know!"

Award Year: 1987–1988
Outstanding Drama Series Writing Team
Winners: Agnes Nixon, Clarice Blackburn, Lorraine Broderick, Susan Kirshenbaum, Kathleen Klein, Karen L. Lewis, Victor Miller, Megan McTavish, Elizabeth Page, Peggy Sloane, Gillian Spencer,

Elizabeth Wallace, Wisner Washam, Mary K. Wells, Jack Wood: *Writers*

Award Year: 1987–1988
Outstanding Supporting Actress In A Drama Series
Winner: Ellen Wheeler as Cindy Parker

Her tender portrayal of AIDS victim Cindy Chandler earned Ellen Wheeler an Emmy as Outstanding Supporting Actress in 1988. The Emmy was Ellen's second. Earlier in her career, she had been awarded Outstanding Ingenue for her dual role as *Another World*'s Marley and Victoria Love.

Award Year: 1988–1989
Outstanding Supporting Actress In A Drama Series
Winner: Debbi Morgan as Angie Hubbard

Debbie Morgan (Dr. Angie Hubbard) won the Emmy for Outstanding Supporting Actress in 1989 and gave this heart-warming speech: 'I would like to dedicate this award to a man I feel is largely responsible for my being here today. I grew up in an environment where great successes, great achievements, were not always within the realm of possibility. But at sixteen this man cast me in a high school production of *A Midsummer Night's Dream* as the character of Puck. Thank you, Jim Mendenhall. It was on that stage and through this man that I found I could have bigger dreams, bigger ambitions, and yes, they were in the realm of possibility."

Award Year: 1988–1989
Outstanding Lead Actor In A Drama Series
Winner: David Canary as Adam and Stuart Chandler

"This is indeed one of the most humbling experiences of my life," said David Canary, accepting his second Emmy Award as Outstanding Lead Actor in 1989. He paid tribute to his colleagues, with "apologies to the so many hundreds of others of us who go out there everyday and dig in the trenches, and give it our best shot in daytime, because it's hard work. I don't deserve this any more than any of you, we all know that, but I've got it, and I'm thrilled to have it!"

Award Year: 1988–1989
Outstanding Achievement In Lighting Direction For A Drama Series

Winners: Donna Larson, Alan Blacher, Dennis M.
Size: *Lighting Director*

Award Year: 1989–1990
Outstanding Supporting
Actress In A Drama Series
Winner: Julia Barr as Brooke
English

Award Year:
1989–1990
Outstanding
Juvenile Female
In A Drama Series
Winner: Cady
McClain as
Dixie Martin

A tearful Outstanding
Juvenile Female win-
ner Cady McClain
(Dixie Cooney) looked
ravishing in 1990 as
she effusively thanked
her "family at *All My Children*...the most generous, loving,
giving, creative, inspiring people that I've ever worked with,"
and expressed her affection for co-star Michael Knight: "I
love you, I adore you, you make my day shine with
happiness!"

Julia Barr (Brooke English), winner of
the 1990 Emmy as Outstanding
Supporting Actress, looked coolly ele-
gant when she won her Emmy and spoke the immortal words,
"Life is not a soap opera, thank God!" She paid special tribute
to husband Richie, and daughter Allison, saying "Yes, mom
won the 'Enemy' Award."

Award Year: 1991–1992
Outstanding Drama Series
Winners: Felicia Minei Behr: *Executive Producer;*
Terry Cacavio, Thomas De Villiers: *Supervising
Producers;* Nancy Horwich: *Coordinating Producer*

Award Year: 1992–1993
Outstanding Lead Actor In A Drama Series
Winner: David Canary as Adam and Stuart Chandler

Award Year: 1989–1990
Outstanding Achievement In Costume Design For
A Drama Series
Winners: Carol Luiken, Charles Clute: *Costume
Designers*

Award Year: 1993–1994
Outstanding Drama Series
Winners: Felicia Minei Behr: *Executive Producer;*
Terry Cacavio, Thomas De Villiers: *Supervising
Producers;* Nancy Horwich: *Coordinating Producer*

In 1994, the Academy's top prize for Outstanding Drama Series was awarded for the second time to *All My Children*. The distinguished producers proudly clutching their Emmys are (from left) Thomas DeVilliers, Terry Cacavio, Executive Producer Felicia Minei
Behr and Nancy Horwich.

Chapter 7

THE *ALL MY CHILDREN* FAMILY

It takes hundreds of dedicated people to bring *All My Children* to life everyday. Over the past 25 years, hundreds more have passed through Pine Valley and contributed greatly to making the show the institution it has become.

The long list of characters who have appeared in Pine Valley and the actors who portray them (sometimes several per character) includes some now famous names, as well as some who are gone and dearly missed. And there are quite a few actors who created their roles and continue to play them after many years.

The current cast of *All My Children* is an international one and is quite distinguished in its theatrical credits. These actors continue to grow as artists by performing on the stage or in other theatrical productions. Their real life pursuits range from athletic activities to devoted charity work. The people who bring the characters on *All My Children* to life have interesting lives of their own.

And last, but certainly not least, are the production staff and crew, who work around the clock to put together the next cherished episode of *All My Children*—and make its millions of viewers so loyal.

The team that puts together *All My Children* every day was well represented when the late makeup artist Sylvia Lawrence, Agnes Nixon, Mary Fickett (Ruth), Ray McDonnell (Joe), Susan Lucci (Erica) and Ruth Warrick (Phoebe) all gathered to cut the cake as *All My Children* celebrated the taping of its 5000th show in 1989.

Character	Actor	Years	Character	Actor	Years
Dr. Russell Anderson	David Pendleton	1978–79	Ted Brent	Mark Dawson	1970
Dr. Russell Anderson	Charles M. Brown	1979–80	Ruth Brent Martin	Mary Fickett	1970–*present*
Steven Andrews	Nicholas Coster	1988–89	Candy Brown	Elizabeth Forsyth	1981–85
Mrs. Bancroft	Dana Ivey	1989	Yvonne Caldwell	Vanessa Bell	1984–85, 87
Laurel Banning	Kristen Jensen	1992–93	Taylor Roxbury Cannon	Ingrid Rogers	1992–*present*
Laurel Banning Montgomery	Felicity LaFortune	1993	Ship's Captain	Michael Landrun	1993
			Elizabeth Carlyle	Lisa Eichhorn	1987 –88
Judy Barclay	Maia Danziger	1983–84	Lynn Carson	Donna Pescow	1983
Tony Barclay	Brent Barrett	1983–84	Adam/Stuart Chandler	David Canary	1983–*present*
Mickey Barlowe	Marie Reynolds	1985	Adam (Jr.) Chandler	Kevin Alexander	1989–*present*
Lucas Barnes	Richard Lawson	1992–94	Julie Chandler	Stephanie Winters	1985–86
Gil Barrett	Stephen McNaughton	1983	Julie Chandler	Lauren Holly	1986–89
Dr. Angie Baxter Hubbard	Debbi Morgan	1982–90	Ross Chandler	Robert Gentry	1983–89
Dr. Angie Baxter Hubbard	Saundra Quarterman	1990–91	Scott Chandler	Philip Amelio	1988–91
Aunt Flora Baxter	Lynne Thigpen	1983	Charwoman	Elizabeth Taylor	1983
Les Baxter	Antonio Fargas	1982–83, 87	An–Li Chen	Irene Ng	1991
Pat Baxter	Lee Chamberlain	1982–91	An–Li Chen	Lindsey Price	1991–93
Donna Beck	Francesca Poston	1976	Dr. Clader	Bob Heitman	1982–*present*
Donna Beck Tyler Cortlandt Sago	Candice Earley	1976–92, 93	Gilles St. Clair	Gilles Kohler	1985–86
			Lt. Cody	Daniel von Bargen	1994–*present*
Mitch Beck	Brian Fitzpatrick	1987–88	Larry Colby	Joseph Warren	1983–84
Rusty Bennett	Obba Babatunde	1987	Liza Colby	Marcy Walker	1981–84
Jerry Benson	Steve Rankin	1980	Liza Colby	Alice Haining	1984
Denny Benton	Kale Browne	1993	Marian Colby	Jennifer Bassey	1983–85, 89
Detective Berniker	Michael Guido	1991–93	Kelly Cole Tyler	Francesca James	1978–80, 81, 83, 84, 86
Carl Blair	John K. Carroll	1977–79	Jamie Coles	Jason Lauve	1975
Carl Blair	Steven James	1979–84	Stacey Coles	Maureen Mooney	1975
Carl (Jr.) Blair	Billy Mack	1980–83	Wyatt Coles	Bruce Gray	1975
Brian Bodine	Gregory Gordon	1990–91	Nurse Collins	France Iann	1991
Brian Bodine	Matt Borlenghi	1991–93	Matt Connolly	Michael Tylo	1986–88
Brian Bodine	Brian Green	1993–94	Matt Connolly	Steve Fletcher	1989
Trask Bodine	Matt Servitto	1989–90	Ceara Connor	Genie Francis	1990–92
Kent Bogard	Michael Woods	1981	Claudia Connor	Bethel Leslie	1991
Kent Bogard	Lee Godart	1982	George Connor	Stephen Joyce	1991
Lars Bogard	William Blankenship	1982	Cookie	Andrea McArdle	1992
Lars Bogard	Robert Milli	1982–83	Dixie Cooney	Kari Gibson	1988
Lars Bogard	Jack Betts	1983	Dixie Cooney Martin	Cady McClain	1989–*present*
Detective Victor Borelli	Anthony Ponzini	1986	Coral	Mary Kane	1987–*present*
Sam Brady	Jason Kincaid	1982–84	Daisy Cortlandt/Monique	Gillian Spencer	1980–87, 89, 90
Charlie Brent	Ian Washam	1972–76	Melanie Cortlandt	Paige Turco	1989–91
Charlie Brent	Brian Lima	1976–80	Michael Cortlandt	Liza Tullis	1989
Charlie Brent	Josh Hamilton	1985	Nina Cortlandt Warner	Taylor Miller	1979–84, 86–89
Charlie Brent	Robert Duncan McNeill	1986–88	Nina Cortlandt Warner	Heather Stanford	1984–85
Charlie Brent	Charles Van Eman	1990–91	Nina Cortlandt Warner	Barbara Kearns	1985–86
Charlie Brent	Christopher Lawford	1992–*present*	Opal Cortlandt	Jill Larson	1989–*present*
Phillip Brent	Richard Hatch	1970–72	Palmer Cortlandt	James Mitchell	1979–*present*
Phillip Brent	Nicholas Benedict	1973–79, 88	Will Cooney Cortlandt	Lonnie Quinn	1988–89

Character	Actor	Years	Character	Actor	Years
Will Cooney Cortlandt	James Patrick Stuart	1989–92	Alf Gresham	Steven Keats	1992
Amanda Cousins	Amanda Bearse	1982–84	Flora Gresham	Katharine Houghton	1992
Laura Cudahy	Ann Delahanty	1984–88	Edmund Grey	John Callahan	1992–present
Laura Cudahy	Kyndra Joy Casper	1989	Robert Grossman	Chip Zein	1994
Sean Cudahy	Alan Dysert	1979–81, 88–91	Verla Grubbs	Carol Burnett	1983
Tom Cudahy	Richard Shoberg	1977–present	Mrs. Gurney	Portia Nelson	1980–90
Cal Cummings	Count Stovall	1989–91	June Hagen	Carole Shelley	1984–86
Mark Dalton	Mark LaMura	1976–85, 86–89, 94	Dr. Stephen Hamill	Andrew Jackson	1991–93
Bitsy Davidson	Ann Flood	1988–89	Dr. Hampton	Lonnie Smith	1988
Cecily Davidson Kelly	Rosa Langschwadt Nevin	1986–89	Alice Hart	Rochelle Oliver	1993, 94
Nick Davis	Lawrence Keith	1970–78, 83, 84, 88, 91, 93, 94	Bill Hart	Bill Raymond	1993, 94
			Kendall Hart	Sarah Michelle Gellar	1993–present
Dean	Sean Christopher Kellman	1993	Helga	Susan Willis	1991–92
Timmy Dillon	Michael Shulman	1989–91	Galen Henderson	Karen Person	1992–93
Timmy Dillon	Tommy Michaels	1991–present	Galen Henderson	Courtney Eplin	1992
Trevor Dillon	James Kiberd	1989–present	Del Henry	Winsor Harmon	1994–present
Eddie Dorrance	Warren Burton	1978–79	Walter Hines	William Swan	1980–present
Eddie Dorrance	Ross Petty	1978	Bill Hoffman	Michael Shannon	1972
Brooke English	Julia Barr	1976–81, 82–present	Edie Hoffman	Marilyn Chris	1972
Brooke English	Elissa Leeds	1976	Eugene Hubbard	Tom Wright	1984–85
Brooke English	Harriet Hall	1981	Frankie Hubbard	Z Wright	1986–91
Peg English	Patricia Barry	1980–81	Jesse Hubbard	Darnell Williams	1981–88, 94
Ethel	Barbara Hooyman	1982	Alexander Hunter	Mitchell Ryan	1985
Nigel Fargate	Alexander Scourby	1976–77	Jeremy Hunter	Jean LeClerc	1985–92
Nigel Fargate	Sidney Armus	1976	Natalie Hunter Dillon	Kate Collins	1985–92
Richard Fields	James A. Stephens	1993	Natalie Hunter Dillon	Melody Anderson	1992–93
Reverend Finney	Jonathan Moore	1979–89	Irma	Christy McGinn	1991
Maggie Flanagan	Paula Trueman	1978	Sgt. Mel Jacobi	Chris Wallace	1978
Harry Flax	Biff McGuire	1975	Stephen Jacobi	Dack Rambo	1982–83
Chateau Maitre'd Freddie	Fred Porcelli	1978–80	Jean	Angela Pietropinto	1988
Derek Frye	William Christian	1991–present	Lettie Jean	Judith Roberts	1979–80
Livia Frye	Tonya Pinkins	1991–present	Lettie Jean	Delphi Harrington	1980, 90
Terrence Frye	Dondre T. Whitfield	1991–present	Jim Jefferson	Paul Falzone	1980–81
Terrence Frye	Akili Prince	1991	Max Jeffries	Larry Pine	1992
Helen Gallagher	Nurse Harris	1994–present	Mrs. Johnson	Carol Burnett	1976
Jenny Gardner Nelson	Kim Delaney	1981–84, 94	Carter Jones	John Wesley Shipp	1992
Opal Gardner	Dorothy Lyman	1981–83	Marta Jones	Jennifer Van Dyck	1992
Ray Gardner	Gil Rogers	1977–79, 82, 93, 94	Nanny Judith	Roberta Maxwell	1988
Bob Georgia	Peter Strong	1984–85	Eric Kane	Albert Stratton	1989–90
Mary Georgia	Geraldine Court	1985	Erica Kane	Susan Lucci	1970–present
Lionel Glynn	Charles Cioffi	1993	Goldie Kane	Louise Shaffer	1988
Mrs. Gonzales	Gloria Irizarry	1982	Mona Kane Tyler	Frances Heflin	1970–94
Keith Gordon	David King	1991	Silver Kane	Debbie Goodrich	1982–83
Dr. Tim Gould	Tim Van Pelt	1985–90	Silver Kane	Claire Beckman	1988
Dr. Tim Gould	Michael Levin	1993	Dr. Christina Karras	Robin Strasser	1976–79
Caroline Grant	Patricia Dixon	1975–79	Noelle Keaton	Rosalind Ingledew	1987
Dr. Frank Grant	Don Blakely	1972	Grace Keefer	Lynn Thigpen	1994
Dr. Frank Grant	John Danelle	1972–82	Noah Keefer	Keith Hamilton Cobb	1994–present
Nancy Grant	Lisa Wilkinson	1973–84	Creed Kelly	James Horan	1988–89
Zach Grayson	Robert LuPone	1984–85	Nico Kelly	Maurice Benard	1987–89
Janet Green	Kate Collins	1990–92	Betsy Kennicott	Carla Dragoni	1979–82
Janet Green	Robin Mattson	1994–present	Dan Kennicott	Daren Kelly	1976–79

Character	Actor	Years	Character	Actor	Years
Katie Kennicott	Greta Lind	1990–91	Tad Martin	Terrell Anthony	1990
Mary Kennicott	Susan Blanchard	1971–75	Tara Martin	Karen Gorney	1970–74, 76–77
Mary Kennicott	Jacqueline Boslow	1971	Tara Martin	Stephanie Braxton	1974–76
Dr. Khademy	Harsh Nayyar	1994	Tara Martin Jefferson	Nancy Frangione	1977–79, 85
Rick Kincaid	Stephen Parr	1981–82	Tara Martin Jefferson	Mary Lynn Blanks	1979–80
Brandon Kingsley	Michael Minor	1980–82, 88	Wade Matthews	Christopher Holder	1986
Pamela Kingsley	Kathy Kamhi	1980–82	Jason Maxwell	Tom Rosqui	1972
Pamela Kingsley Blackthorne	Kathleen Rowe McAllen	1988	Jason Maxwell	John Devlin	1972–73
			Robin McCall	Deborah Morehart	1985–87
Sara Kingsley	Tudi Wiggins	1980–82	Bonnie McFadden	Daniella & Francesca Serra	1981
Roy Kramer	Mark McCoy	1986	Wally McFadden	Jack Magee	1978–80
Michael LaGuardia	Josh Dubinsky	1986–87	Wally McFadden	Nigel Reed	1980
Anton Lang	Rudolf Martin	1993–*present*	Wally McFadden	Patrick Skelton	1980–81
Corvina Lang	Margaret Sophie Stein	1992–93, 94–*present*	Alec McIntyre	Grant Aleksander	1993–*present*
			Barbara Montgomery	Susan Pratt	1987–91
Craig Lawson	Scott Thompson Baker	1991–92	Bianca Montgomery	Jessica Leigh Falborn	1988–91
Bruno Lazario	Robert Cuccioli	1994	Bianca Montgomery	Caroline Wilde	1991
Dr. Damon Lazarre	Charles Keating	1987–88	Bianca Montgomery	Lacey Chabert	1993
Elena Lazlo	Christina Belford	1992	Bianca Montgomery	Gina Gallagher	1993–*present*
Judge Lerner	Franklin Cover	1987	Claudette Montgomery	Paulette Breen	1975
Lily	Michelle Trachtenberg	1993–*present*	Claudette Montgomery	Susan Plantt-Winston	1977–80
Nils Lindstrom	Patrick Wayne	1990	Jackson Montgomery	Walt Willey	1989–*present*
Lucy	Kelly Clarke	1992–*present*	Travis Montgomery	Larkin Malloy	1987–91
Myrtle Lum Fargate	Eileen Herlie	1976–*present*	Travis Montgomery	Daniel Hugh Kelly	1993, 1994
Mrs. Manganaro	Morgana King	1993	Peggy Moody	Anne Meara	1992–*present*
Angelique Marick	Season Hubley	1992–93, 94	Myra Murdoch Sloane	Elizabeth Lawrence	1979–92
Dimitri Marick	Michael Nader	1991–*present*	Enid Nelson	Natalie Ross	1981–86, 91
Hugo Marick	Fritz Weaver	1992	Greg Nelson	Laurence Lau	1981–86
Wilma Marlowe	Jo Henderson	1985–86	Greg Nelson	Jack Armstrong	1986
Wilma Marlowe	Ruby Holbrook	1986–87	Joseph Orsini	Sam Groom	1993
Wilma Marlowe	Dena Dietrich	1994–*present*	Nola Orsini	Barbara Rush	1992–93, 94
Gloria Marsh Chandler	Teresa Blake	1991–*present*	Ted Orsini	Michael E. Knight	1993
Helen Marsh	Joyce Van Patten	1993	Cindy Parker	Ellen Wheeler	1987–89
Bobby Martin	Mike Bersell	1970	Karen Parker	Ellen Wheeler	1989–90
Dr. Joseph Martin	Ray MacDonnell	1970–*present*	Skye Patterson	Antoinette Byron	1986–87
Dr. Jeff Martin	Charles Frank	1970–75, 88	Skye Patterson	Robin Christopher	1987–91
Dr. Jeff Martin	Christopher Wines	1970	Dr. Sally Perkins	Susanna Dalto	1983
Dr. Jeff Martin	Robert Perault	1976–77	Pilar	Terri Eoff	1988
Dr. Jeff Martin	James O'Sullivan	1977–79	Andrew Preston	Steve Caffrey	1984–86
Dr. Jeff Martin	Jeffrey Byron	1986–87	Cynthia Preston	Jane Elliot	1984–86
Joey Martin	Michael Scaleri	1983–88	David Rampal	Trent Bushey	1989–91
Joey Martin	Michael Brainard	1989–91, 94	Marissa Rampal	Nicole Orth–Pallavicini	1988
Kate Martin	Christine Thomas	1970	Marissa Rampal	Nancy Addison	1988
Kate Martin	Kate Harrington	1970	Mimi Reed	Shari Headley	1991–*present*
Kate Martin	Kay Campbell	1970–85	John (Remy) Remington	Eddie Earl Hatch	1988–89
Margo Flax Martin	Eileen Letchworth	1972–76	Dr. Rosenstein	Tony Roberts	1994
Paul Martin	Ken Rabat	1970–72	Mike Roy	Nicholas Surovy	1983–84, 88
Paul Martin	William Mooney	1972–82, 84–85	Mike Roy	Hugo Napier	1984–85
Tad Martin	Matthew Anton	1973–77	Sabrina	Marlo Marron	1992
Tad Martin	John E. Dunn	1978–81	Benny Sago	Larry Fleischman	1976–79
Tad Martin	Michael E. Knight	1982–86, 88–90, 92–*present*	Benny Sago	Vasili Bogazianos	1980–90
			Emily Ann Sago	Amber Barretto	1988

Character	Actor	Years	Character	Actor	Years
Emily Ann Sago	Liz Vassey	1988–91	Ann Tyler	Diana DeVegh	1970
Bryan Sanders	Curt May	1985–86	Ann Tyler	Joanna Miles	1970–71
Carrie Sanders Tyler	Andrea Moar	1980–83	Ann Tyler	Judith Barcroft	1971–77
Kurt Sanders	William Ferriter	1980–81	Ann Tyler	Gwyn Gillis	1979–81
Leora Sanders	Lizbeth MacKay	1980–81	Dr. Charles Tyler	Hugh Franklin	1970–83, 85
Dr. Maria Santos	Eva LaRue	1993–present	Dr. Chuck Tyler	Jack Stauffer	1970–72
Hector Santos	Raul Davila	1993–present	Dr. Chuck Tyler	Gregory Chase	1972–73
Isabella Santos	Socorro Santiago	1993, 94	Dr. Chuck Tyler	Chris Hubbell	1973–75
Julia Santos	Sydney Penny	1993–present	Dr. Chuck Tyler	Richard Van Vleet	1975–84, 86, 89–92
Detective Saunders	Leo Finney	1993	Lincoln Tyler	Paul Dumont	1970–71
Judith Sawyer	Gwen Verdon	1982	Lincoln Tyler	James Karen	1970
Melanie Sawyer	Carol McCluer	1981–82	Lincoln Tyler	Nicholas Pryor	1971
Kitty Shea Davis Tyler	Francesca James	1972–77	Lincoln Tyler	Peter White	1974–80, 81, 84, 86
Devon Shepherd McFadden	Tricia Pursley Hawkins	1977–81, 83–84	Phoebe Tyler Wallingford	Ruth Warrick	1970–present
Ellen Shepherd Dalton Chandler	Kathleen Noone	1977–89	Tyrone	Roscoe Orman	1976
Hal Short	Dan Hamilton	1975	Stan Ulatowski	Eugene Anthony	1988–91
Simone	Viveca Lindfors	1983	Mrs. Valentine	Alyce Webb	1980–present
Lois Sloan	Hilda Haynes	1970	Alfred Vanderpoole	Bill Timoney	1983–86, 89
Jasper Sloane	Ronald Drake	1982–92	Arlene Vaughan	Phyllis Lyons	1990–93
Jane Smith	Sasha von Schoeler	1986	Hayley Vaughan	Kelly Ripa	1990–present
Agent Starling	Josie deGuzman	1994	Josh Waleski	Stan Albers	1988–89
Stella	Judy Kaye	1994	Langley Wallingford/ Lenny Wlasuk	Louis Edmonds	1979–present
Dr. Amy Stone	Catherine Christianson	1986	Dr. Walsh	Laurence Luckenbill	1994
Olga Svenson	Peg Murray	1982–present	Bobby Warner	Matthew MacNamara	1981–88
Austin Sweeney	Clark Reiner	1993	Bobby Warner	Chris Mazura	1988–89
Terry	Debbie Governor	1975	Cliff Warner	Peter Bergman	1979–87, 88–89
Sheila Thomas	Cynthia Sullivan	1984–85	Linda Warner	Melissa Leo	1984–85
Sybil Thorne	Linda Gibboney	1979–81	Peggy Warner	Amy Steele	1980
Dottie Thornton	Dawn Marie Boyle	1977–80	Clayton Watson	Reuben Green	1977
Dottie Thornton	Tasia Valenza	1983–86	Leo Webb	Timothy Jerome	1994
Dr. David Thornton	Paul Gleason	1976–78	Syd Weber	Lisa Howard	1987
Edna Thornton Sago	Sandy Gabriel	1977–80, 83–86	Giles Westfall	Gerry Becker	1993
Jeb Tidwell	Robert Swan	1988	Olive Whelan	Maureen O'Sullivan	1981
Father Tierney	Mel Boudrot	1977–present	Celia Wilson	Cynthia Ruffin	1994
Dr. Anna Tolan	Courtney Sherman	1990–92	Hillary Wilson Martin	Carmen Thomas	1984–88
Dr. Anna Tolan	Lois Robbins	1992–present	Jamal Wilson	Amir Jamal Williams	1993–present
Lt. Toland	Paul Hecht	1983–85	Jamal Wilson	James Wiggins	1993
Harlan Tucker	William Griffis	1977–81, 83	Winifred	Cheryl Hulteen	1991–present
Billy Clyde Tuggle	Matthew Cowles	1977–80, 84–90	Joanna Yaeger	Meg Myles	1983–84, 87
Estelle Tuggle	Kathleen Dezina	1978–82	Z	Brian McReady	1991
Amy Tyler	Rosemary Prinz	1970			

Grant Aleksander

GRANT ALEKSANDER (Alec McIntyre)

Birthplace: Baltimore, Maryland   Birthdate: August 6
Height: 6'2"   Hair: Blond   Eyes: Blue

Grant Aleksander joined the cast in August 1993 as Alec McIntyre, a successful businessman who came to Pine Valley to help run Chandler Enterprises. Mixing business with pleasure, he seduced Adam Chandler's beautiful and vulnerable wife, Gloria, blackmailed her about their affair, then stole Erica Kane's company, Enchantment, out from under her nose. Later, after learning about a son, Jamal, whom he never knew he had, Alec turned over a new leaf.

Grant was born and raised in Baltimore, Maryland, where he planned on a career in sports until a drama teacher encouraged him to try out for a school production. He went on to attend Washington and Lee University in Virginia and became heavily involved in the theater program, where he appeared in *The Crucible*, *The Owl And The Pussycat* and *The Glass Menagerie*, and played the title roles in both *Manson* and *Hamlet*. He also appeared on the Baltimore stage in *The Prime Of Miss Jean Brodie* and *Cat On A Hot Tin Roof*.

After studying drama in New York at New York University and Circle in the Square, he went on to play Phillip Spaulding on *Guiding Light* for a total of seven years between 1982 and 1991. Other television credits include *Hardcastle And McCormick*, *Who's The Boss?*, *Fall Guy*, *Dark Mansions*, *Capitol* and the ABC Afterschool Special presentation, *A Very Delicate Matter*.

Grant lives in New York City with his actress wife, Sherry Ramsey. They are active members of People for the Ethical Treatment of Animals (PETA) and are the nurturing owners of many cats and dogs.

JULIA BARR (Brooke English)

Birthplace: Fort Wayne, Indiana   Birthdate: February 8
Height: 5'1"   Hair: Blond   Eyes: Blue

Julia Barr joined the cast of *All My Children* in 1976 as impetuous teenager Brooke English, the spoiled, rich niece of Phoebe Tyler. Over the years, Brooke has survived her share of trials and tribulations, emerging as a true soap heroine. And Julia's portrayal of Brooke has earned her not only six Emmy nominations but, in 1991, the award as Outstanding Supporting Actress in a Daytime Drama Series.

Julia grew up in Indiana, where she worked with the Fort Wayne Community Theater before attending Purdue University, where she appeared in such productions as *Our Town*, *A Streetcar Named Desire* and *Endgame*. Among her other television credits are *Gathering Of One*, *The Adams Chronicles* and *Ryan's Hope*. Julia also played Norma Childs in the film, *I, The Jury*.

In 1981, she left *All My Children* for fifteen months to tour with

Julia Barr

Katharine Hepburn and Dorothy Loudon in *West Side Waltz*. Also on this hiatus, she married oral surgeon Dr. Richard Hirschlag. Recently, Julia became the spokesperson for The Company of Women, a national merchandise catalog whose proceeds help fund the Rockland Family Shelter, a New York-based facility that provides assistance to battered women and their children, rape survivors and the homeless. Julia lives in New Jersey with her husband and their ten-year-old daughter, Allison Jane. She enjoys theater, studies voice and takes cooking classes in her spare time.

TERESA BLAKE (Gloria Marsh)

Birthplace: Tuscaloosa, Alabama   Birthdate: December 12
Height: 5'6-1/2"   Hair: Blond   Eyes: Blue

Teresa Blake joined the cast October 1991 as nurse Gloria Marsh, who came to Pine Valley with a vendetta against her former fiancé, but circumstances caused her to turn over a new leaf. Meeting her match, she married wealthy businessman Adam Chandler, but Adam's duplicity finally drove her away. Teresa has received critical acclaim for her realistic portrayal of this troubled woman who has regained control of her life, and was nominated for a 1993 Soap Opera Award as Outstanding Female Newcomer.

Off camera, Teresa has certainly taken control of her life. A native of Tuscaloosa, Alabama, she launched her career after victory in a contest for a suntan lotion company led to a succession of modeling jobs. Following high school, she moved to Miami and continued modeling. She also began acting. While in Florida, she guest-starred in several television series, including *Miami Vice* and *B.L. Stryker* with Burt Reynolds, whom she refers to as "the kindest, most gentle man I've ever worked with."

Moving to Los Angeles, she co-starred in the television movie *Prize Pulitzer* and was featured in the theatrical releases *Revenge Of the Nerds*, *Payback*, *It Had To Be You* and the James Bond thriller *License To Kill*. Then she moved to New York and landed her role on *All My Children*.

Her many interests include karate, music and all types of dancing. She also enjoys learning new languages. While in Los Angeles, she learned sign language from hearing-impaired friends and hopes to become proficient at that as well.

Teresa Blake

JOHN CALLAHAN (Edmund Grey)

Birthplace: Brooklyn, New York   Birthdate: December 23
Height: 6'   Hair: Brown   Eyes: Blue

John Callahan joined *All My Children* in April 1992 in the role of Edmund Grey, a dashing, world-renowned reporter who later married Dr. Maria Santos and began a career in politics. A familiar face to television audiences, Callahan came to *AMC* from the daytime drama *Santa Barbara*, on which he played the highly charged role of Craig Hunt. Before that, he portrayed Eric Stavros, the playboy son of Cesar Romero, on the prime-time serial *Falcon Crest* for nearly three years. And earlier still, he appeared on ABC's *General Hospital* as Leo Russell, a master masseur.

John Callahan

The All My Children Family

A native of New York City, Callahan moved west to attend the University of California in Berkeley as a pre-law student. After working through college as a bartender, he was working as a nightclub manager when he decided on a career in entertainment. Shortly afterward he appeared as Petruchio in the Bay Area stage production of *The Taming Of The Shrew*, in *The Rainmaker* at the Berkeley Stage Company and *Tequila* at the Eureka Theater in San Francisco.

Married for twelve years to his wife, Linda, Callahan has helped raise her two sons, Matthew and Josh. He's an avid golfer, enjoys softball, reading and traveling, and is active in several charities.

David Canary

DAVID CANARY (Adam/Stuart Chandler)

Birthplace: Elwood, Indiana   Birthdate: August 25
Height: 5'11"   Hair: Gray   Eyes: Blue

This four-time Emmy winner, who began his career on the Broadway stage and in Hollywood film and television productions, has won his acting awards for his portrayal of the powerful and mercurial Adam Chandler as well as Adam's shy, gentle twin, Stuart.

Canary attended the University of Cincinnati on a football scholarship, and graduated as a music major specializing in voice in a unique university program that combined study at the Cincinnati Conservatory of Music. A native of Elwood, Indiana, he grew up in Massillon, Ohio, not far from the Football Hall of Fame in Canton.

But he gave up both football and singing to become an actor, making his Broadway debut with Colleen Dewhurst in Jose Quintero's production of *Great Day In The Morning*. Prime-time television audiences remember him as Candy in *Bonanza*, as Russ Gehring in *Peyton Place* and from numerous guest appearances on other programs, including the made-for-television film, *The Dain Curse*. He has also appeared on daytime television as Stephen Frame in *Another World*. Among his feature films are *Hombre*, *The St. Valentine's Day Massacre* and *End Of A Dark Street*.

Since he joined the cast of *All My Children* in 1983, Canary has returned to the stage in Tennessee Williams' *Clothes For A Summer Hotel*, Strindberg's *The Father*, *The Fantasticks*, *The Happiest Girl In The World* and *Blood Moon*.

William Christian

WILLIAM CHRISTIAN (Detective Derek Frye)

Birthplace: Washington, D.C.   Birthdate: September 30
Height: 5'11"   Hair: Dark Brown   Eyes: Brown

When William Christian first appeared on *All My Children* in July 1990, as Detective Derek Frye, he felt he had a few days of work ahead of him and made the most of the role. His work paid off. Three months later, Christian became a regular on the program. In May 1991, he was nominated for a Daytime Emmy Award as Outstanding Supporting Actor in a Drama Series.

After graduating in drama from Catholic University, he continued studying through graduate school at American University, earning a

Master's degree. Paying his post-graduate dues, he appeared off-Broadway with actress Esther Rolle in *A Member Of The Wedding* at the Roundabout Theater, then in *Black Eagles* at the Crossroads Theater Company in New Brunswick, New Jersey. During a break from the show in April 1993, he co-starred in the off-Broadway play *Them That's Got*.

Although he enjoyed his other roles, Christian has particularly fond memories of his first appearance on *All My Children*. As a day player, he portrayed one of several rowdy wrestlers invited to dinner at the Chateau by the character Bob Georgia. "They caused quite a ruckus," according to Christian, who watches the videotape of the scene on occasion for a laugh.

In 1993 and 1994, he received an NAACP Image Award nomination, in the category of Featured Male in Daytime.

MARY FICKETT (Ruth Brent Martin)

Birthplace: Bronxville, New York   Birthdate: May 23
Height: 5'8"   Hair: Blond   Eyes: Blue

Mary Fickett and Ray MacDonnell

As nurse Ruth Brent Martin, Mary Fickett has been with the show since its inception in 1970. Ruth has endured the death of a husband, a second marriage, the death of her adopted son, an extramarital affair, the adoption of another son, a kidnapping, a brutal rape, a mid-life pregnancy and the return from the dead of her second adopted son, Tad. For her portrayal of Ruth, Fickett was the first daytime performer to be honored with an Emmy Award.

Past performances have earned her the first annual Theatre Guild Award and a Tony Award nomination for her portrayal of Eleanor Roosevelt in *Sunrise at Campobello*. Among her other Broadway credits: *I Know My Love*, *Tea And Sympathy* and *Love And Kisses*. And her track record on television is even more extensive: *Studio One*, *Kraft Theatre*, *Philco Playhouse*, *The FBI*, *Bonanza*, *The Defenders* and the acclaimed ABC special, *Pueblo*. Other daytime series in which she has appeared are *Edge Of Night* and *The Nurses*.

Daughter of the late Homer Fickett, one of radio's foremost directors, Mary recalls that when she was growing up there were always a lot of writers and actors in the house. "It was then," she says, "that I decided all I ever wanted to be was an actress."

SARAH MICHELLE GELLAR (Kendall Hart)

Birthplace: New York, New York   Birthdate: April 14
Height: 5'3"   Hair: Brown   Eyes: Green

Sarah Michelle Gellar

Sarah Michelle Gellar has played Kendall Hart on *All My Children* since March 1993, and within a year received her first Emmy nomination for the role. The bad-seed daughter whom Erica Kane had given up at birth for adoption, Kendall and her machinations prompted Erica to stab her husband—an assault that cost her a month in prison.

By the age of seventeen, Gellar had amassed a long and impressive list of acting credentials. She is best known for her starring role as Sydney Rutledge in the syndicated soap opera *Swan's Crossing*, but her

The All My Children Family

other television work includes the role of young Jackie Kennedy in the television miniseries *A Woman Named Jackie*. She was also a series regular on the syndicated program *Girl Talk*, and made guest appearances on *Spenser: For Hire*, *Love, Sydney* and *Guiding Light*. Her first professional role was in the television movie *Invasion Of Privacy*, which co-starred Valerie Harper, Jeff Daniels and Carol Kane.

Gellar has also compiled an impressive record on the big screen as well as on the stage, featured in the theatrical movies *High Stakes*, *Over The Brooklyn Bridge* and *Funny Farm*, and starring in the original (pre-Broadway) cast of Neil Simon's play *Jake's Women*, and opposite Matthew Broderick in New York City's Circle in the Square production of *The Widow Claire*.

Before she became an actress, Gellar was a competitive ice skater for three years and ranked third in a New York State regional competition.

Keith Hamilton Cobb

KEITH HAMILTON COBB (Noah Keefer)

Birthplace: North Tarrytown, New York   Birthdate: January 28
Height: 6'3"   Hair: Dark Brown   Eyes: Brown

He joined the cast in July 1994 as Noah Keefer, a guy from the wrong side of town who took in runaway Julia Santos and began to care for her. Cobb was born and raised in Tarrytown, New York, where he attended Sleepy Hollow High School. A 1987 graduate of the New York University Tisch School of the Arts, he also received theatrical training at the Circle in the Square and Playwright's Horizons.

His first professional job was in a production of Cocteau's *The Infernal Machine* at the Jean Cocteau Repertory in lower Manhattan. Since then, he has appeared in productions of *Othello*, *The Beaux Stratagem*, *Cymbeline*, *Hamlet* and *Coriolanus* for the New Jersey Shakespeare Festival, the Actors Theatre of Louisville, the Huntington Theatre Company and the North Shore Music Theatre. Most recently, he appeared as Tybalt in *Romeo And Juliet* and *Octavius* in Julius Caesar, both at the Shakespeare Theatre.

Cobb also teaches acting at Youth Theatre Interactions, Inc., and participates in a performing arts program for children in South Yonkers, New York. As both actor and director, he has worked for the past several seasons with the Playwright's Theatre of New Jersey in their Special Needs Program, teaching playwriting and performing the plays of youthful offenders within the New Jersey correctional system.

Single, he lives in New York state, enjoys cycling, swimming and fencing, and admits to a passion for all things Shakespearean.

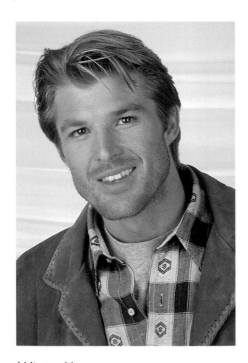

Winsor Harmon

WINSOR HARMON (Del Henry)

Birthplace: Crowley, Louisiana   Birthdate: November 22
Height: 6'   Hair: Blond   Eyes: Brown

Winsor Harmon joined the cast of *All My Children* in February 1994, as Del Henry , a writer with a hidden agenda that included getting to know his half-sister, Dixie Cooney Martin. Del now suffers from degenerative kidney disease and needs a compatible donor in order to save his life. To pay his mounting hospital bills, he has reluctantly joined forces with Pine Valley's bad girl, Kendall Hart, to write a tell-all book about her mother, Erica Kane. To further complicate matters, his college sweetheart, Dr. Maria Santos Grey, believes he has returned to town to cause trouble in her life.

Winsor was born in Crowley, Louisiana, and raised in Rockwall, Texas. After graduating from Rockwall High School, he attended Texas A&M on a football scholarship. Before joining *All My Children*, his first professional acting job was as "the Marlboro Man" in South America for two years.

His many interests include most sports, martial arts, wildlife and writing. He also enjoys singing country music and riding motorcycles.

EILEEN HERLIE (Myrtle Lum Fargate)

Birthplace: Glasgow, Scotland   Birthdate: March 8
Height: 5'4"   Hair: Chestnut brown   Eyes: Brown

Eileen Herlie

In 1976, Eileen Herlie joined the cast as Myrtle Lum Fargate, a salt-of-the-earth woman with a carnival background, who operates a boarding house and runs a fashion boutique. Born and raised in Glasgow, Scotland, she worked for several years in the Scottish National Theatre and in the English theater in the company of Tyrone Guthrie. Among her first hit plays on the London stage was Jean Cocteau's *The Eagle Has Two Heads*.

On Broadway, she starred as Queen Gertrude opposite Richard Burton's *Hamlet* and played the same role in the film with Sir Laurence Olivier. She also starred on Broadway with Ruth Gordon in *The Matchmaker*, with Jackie Gleason and Walter Pidgeon in *Take Me Along*, with Ray Bolger in *All American*, and as Queen Mary in *Crown Matrimonial*. Herlie's other film credits include *Freud* with Montgomery Clift and Sidney Lumet's *The Seagull* with Simone Signoret.

Ms. Herlie, who is no longer married, lives in Manhattan.

JAMES KIBERD (Trevor Dillon)

Birthplace: Providence, Rhode Island   Birthdate: July 6
Height: 6"   Hair: Light brown   Eyes: Brown

James Kiberd

James Kiberd joined the cast June 1989 as offbeat detective Trevor Dillon, in what was originally intended as a five-day stint, but his creation of this wildly unique character earned him a contract role on his first day, and Trevor has now graduated from detective to lawyer.

An artist since the age of four, when he began drawing portraits, Kiberd studied at the Rhode Island School of Design, the Graduate School of Fine Arts at the University of Pennsylvania and most of Europe's major museums. But he chose to become an actor after his portrayal of Macbeth at the Pennsylvania Shakespeare Festival topped all attendance records. His regional and off-Broadway credits include *Death Of A Salesman*, *The Seagull*, *Who's Afraid Of Virginia Woolf?*, *Dracula*, Thurber's *The Male Animal* and the world premiere of Donald Freed's *Veteran's Day*. He also starred in the 1983 movie *Loving* with Geraldine Page in the role of Mike Donovan, an emotionally scarred Vietnam veteran, then continued with the role when *Loving* became a daytime drama on ABC, winning for him a Soap Opera Award as Best Actor.

He met his wife, actress Susan Keith, when she was hired to play his love interest on the serial, but it wasn't love at first sight. After screen-testing with twenty women to be his new romantic partner, Kiberd told the producers, "They're all fine except her, please don't hire her." They now share a glorious 130-year-old Victorian home in upstate New York with a Siamese cat and two Rottweilers.

Michael E. Knight

MICHAEL E. KNIGHT (Tad Martin)

Birthplace: Princeton, New Jersey   Birthdate: May 7
Height: 6'1"   Hair: Light Brown   Eyes: Blue

Michael E. Knight took the role of Tad Martin in 1983 and was honored with two Emmy Awards for Outstanding Younger Leading Man in a Drama Series (1986 and 1987) before leaving the show to spread his wings in other acting arenas. He starred in *Run For Your Wife* on the Los Angeles stage, played a lead role in the Columbia Pictures feature film *Hexed* and guest-starred in a variety of prime-time series, including *Murder, She Wrote*, *Dear John* and *Grapevine*. Just before returning to his role as Tad on *AMC* in December 1992, he co-starred in the off-Broadway play *Wrong Turn At Lungfish*.

An acting career had been Knight's ambition since the age of twelve, and he earned his degree in theater arts in only three years at Wesleyan University in Middletown, Connecticut. After further training at the Circle in the Square Theater, he went on to appear in stage productions of *Absurd Person Singular* and *Enemies* as well as in the feature film *Baby, It's You*. He also produced and starred in the off-off-Broadway production of *Call Back, A Duel In One Act* in the spring of 1984.

Born in Princeton, New Jersey, Knight nevertheless considers himself a Californian. He spent his early years in Ojai in Southern California, where his father was a faculty member of a boys' preparatory school, which Michael also attended. The family later moved to San Francisco. He is the only one of three sons in his family to pursue an acting career. Michael and his wife, actress Catherine Hickland, live in New York.

Felicity LaFortune

FELICITY LaFORTUNE (Laurel Banning Montgomery)

Birthplace: Oak Park, Illinois   Birthdate: December 15
Height: 5'7"   Hair: Brown   Eyes: Gray

Felicity LaFortune took on the challenging rolle of Laurel Banning in March 1993 and has made it her own. Laurel, a woman driven to steal for the sake of her child, reformed to marry handsome attorney Jackson Montgomery—but she now faces losing him to another woman: Erica Kane.

LaFortune dreamed of being a performer since childhood. When she was thirteen, she chose to concentrate on opera, and later studied voice at the American Conservatory of Music in Chicago.

With her beautiful mezzo-soprano voice, she began her professional career with the Repertory Opera Theater in Chicago, moved on to the San Francisco Opera chorus, then joined the prestigious Santa Fe Opera Company.

Making the transition to the theatrical stage, she appeared in productions throughout the nation, working with such distinguished actors and directors as Jason Robards, Jose Ferrer, Gene Saks, Jerome Robbins and John Guare. Her television credits include a recurring role on the series *thirtysomething* and guest-starring appearances on *L.A. Law*, *Midnight Caller*, *Murphy Brown*, *Crossbow* and *D.E.A.* Before *All My Children*, LaFortune was well-known to daytime television viewers for her portrayal of media magnate Leigh Kirkland on ABC's daytime drama *Ryan's Hope*.

In her spare time, she works with new composers at New York University's musical theater MBA program, and in addition to attending classical concerts and recitals, enjoys gardening, cooking and playing with her cat, Jacques. She and her husband, writer Steven Gilbert, live in New York and Los Angeles.

Jill Larson

JILL LARSON (Opal Cortlandt)

Birthplace: Minneapolis, Minnesota   Birthdate: October 7
Height: 5'8-1/2"   Hair: Strawberry blond   Eycs: Blue/Green

When Jill Larson joined the cast of *All My Children* in November 1989, she breathed new life into the character of flamboyant, exasperating Opal Gardner Purdy Cortlandt. It's a role for which Larson has been nominated for an Emmy as Outstanding Supporting Actress in 1991 and in 1993.

Born and raised in Minnesota, she earned a degree in communications from New York City's Hunter College. She also studied drama at the Circle in the Square Professional Theater Program. Primarily a stage actress, Larson went on to star in regional theater as Laura in *The Glass Menagerie*, as Vinnie in *Day In Life With Father* and the title role in *Agnes Of God*. Other projects for ABC include a longterm role as the psychotic kidnapper Ursula Blackwell on *One Life To Live*, and the ABC Afterschool Special presentation *Over The Limit*.

Larson is a founding member and president of GLM Productions, a theatrical production company through which she produced the off-Broadway comedy revue *Serious Bizness* and co-produced the documentary film *Gibbs Garden*.

Single, she divides her time between her New York City apartment and a weekend home in Pennsylvania. When time allows, this busy actress says, "I love home improvement projects, especially carpentry," she explains, "but my one true love is indulging in anything related to food!"

Eva LaRue

EVA LaRUE (Dr. Maria Santos)

Birthplace: Long Beach, California   Birthdate: December 27
Height: 5'7-1/2"   Hair: Brown   Eyes: Brown

Eva LaRue joined the cast in March 1993 as Dr. Maria Santos, a skilled young neurologist. The beautiful doctor tied the knot with journalist Edmund Grey, but secrets have threatened her happiness.

The All My Children Family

A native Californian, Eva began her acting career at the age of six, singing jingles and appearing in television commercials. She's come a long way since then: guesting in such prime-time series as *Nurses*, *Married...With Children*, *Perfect Strangers*, *Dallas* and *Freddy's Nightmares*, and starring in feature films that range from *Robocop III* and *Heart Condition*, to *Crash N' Burn* and *The Barbarians*.

Before *All My Children*, she also paid her dues on daytime television in the short-term role of Margo on *Santa Barbara*, and she even served a stint as co-host to Dom DeLuise on *The New Candid Camera*.

When she's not working on *AMC*, LaRue sings professionally whenever the opportunity arises. While living in Los Angeles, she found the time to sing the national anthem at several L.A. Kings hockey games and L.A. Raiders football games. She's also been riding and showing horses for ten years and likes to stay in shape with Tae Kwon Do.

Christopher Lawford

CHRISTOPHER LAWFORD (Charlie Brent)

Birthplace: Los Angeles   Birthdate: March 29
Height: 6'2"   Hair: Brown   Eyes: Hazel

Christopher Lawford attracted admiring attention on *All My Children* in his first appearance on the show in July 1992 when he assumed the role of Charlie Brent, former cosmetics model, "Man of Enchantment" and ex-boyfriend of Erica Kane. Today, Charlie runs a detective agency and spends his spare time with girlfriend Hayley Vaughan.

Lawford's journey to Pine Valley was a circuitous one. The son of famed movie actor Peter Lawford and Patricia Kennedy, he had planned to become a lawyer, taking his Bachelor of Arts degree from Tufts University and a Doctorate in law from Boston College. But when he realized that acting was his true calling, he began dramatic training and quickly landed a succession of major movie roles, appearing in the John Huston film *Mr. North*, then *The Doors*, *Russia House*, *Spellbinder*, *Impulse* and most recently, *Jack The Bear* with Danny DeVito.

Equally busy on television, he has guest-starred in several series: *Midnight Caller*, *Silk Stalkings* and *Tales From The Crypt*. He even had the chance to work with Arnold Schwarzenegger—his cousin via marriage—in the made-for-television movie *Christmas In Connecticut*.

He lives with his wife, Jeannie, and their two children, David and Savannah, in New York.

SUSAN LUCCI (Erica Kane Marick)

Birthplace: Westchester, New York   Birthdate: December 23
Height: 5'3"   Hair: Chestnut   Eyes: Dark brown

She's sexy, sassy, beautiful—"the woman you love to hate." She's Erica Kane Martin Brent Cudahy Chandler Montgomery Montgomery Marick. *TV Guide* called her "unequivocally the most famous soap opera character in the history of daytime TV." Susan Lucci, the actress who has made this scheming temptress a household name, says, "Erica is probably the best part ever written for a woman."

Susan Lucci

In addition to her fourteen Emmy nominations as Best Actress, Lucci has won a 1992 People's Choice Award, the 1993 *Soap Opera Digest* Award for Outstanding Lead Actress, the 1994 Crystal Apple Award, the 1985 *People* magazine poll as Best Soap Actress, the 1988 *Soap Opera Digest* Editor's Award for Outstanding Contribution to Daytime Television, and the 1989 Canadian *TV Guide* People's Choice Award for Best Soap Actress.

A familiar face on prime-time TV as well as daytime, Lucci has headlined in numerous made-for-television movies: *Lady Mobster*, *Mafia Princess*, *Invitation To Hell*, *Anastasia*, *Haunted By Her Past*, *French Silk*, *Between Love And Hate*, *The Woman Who Sinned* and *Double Edge*. She has also hosted *Saturday Night Live* and starred in both the final season of *Dallas* and the highest-rated ABC television movie during the 1990–91 season, *The Bride In Black*.

She has kept equally busy off camera. In 1991, she launched the Susan Lucci Collection of beauty products, marketed through the QVC home shopping network. And during her infrequent leisure hours, she enjoys tennis, skiing and traveling.

Mary Fickett and Ray MacDonnell

RAY MacDONNELL (Dr. Joe Martin)

Birthplace: Lawrence, Maine   Birthdate: March 5
Height: 6"   Hair: Brown   Eyes: Blue

Ray MacDonnell has been with *All My Children* since its inception in 1970, playing the role of Dr. Joe Martin. Dr. Joe remains one of Pine Valley's most upstanding citizens as he and his wife Ruth struggle to rebuild their family home, which was destroyed in a recent tornado.

Before joining the show, MacDonnell appeared as the popular character Philip Capice on *Edge Of Night* for nearly eight years. Ray's other television credits include *Studio One* and *Armstrong Circle Theatre*. He has also starred on Broadway in *Mame* with both Angela Lansbury and Ann Miller, and in numerous off-Broadway productions.

Born and raised in Lawrence, Massachusetts, MacDonnell went to nearby Amherst College before transferring to the Royal Academy in London as a Fulbright scholar. Today, he lives in Westchester with his wife Patricia. They have three children: Kyle, Sarah and Daniel.

RUDOLF MARTIN (Anton Lang)

Birthplace: West Berlin, Germany   Birthdate: July 31
Height: 6'2"   Hair: Brown   Eyes: Brown

Rudolf joined *All My Children* in August 1993 in the role of Anton Lang, a medical exchange student from Hungary who was sponsored by Dimitri Marick. Anton was later revealed to be Dimitri's son from his youthful affair with Anton's mother, Corvina Lang. Martin originally auditioned for another role on the show, making such an impression on the producers that the character of Anton was created for the talented young actor.

Born and raised in West Berlin, he moved with his family from Berlin to Paris to Italy, arriving in the United States a short time after

Rudolf Martin

his high school graduation from the Université de Paris. While studying at the Lee Strasberg Theatre Institute, he landed his first professional role in the Susan Seidelman short film *The Dutch Master*, which was nominated for a 1994 Academy Award. He went on to appear in the off-Broadway plays *Murder In Disguise*, *The Dumb Waiter* and *Front Page*.

The multi-lingual actor, who speaks German, French, Italian and English fluently, lives in Manhattan and is single.

ROBIN MATTSON (Janet Green)

Birthplace: Los Angeles   Birthdate: June 1
Height: 5'7 1/2"   Hair: Blond   Eyes: Blue

Robin Mattson

As the new Janet Green on *All My Children*, Robin Mattson has made Janet an integral part of Pine Valley life after serving a jail sentence for the murder of Will Cortlandt.

A familiar face on daytime television, she is remembered for her portrayals of Heather Webber on *General Hospital* and Gina Timmons on *Santa Barbara*. By infusing her roles with an off-beat sense of humor as well as her own brand of wicked mischief, Mattson has achieved wide popularity with viewers, and her performances have garnered four Emmy Award nominations and six *Soap Opera Digest* Awards—three for Best Comedic Performance and three for Best Villainess.

A native of Los Angeles, she began to act professionally at the age of six. After appearances on numerous series, including *Daniel Boone* and *The John Forsythe Show*, she made her feature film debut as the star of *Namu, The Killer Whale* for producer Ivan Tors. As a child actress, she was placed under contract by Tors and went on to appear in *Gentle Ben*, *Flipper* and *Island Of The Lost*.

Her motion pictures for television include *Mirror, Mirror, Are You Alone In The House?*, *Doctors' Private Lives*, *False Witness* and *Murder At The PTA*. Robin has also appeared in the feature films *Return To Macon County* opposite Nick Nolte and Don Johnson, *In And Out*, *Take Two* and *Wolf Lake* with Rod Steiger.

Recently, Mattson chose to pursue her lifelong passion for cooking by graduating from the Gastronomic Directives Course at the Los Angeles International Culinary Institute. She and the special man in her life, Henry Neuman, live in Manhattan.

CADY McCLAIN (Dixie Cooney Martin)

Birthplace: Burbank, California   Birthdate: October 13
Height: 5'3"   Hair: Blond   Eyes: Blue

Cady McClain

Cady McClain joined the cast October 1988 as Dixie Cooney, the niece of wealthy Palmer Cortlandt. Reunited with her true love, Tad Martin, she married him for the second time in 1993.

McClain was born and raised in Southern California. She began her career at the age of nine with a popular commercial for Band-Aids. Other commercials followed, as well as roles in such series as *Cheers*, *St. Elsewhere*, *Spenser: For Hire* and *Lou Grant*. She also appeared in the television movies *Who Will Love My Children*, *Home Fires*, *A Father's*

Homecoming and the ABC Afterschool Special presentation *Just A Regular Kid*. Among her film credits are *My Favorite Year* (as Peter O'Toole's daughter, Tess), *Pennies From Heaven* and *Simple Justice*.

In 1990, she won an Emmy Award for her portrayal of Dixie, and received a nomination in 1992. In 1991, she won *Soap Opera Digest*'s award for Best Heroine, and in 1994, she and Michael Knight won *Soap Opera Update*'s MVP Award for Best Couple.

Despite her heavy schedule on *All My Children*, McClain has taken time out to appear on the stage in *Barefoot In The Park* for Music Fair at Valley Forge and Westbury, and in *Quiet On The Set* at the Westbeth. Last winter, she starred as Hero in a Lincoln Center production of *Much Ado About Nothing* and in 1994 starred in the Rogue Repertory Company's production of *Comedy Of Errors*. Her other theatrical credits include *A Little Night Music* for the New York City Opera Ensemble and Judith Viorst's *Happy Birthday And Other Humiliations* for the John Drew Theater and the L.A. Workshop Production. A dedicated professional, she continues to study at Michael Howard Studios in New York.

In her spare time, Cady enjoys drawing, singing and chowing down on Mexican food—especially "sloppy burritos."

Tommy Michaels

TOMMY MICHAELS (Tim Hunter)

Birthplace: Staten Island, New York   Birthdate: February 8
Height: 5'1"   Hair: Sandy blond   Eyes: Blue

Tommy joined the cast in 1989 as Timmy Hunter, a teenager who developed a drug problem after struggling to cope with the death of his mother. His portrayal has earned the young actor a 1993 Youth in Film Award.

A veteran of the Broadway stage before he came to the show, Michaels played Winfield Joad in *The Grapes Of Wrath*, then Gavroche in *Les Miserables* for a year. And during a hiatus last year, he played the title role in a new musical, *Romulus Hunt*, written by Carly Simon for the Metropolitan Opera Guild. He has also just completed his first film role in *Quiz Show*, directed by Robert Redford.

Michaels is proud to be the Honorary Chairman of the Make-A-Wish Foundation's Kids Helping Kids program. He also recorded a new song for the foundation, "Just Make That Wish." He lives in New York with his family and actively participates in his favorite sport, soccer. He also enjoys ice hockey, basketball and skiing.

James Mitchell

JAMES MITCHELL (Palmer Cortlandt)

Birthplace: Sacramento, California   Birthdate: February 29
Height: 5'10"   Hair: Gray   Eyes: Brown

Since joining the cast of *All My Children* in 1979, James Mitchell has earned seven Emmy nominations for is portrayal of haughty, domineering Palmer Cortlandt, a tycoon with a smile on his face and a scheme up his sleeve.

Mitchell came to the show from a distinguished screen and stage career. His films include *The Turning Point*, in which he played the

The All My Children Family

artistic director, *The Bandwagon, Oklahoma!* and *Deep In My Heart* with Cyd Charisse. Earlier in his career, an accomplished dancer, he played leading roles in a number of Broadway musicals: *Carnival, Paint Your Wagon, Brigadoon* and *Bloomer Girl*. He toured with the American Ballet Theater in New York, Europe and South America, and with the Agnes DeMille Dance Theater throughout the United States. He has also starred on tour in *Funny Girl* with Carol Lawrence, in *The Threepenny Opera* with Chita Rivera and in *The King And I* with Ann Blyth.

In addition to serving as assistant to the director of the Los Angeles Civic Light Opera production of *Annie Get Your Gun* with Debbie Reynolds, Mitchell has taught movement for actors to theater arts students, which he describes as an exchange of the disciplines of dancing and acting. He has also taught at Yale University and at Drake University, which awarded him an honorary doctorate in fine arts.

Michael Nader

MICHAEL NADER (Dimitri Marick)

Birthplace: St. Louis, Missouri   Birthdate: February 19
Height: 6'2"   Hair: Brown   Eyes: Brown

Michael joined *All My Children* in September 1991 as the wealthy, mysterious and dashing Dimitri Marick. Nader had already established himself in the ABC prime-time soap *Dynasty* in his role as Dex Dexter, whom he portrayed from November 1983 to May 1989.

Nader began his acting career when, while attending Santa Monica College in Los Angeles, he was tapped to appear in a successful series of beach movies starring Annette Funicello and Frankie Avalon. After a stint as a semi-regular with Sally Field on the television series *Gidget*, Nader decided to move to New York to pursue his craft.

Studying at the prestigious Actors Studio and the Herbert Berghof Studio, he appeared in several off-Broadway plays before returning to the screen as Kevin Thompson on the daytime serial *As The World Turns*. Returning to Los Angeles after three years on that show, he quickly landed the part of Alexi Theodopolous on the series *Bare Essence*. Nader's television work also includes starring roles in numerous made-for-television movies, most notably *Lady Mobster*, which co-starred his *All My Children* castmate Susan Lucci.

He lives in New York City with his wife and dog.

SYDNEY PENNY (Julia Santos)

Birthplace: Nashville, Tennessee   Birthdate: August 7
Height: 5'4"   Hair: Brown   Eyes: Brown

Her eye-catching first appearance on *All My Children* aired in September 1993: Portraying the sexy schemer Julia Santos, Penny made her debut clad only in a towel. In 1994, Julia's story took a serious turn when she received a disfiguring scar, sustained during a tornado that ripped through Pine Valley.

Like her character, Penny has been attracting attention for many years despite her youth. She received critical acclaim for her perfor-

Sydney Penny

mance as young Meggie in the hit ABC miniseries *The Thorn Birds*. More recently, she played the popular role of B.J. Walker in the daytime serial *Santa Barbara*, earning herself an Emmy nomination.

Penny's entrance into show business came early. Her parents, country and western entertainers Hank and Shari Penny, took their daughter to many of their performances. On one occasion—and without prompting—three-and-a-half-year-old Sydney jumped up on stage and sang her own composition, "My Little Pony." Three years later, she landed her first paying gig—in a toy commercial.

Penny's long list of credits include a co-starring role in a syndicated series, *The New Gidget*, and featured parts in the movies *Pale Rider* with Clint Eastwood, *Running Away* with Sophia Loren and the French film *Bernadette*.

Off camera, she enjoys horseback riding, cooking and has a passion for anything to do with the era of the 1930s and 1940s.

TONYA PINKINS (Livia Frye Cudahy)

Birthplace: Chicago, Illinois   Birthdate: May 30
Height: 5'7"   Hair: Brown   Eyes: Brown

In the role of Livia Cudahy, Tonya Pinkins joined the cast May 1991. A successful attorney and single mother, Livia later entered into an interracial marriage with health club owner Tom Cudahy.

A native of Chicago, Pinkins attended Carnegie Mellon University in Pittsburgh, where she studied theater, music and dance. Leaving school, she moved to New York after landing a role in Stephen Sondheim's *Merrily We Roll Along*, then went on to appear in *An Ounce Of Prevention*, *Just Say No*, *Caucasian Chalk Circle* and *Little Shop Of Horrors* on the New York stage.

Pinkins' portrayal of Sweet Anita in the Broadway musical *Jelly's Last Jam* earned her a Tony Award, a Drama Desk Award and the Clarence Derwent Award. In the summer of 1994, during a hiatus from the show, she starred as Mistress Ford in the New York Shakespeare Festival's production of *The Merry Wives Of Windsor*.

She compiled an equally impressive record on television before joining *All My Children* with featured roles on *The Cosby Show*, *Law And Order*, *As The World Turns* and *Crime Story*. And she was seen in 1994 in the made-for-television movie *Women In Prison* on ABC. She has also appeared in the feature films *Above The Rim*, *See No Evil, Hear No Evil*, *Hot Shots* and *Bean Street*.

Pinkins, who is divorced, is the mother of two young sons, Myles and Maxx.

Tonya Pinkins

KELLY RIPA (Hayley Vaughan)

Birthplace: Stratford, New Jersey   Birthdate: October 2
Height: 5'4"   Hair: Blond   Eyes: Blue

Kelly Ripa joined the cast of *All My Children* in the role of feisty Hayley Vaughan in November 1990. Ripa, who sees a little bit of herself in Hayley, had been performing in her senior high school play,

Kelly Ripa

The Ugly Duckling, when she was approached by her current manager, Cathy Parker, who encouraged her to pursue acting. After attending New Jersey's Camden Community College, she performed in local theater productions before coming to the show.

Kelly has become one of *All My Children*'s most popular young actors, gracing the covers of numerous fan magazines and receiving nominations for a 1993 Daytime Emmy Award and a 1993 Soap Opera Award.

Kelly, with one sibling, is the first in her family to enter the acting profession. She had studied ballet since age three, plays the piano and, in her words, is "no Barbra Streisand," but can carry a tune. On the side, she currently co-hosts *Music Scoop*, a syndicated music video series.

Ingrid Rogers

INGRID ROGERS (Taylor Cannon)

Birthplace: Toronto, Canada   Birthdate: April 27
Height: 5'7"   Hair: Dark Brown   Eyes: Brown

Ingrid Rogers made her professional acting debut on *All My Children* in May 1992 as the manipulative, attractive, upscale teenager Taylor Roxbury Cannon, who later became a police officer.

The Toronto native, who spent her early years in Jamaica before moving back to Canada, first studied acting in high school and fell in love with it. Rogers then went to the University of Toronto and became a business major, at the suggestion of her father, but soon realized that her heart wasn't in it. Shortly afterward she transferred to the American Academy of Dramatic Arts, and after graduation, joined the American Academy of Dramatic Arts Theater Company and performed in a number of plays. A screen test for the role of Taylor followed, and the rest, as they say, is history.

In 1993, Rogers appeared in her first feature film, *Carlito's Way*, in which she co-starred with Al Pacino, Sean Penn and Penelope Ann Miller.

For relaxation, she enjoys reading, dancing and watching sunsets. She and her husband, David Fryberger, live in New York City.

Richard Shoberg

RICHARD SHOBERG (Tom Cudahy)

Birthplace: Grand Rapids, Michigan   Birthdate: March 1
Height: 6'   Hair: Brown   Eyes: Blue

Richard Shoberg originated the role of Tom Cudahy when he joined the cast in 1977. Cudahy's interracial marriage to attorney Livia Frye was strengthened by their fight to retain custody of their foster child, Jamal. Shoberg won an Emmy nomination for Outstanding Actor for his portrayal of Tom in 1992.

Born in Grand Rapids, Michigan, Richard grew up on a family-owned hunting and fishing resort in the Les Cheneaux Islands in the upper peninsula of Michigan. In high school, he excelled at many sports, including football, and was recruited to play at nearby Albion College, where he also developed an interest in theater. As part of the college's outside studies program, Richard was able to study theater in New York for a semester with Lee Strasberg at the Actors Studio.

Deciding to remain in New York and pursue his acting career, he landed his first television role in 1971 as Mitch Farmer on *Somerset*, going on to portray Kevin Jamison on *Edge Of Night* and play a featured role in the television movie *The Silence* with Richard Thomas.

Even after taking his role on *All My Children*, Shoberg has remained active in the New York theater community, favoring experimental and original works. He is also a talented singer/guitarist and has written a number of songs. He lives in New York with his wife, Varaporn, a native of Thailand, with whom he has had two sons, Zachary and Maxwell. The family divides their time off between vacations in Michigan and Thailand.

RUTH WARRICK (Phoebe Tyler Wallingford)

Birthplace: St. Joseph, Missouri   Birthdate: June 29
Height: 5'6 1/2"   Hair: Auburn   Eyes: Blue

Ruth Warrick

When movies are discussed, whether at film festivals or in front of the television set—one film is consistently acclaimed as perhaps the finest ever made: *Citizen Kane*. The young, theater-trained actress who played Orson Welles' wife was Ruth Warrick.

Born in St. Joseph, Missouri, Warrick moved to Kansas City while she was in high school and later attended the University of Kansas City. A promotional tour brought her to New York, where her interest in acting brought her to the Mercury Theater, headed by Welles, with whom she ultimately headed to Hollywood.

After Kane, she went on to appear in twenty other movies before moving on to daytime television, starting with a long run as Hannah Cord in *Peyton Place*, then five years on *As The World Turns* before joining the cast of *All My Children* in its first year as Phoebe Tyler.

Long active in arts-in-education programs, including programs for the disadvantaged in the Watts area of Los Angeles, Warrick received the first national Arts in Education Award in 1983 from the Board of Directors of Business and Industry for Arts in Education, which cited her for leadership in helping to make the arts more central to the schooling process. The award was then named the Ruth Warrick Award for Arts in Education and is now given annually.

Warrick, who lives in Manhattan, holds certification as a licensed metaphysics teacher from Unity School of Practical Christianity in Lees Summit, Missouri. Married several times, she is currently single. Her popular and fascination autobiography, *The Confessions of Phoebe Tyler*, discusses the character of Phoebe as well as her own life as an actress in New York and Hollywood. The book, which she wrote with Don Preston, was published in 1980 by Prentice-Hall.

Dondre T. Whitfield

DONDRE T. WHITFIELD (Terrence Frye)

Birthplace: Brooklyn, New York   Birthdate: May 27
Height: 6'   Hair: Dark brown   Eyes: Brown

The All My Children Family

Dondre T. Whitfield joined *All My Children* in October 1991 in the role of Terrence Frye, a young man who was later the victim of a racial attack. Terrence is now finding happiness with police officer Taylor Cannon. Praised by an industry publication as one of the best young actors on daytime, Dondre is a three-time Emmy nominee, and his performance on AMC has earned him two nominations for the NAACP Image Award. Before joining the show, he was known to prime-time audiences for his role as Robert on *The Cosby Show*. He also co-starred in the critically acclaimed ABC Afterschool Special presentation *All That Glitters*, appeared as Jesse Lawrence on the daytime drama *Another World* and was featured in the theatrical film *Bright Lights, Big City*.

When he's not on the set of *All My Children*, Dondre devotes much of his time to working with underprivileged children. To unwind, he loves to participate in athletics, thriving on the competition in basketball or baseball. He's single and lives in New Jersey.

Walt Willey

WALT WILLEY (Jackson Montgomery)

Birthplace: Ottawa, Illinois   Birthdate: January 26
Height: 6'3"   Hair: Blond   Eyes: Blue

Walt Willey plays the charming lawyer/entrepreneur Jackson Montgomery, who has a taste for trouble and a talent for success. The actor started out as a sculptor, working in concrete and cast aluminum, as an undergraduate at Southern Illinois University, where he also became proficient at drawing and painting. But in his senior year, he began to act in school plays, and after touring with an improvisational group, decided to pursue an acting career in New York. His first professional assignment there was as an extra on *All My Children* before going on to play Joe Novak on *Ryan's Hope* and honing his craft in off-Broadway productions. He came back to become a regular on *AMC* in 1989.

Off camera, Walt is writing a children's book. He also performs as a stand-up comic and pursues his interest in art, developing his own line of tee-shirts and doing cartoons. In 1994, he even appeared as himself in comic-book form in "The Second Life of Dr. Mirage," from Valiant Comics. For relaxation, he enjoys scuba diving and chess.

1994 Show Credits

Created by: Agnes Nixon

Executive Producer: Felicia Minei Behr

Directed by: Jim Baffico, Christopher Goutman, Henry Kaplan, Conal O'Brien

Head Writer: Megan McTavish

Writers: Hal Corley, Frederick Johnson, Gail Lawrence, Jeff Beldner, Karen Lewis, Elizabeth Smith, Michelle Patrick, Bettina F. Bradbury, Ralph Wakefield, Pete T. Rich

Supervising Producer: Terry Cacavio

Coordinating Producers: Nancy Horwich, Lisa S. Hesser

Associate Producer: Carole Shure

Associate Directors: Barbara M. Simmons, Shirley Simmons

Scenic Designer: Kevin Rupnik

Associate Scenic Designers: Paul D. Robinson, Tarrant Smith

Costume Designer: Carol Luiken

Assistant Costume Designer: Charles Clute

Casting Director: Judy Blye Wilson

Assistant Casting Director: Elias Tray

Music Produced by: Narwal Productions, Inc.

Music Composed by: Earl Rose, Billy Barber

Music Directors: Sybil Weinberger, Pamela Magee, A.J. Gundell

Production Managers: Michael M. Luzzi, Patricia Nesbitt, Ronald P. Rhodes

Technical Directors: Howard Zweig, Michael V. Pomarico

Lighting Directors: Donna Larson, Daniel A. Kinsley, Thomas Winberry

Video: Len Walas

Cameras: Robert Ambrico, Robert Bellairs, Paul Martens, Chris Mauro, Greg Saccaro, Trevor Thompson, Joseph Puleo, Vincent Senatore

Audio: Dominick Maldari, Chuck Eisen

Boom: Melvin Jackson, David Gordon, Stan Talarek

Sound Effects: Glen Heil, Serge Ossorguine

Videotape Editors: Roger Haenelt, Jack Hierl, Nat Rogers

Electronic Maintenance: Myron Kohut, Bob Bovino, Bob Dietzsch, Peter Blangiforti, Steve Francis

Technical Manager: Richard Reid

Business Manager: Helen Tunkiar

Stage Managers: Penny Bergman, Tamara Grady, Rose Riggins, Rusty Swope

Production Assistants: Robin Moger Maizes, Sonia Blangiardo

Studio Coordinators: Linda Burstion, Rhoda Gilmore

Production Administrator: Lance Hodges

Production Propertymen: Jim Balzaretti, Andrew Abamonte

Wardrobe: Marilyn Putnam, Mark Klein, Curtis Hay

Assistant to the Producer: Ginger Smith

Writers' Associates: Jane Murphy, Iris DeVita

Production Associates: Joann Busciglio, Jennifer Minda, Adam Harris, Samantha Walker

The All My Children Family

Photo Credits

All photos and video images are copyright © Capital Cities/ABC. Photographer credits are as follows:

16	Ken Regan
17	Owen Franken
18	Capital Cities/ABC
19	Capital Cities/ABC
23	Ken Regan
27	Owen Franken
29	Owen Franken
31	Capital Cities/ABC
35	Ann Limongello
43	Capital Cities/ABC
45	Capital Cities/ABC
47	Ann Limongello
49	Ann Limongello
55	Steve Fenn
56	Steve Fenn
57	Ann Limongello
59	Steve Fenn
60	Ann Limongello
61	Steve Fenn
62	Steve Fenn
63	Capital Cities/ABC
64	Steve Fenn
65	Capital Cities/ABC
66	Ann Limongello
68	*top left*, Capital Cities/ABC
	middle left, Capital Cities/ABC
69	Ann Limongello
70	Steve Fenn
71	Steve Fenn
72	*top left*, Steve Fenn
	middle left, Capital Cities/ABC
73	*top right*, Capital Cities/ABC
	bottom right, Bob Sacha
74	*top left*, Ann Limongello
	bottom left, Steve Fenn
77	Gary Miller
78	Capital Cities/ABC
80	Gary Miller
81	Steve Fenn
82	Ann Limongello
83	Joe McNally
84	Ann Limongello
85	Ann Limongello
86	Capital Cities/ABC
88	Ann Limongello
89	L. Corbett
90	*top left*, Ann Limongello
	bottom left, Ann Limongello
91	Ann Limongello
92	Ann Limongello
93	Capital Cities/ABC
94	Capital Cities/ABC
95	Capital Cities/ABC
96	*top left*, Capital Cities/ABC
	bottom left, Scott Humbert
97	Mike Fuller
98	Capital Cities/ABC
99	Ann Limongello
100	Capital Cities/ABC
101	Ann Limongello
102	Ann Limongello
103	*top right*, Capital Cities/ABC
	bottom right, Ann Limongello
104	*all*, Ann Limongello
105	*all*, Ann Limongello
106	Ann Limongello
108	Cathy Blaivas
110	*all*, Cathy Blaivas
111	Cathy Blaivas
113	Cathy Blaivas

114	Ann Limongello
115	Capital Cities/ABC
116	Ann Limongello
117	Ann Limongello
118	Donna Svennevik
119	Capital Cities/ABC
120	Ann Limongello
121	Ann Limongello
122	Kimberly Butler
123	Kimberly Butler
124	Kimberly Butler
125	Ann Limongello
126	*top left*, Ann Limongello
	bottom left, Kimberly Butler
127	Donna Svennevik
128	Steve Fenn
130	*top*, Owen Franken
	bottom, Steve Fenn
131	*top left*, Owen Franken
	top right, Ann Limongello
	bottom, Ken Regan
132	Owen Franken
133	*top left*, Karen Epstein
	top right, Sy Friedman
	middle, Owen Franken
	bottom, Ann Limongello
134	*top left*, Donna Svennevik
	bottom right, Ann Limongello
135	*top left*, Capital Cities/ABC
	top right, Ken Regan
	middle left, Steve Fenn
	bottom right, Owen Franken
136	*top left*, Steve Fenn
	top right, Capital Cities/ABC
	bottom, Steve Fenn
137	*top*, Capital Cities/ABC
	bottom, Steve Fenn
138	*top left*, Steve Fenn
	top right, Donna Svennevik
	bottom, Capital Cities/ABC
139	*left*, Ann Limongello
	top right, Cathy Blaivas
	bottom right, Donna Svennevik
140	*top left*, Donna Svennevik
	middle left, Ann Limongello
	middle center, Capital Cities/ABC
	bottom center, Steve Fenn
140-141	*bottom*, Owen Franken
141	*top*, Ann Limongello
	middle right, Ann Limongello
	middle center, Cathy Blaivas
	bottom right, Ann Limongello
142	*top left*, Steve Fenn
	bottom, Steve Fenn
143	*top left*, Steve Fenn
	bottom left, Steve Fenn
	top right, Bob Sacha
	bottom right, Christopher Little
144	*top*, Ann Limongello
	middle center, Donna Svennevik
	middle right, Bob Sacha
	bottom left, Bob Sacha
145	*top left*, Ann Limongello
	bottom left, Ann Limongello
	right, Cathy Blaivas
146	*top left*, Cathy Blaivas
	top right, Ann Limongello
	bottom, Ann Limongello
147	*top*, Steve Fenn
	bottom, Ann Limongello
148	*top left*, Donna Svennevik
	bottom, Ann Limongello

149	*left*, Ann Limongello
	top right, Cathy Blaivas
	middle right, Ann Limongello
	bottom right, Ann Limongello
150	*top left*, Ann Limongello
	top right, Donna Svennevik
	bottom, Ann Limongello
151	*all*, Ann Limongello
152	*top left*, Stephan Churchill
	middle left, Robert Milazzo
	bottom, Ann Limongello
153	*all*, Ann Limongello
154	*top*, Steve Fenn
	bottom left, Ann Limongello
154-155	Ann Limongello
155	*top left*, Robert Milazzo
	top right, E.J. Carr
156	Steve Fenn
158	*top left*, Ann Limongello
	middle left, Capital Cities/ABC
	bottom right, Steve Fenn
159	Donna Svennevik
160	*middle*, Donna Svennevik
	bottom left, Ann Limongello
160-161	*top*, Ann Limongello
161	*top right*, Steve Fenn
	bottom, Ann Limongello
162	*top left*, Steve Fenn
	middle left, Ann Limongello
	middle right, Leslie Wong
	bottom right, Bob Sacha
163	*middle left*, Ann Limongello
	top right, Gary Miller
	middle center, Leslie Wong
	middle right, Ann Limongello
	bottom left, Gary Miller
	bottom right, Ann Limongello
166	*top left*, Ann Limongello
	bottom, Donna Svennevik
167	*top left*, Ann Limongello
	top right, Cathy Blaivas
	bottom, Ann Limongello
168	*top*, Ann Limongello
	bottom left, Donna Svennevik
	middle right, Steve Fenn
169	*top left*, Donna Svennevik
	right, Steve Fenn
170	*top left*, Ken Regan
	middle, Sy Friedman
	bottom left, Ann Limongello
	bottom right, Steve Fenn
171	*top*, Steve Fenn
	bottom left, Steve Fenn
	middle right, Ann Limongello
172	*top*, Steve Fenn
	bottom left, Steve Fenn
	middle right, Ann Limongello
173	*top*, Ann Limongello
	bottom left, Bob Sacha
	middle right, Ann Limongello
174	*left*, Ann Limongello
	middle right, Kimberly Butler
175	*all*, Ann Limongello
176	*top*, Ann Limongello
	middle left, Robert Milazzo
	bottom right, Kimberly Butler
177	*all*, Ann Limongello
178-179	*all*, Steve Fenn
180	Kimberly Butler
182	*top left*, Ann Limongello
	bottom left, Cathy Blaivas
	middle right, Ann Limongello

The All My Children Family

Index